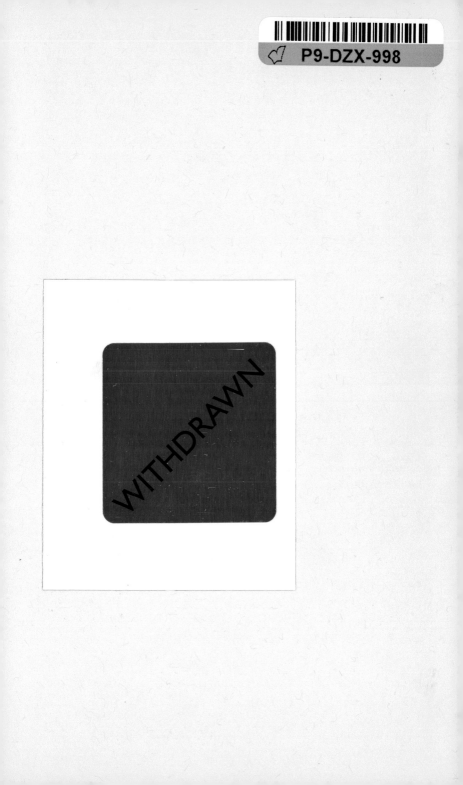

The South and the Southerner

The South
and the
Southerner

BY RALPH McGILL

An Atlantic Monthly Press Book

LITTLE, BROWN AND COMPANY · BOSTON · TORONTO

LIBRARY OF CONGRESS CATALOG CARD NO. 63-8314

FIFTH PRINTING

The author wishes to thank the following for permission to use excerpts
from copyrighted material:

HOLT, RINEHART & WINSTON, INC. for 38 lines from *John Brown's Body*
by Stephen Vincent Benét © 1927, 1928 by Stephen Vincent Benét.
Copyright renewed 1955, 1956 by Rosemary Carr Benét.

OXFORD UNIVERSITY PRESS, INC. for four lines from Richard Eberhart's "If
I Could Only Live at the Pitch That Is Near Madness" from *Collected
Poems 1930–1960* by Richard Eberhart. © Richard Eberhart 1960.

TWAYNE PUBLISHERS, INC. for a poem "Mrs. Broderick was a very unusual woman" from Merrill Moore's *Clinical Sonnets.*

THE VIKING PRESS, INC. for ten lines from a poem "Bohemia" from *The
Portable Dorothy Parker.* © 1927, 1954 by Dorothy Parker. This poem
originally appeared in the *New Yorker.*

ATLANTIC–LITTLE, BROWN BOOKS
ARE PUBLISHED BY
LITTLE, BROWN AND COMPANY
IN ASSOCIATION WITH
THE ATLANTIC MONTHLY PRESS

*Published simultaneously in Canada
by Little, Brown & Company (Canada) Limited*

PRINTED IN THE UNITED STATES OF AMERICA

In memory of Mary Elizabeth and to my son Ralph, Jr., and Jack Tarver — three who have meant so much to me.

Acknowledgments

In writing this book I have been helped at various stages by the editorial counsel of Edward Weeks and Peter Davison of the *Atlantic;* by the steadfast encouragement of James M. Cox, Jr.; and by the stimulus of Grace Lundy, without whose painstaking and intelligent collaboration this book could never have been written.

Contents

Contents

The South and the Southerner

I

There Are Many Souths

IT WAS RAW and cold in Rome that January, 1945, with the great war echoing from the north. On that particularly harsh morning of my first day there the last thing I would have expected was a discussion of Erskine Caldwell, *Tobacco Road*, and the problems of the South. With a friend I had been to the Keats Museum and we had paid our respects to the calm, wonderful woman who, all through the German occupation, had kept the place in order. Now as we left and climbed the Spanish Steps, we came to a bookstore with the name *C. E. Rappaport* on the door. Within was an elderly man, wearing a topcoat and a hat, with a shawl across his knees; he was seated with his feet stretched towards a small electric heater not much larger than a bread toaster. I did not then know him to be one of the world's most respected dealers in rare books.

In answer to my question, he directed me to his shelf of English titles, and after some scrutiny I chose *Men and Manners in America*, by Thomas Hamilton. According to the foreword, it was a new edition, dated April, 1843. Mr. Rappaport, who seemed amused by my choice, told me that Sir Thomas Hamilton was quite a lion in his day, a great Tory and an arrogant aristocrat who found little on his American visit which did not suffer in comparison with Great Britain. The bookseller asked where I came from, and when I said

Georgia, he made me smile by saying that I would find Sir Thomas was the first Erskine Caldwell to portray my home country.

Sir Thomas, as I soon learned, was, indeed, an unsparing critic. But it was his journey northward from New Orleans, much of it by stagecoach, which provoked his harshest strictures. Even so, one could not avoid being amused by, and admiring, the forthright dash of his style. Of Georgia he wrote:

Our road lay through unbroken pine forests and the roads were mere sand in which the wheels sank half up to the axels . . . We traveled all night and on the evening of the following day reached Macon, a considerable village . . . About ten at night we reached Milledgeville, where I was obliged to remain through illness . . . Milledgeville has seen better days, and presents the appearance, not of a decayed gentleman, but of a starving mechanic. Many houses have already gone to decay . . .

A journey through Georgia leaves little to record. The inhabitants bear a bad character in other parts of the Union . . . I traveled with three attorneys, two store keepers, a cotton planter and a slave dealer. My notions of the sort of conversation prevalent in Newgate may not be very accurate, but I much doubt whether it would be found to indicate such utter debasement, both of thought and principle, as that to which I was condemned to listen . . .

Georgia receives large accessions of population in the off-scourings of other slave states. The restraints of law are little felt, and it is the only state in the Union in which I heard it publicly asserted that justice is not purely administered . . . A Georgian with whom I conversed a great deal about his native state, declared that, with plenty of money, he could, with facility, escape punishment for any crime, however heinous . . . He would, he said, have a touch at the sheriff, bribe the prosecutor's counsel to keep back evidence or leave some flaw by which the proceedings could be vitiated . . .

The climate of South Carolina disturbed Hamilton, but he did find gentlemen there. He wrote:

I proceeded from Augusta by coach to Charleston . . . In point of climate, I believe Charleston is fully worse than New Orleans . . . at one season the town is unhealthy and all who can afford it fly to their estates. At another, the country is unhealthy and they take up their abode in the pine barrens . . . In New Orleans a man runs a certain risk, and has done with it. If he live, he continues to eat crawfish in a variety of savoury preparations. If he die, the crawfish eat him without cookery of any sort . . . But in Charleston a man must be continually on the alert; for, go where he may, there is fever at his heels . . .

Mr. Rappaport, who had read the book, asked of the South, and I sought to answer: I told him of the real Tobacco Road which I had seen, and of Erskine Caldwell's gentle, saintlike father, Ira, a Presbyterian minister of Wrens, Georgia, a tall, gaunt man with deep-set eyes. He always had his say, popular or not, and he took quiet pride in his son. Much of his time was given to trying to bring something of Christ to the small eddy of depressed humanity along Tobacco Road in the old plantation areas. He solicited clothing from friends in Northern churches. Once, to his great disgust, he received a handsomely tailored dinner suit. "This for a man who never owned a whole pair of britches in his life," he said, with a wry smile.

When the play, *Tobacco Road,* came to nearby Augusta, Dr. Caldwell, with no notice to newspapers, took some of the road's characters whom Erskine had used in the book to see it. The real Jeeter Lester had died and the good pastor drew deep satisfaction from hearing one of the men say, "Wouldn't Jeeter have purely loved to see it!"

Tobacco Road is to me Caldwell's best book because the characters in it have such warmth and life. I will always believe this is true because he had known them, in part at least, through the honest eyes and compassionate heart and words of his father.

I tried to explain to Mr. Rappaport that there were many

Souths, not one, and that they were changing long before the Second World War began and that this process would be more accelerated when peace came. As for Georgia, I said, it was something like his own Italy, which had a north and a south. The American South was a regional abstraction with a capital S. It possessed, like his Naples and Sicily, a stubborn, often unjustified, pride; it was easygoing and yet violent when it chose to be; it shared, as did southern Italy, a common mystique in which there is grandeur, and pathos, and a note of falseness too. It was something, I said, that I had been born in and to which I had given all my years, but the complexities of it were often too much for me. Now fluid as quicksilver, now rigid and cruel in its adamant injustice and wrongs, now soft and merry, it was difficult to put in words.

I reached around for a Southern story with an Italian angle and I closed out my visit with it. Once, years before, I had read sections of Virgil's *Georgics* to a meeting of small farmers in a combination rural church and schoolhouse, lighted for the evening by kerosene lamps. I stood at the pulpit and told them that Virgil had written of farming and how, in the years before Christ, the Romans had known about plowing under peas, planting vetch and bitter lupin, and the inoculation and selection of seed. I read the lines relating to those things and the audience was entranced. A year later I met one of the farmers at a county political rally. He came up to me and said, "I never will forget you reading about that Italian feller. Imagine him knowing all that way back then."

I told Mr. Rappaport he was one Roman I'd always remember, and I have. For he made me think about the different Souths at a vulnerable time.

A good two years after that meeting, a friend and I decided to locate the source of the Chattahoochee River in the southerly thrust of the Appalachians into northern Georgia where they are called the "Blue Ridges." I mention this here because when a talk touches home as did that one in Rome a man keeps vindicating his part in it.

There is something of the mountains in me, and I am drawn to them. The Chattahoochee, of which Sidney Lanier wrote so beautifully, is at its best in its Blue Ridge stages. The Cherokees put the name on it — River of the Painted Rocks. We drove deep into the Chattahoochee National Forest along an old logging road, parked the car, and began our climb.

We had gone no more than a quarter mile when, well up the slopes which become the southwestern border of the great Highland area, a turkey hen got up heavily and flew with gathering speed deep down into the darkness of the wild gorge to our right. Ahead we could see the rough rock rim of the ridge which completely encloses the headwaters of the river. We strove toward it. Along the way were numerous deer tracks, freshly made, and some revealing that fawns were with the does.

The second growth, the successors to the noble trees of the past, had come back well after the ruthless logging periods of the 1880's and the First World War. Their names are like poems and ballads — sour wood and scarlet oak, black gum and birch, basswood and beech, black walnut and black locust, red maple and white oak, sweetgum and sycamore, yellow poplar and red oak, hemlock and hickory, Virginia pine and the white, short leaf pine, buckeye and the mountain cucumber, the wild black cherry and the mountain magnolias, spruce and silver-bell, white ash and the chinquapin. Many of their names are in old fiddle tunes and mountain songs.

Stark among them stood the white dead trunks of the giant chestnuts, white as old bone, accusing memorials to the blight which took them and a reminder that if man does not become more of a conservationist others of his trees will go. The chestnut keeps trying to come back. It has a will to live. It grows up from the old stumps and beside the dead, ghostly trunks and lives from two to four years before it fades and dies. In one place we found such a chestnut with a trunk a good four inches in diameter, but already the hand of blight had touched its leaves and it soon would be dead.

Laurel and rhododendron were in great plenty, along with sweet shrub and witch hazel, wild sweet william and holly, alder and sassafras, sumac and buckeye. The herbs were there, too. "Yarb" doctors have dug them up for generations. There still are those in the hollows who know how to brew for distempers and aches — dog hobble and mullein, horse-mint and wild cherry, boneset and queen of the meadow, ginseng and lady-slipper, cherry bark bitters with whiskey, yellow root and balsam tea for the kidneys; ivy tea and sage for colds, and pennyroyal tea for the "pneumonia fever."

Here and there, as we plodded upward, were long-abandoned farm sites in a valley or hillside, with occasional stubborn gnarled fruit trees still standing on a nearby slope with the pathos of all old, neglected things. Now and then the ruins of an ancient rock chimney sprawled across the route, with small trees pushing up through the stones. Once we came on a whole chimney, still standing, with every stone intact, but lonely, as must have been those at the moment of turning away from its hearthstone. There had never been any pillared mansions in those remote slopes and valleys. Nor had there been ease from labor. The cabins had been not much better than those of slave quarters on the plantations. Yet this, too, was a part of the South.

In Union County, high above Poplar Stump Gap, we found, near the top of the divide, a small spring flowing out of the huge rocks. It splashed down lichen-covered boulders below to form a pool, where a coon had scraped himself a small space clear of leaves to wash his food. The water here freed itself in two modest trickles to go hurrying down the slope into a deep and dark ravine below us. This was the highest flow of water that went chuckling down into the laurel thickets to meet, finally, with others, and to form the headwaters of the branches which join to make the Chattahoochee.

These tributary streams, discovered in the damp thickets, dash with gathering speed, clear and cold, toward the valley below. The divide, from which they are fed, is the crest of the Blue Ridge, the last southward thrust of the ancient, eroded Appalachians.

Geologists, happily untouched by political or social clamor over boundaries, have established twenty-five natural geologic divisions for our country. One of these is in the Blue Ridge Province. It extends from a point near Gettysburg, Pennsylvania, six hundred miles southwesterly to a point a few miles north of Atlanta, Georgia. A natural barrier, much of it a mass of mountains seventy miles wide, it was long a hindrance to westward migration, as it was to de Soto's gold seekers when they wandered for days, lost in its many, thickly wooded, tangled valleys. These mountains are the Appalachians, called the Apalache by de Soto after an Indian tribe he met with on the coast. The Southern Appalachians were never glaciated. No great lakes were created in the valleys. It is a region of forest and small springs and streams.

Jim Roberts, who lives near the river and who is handy at whittling things, remembered what his grandfather, who "packed in" from Pennsylvania in 1823, had to say about the Appalachians.

"My old granddad said that when he had at last made his way to the top of the big rim where he could see over into the Carolina Piedmont, he expected to start down the mountain slope. But, when he got there and looked, all he could see was a great blue ocean of peaks stretching out into the haze of the distance as far as he could see. 'I just stood there lookin' at it and tremblin' like I had the ague,' he told us. 'I dreaded to start across it. And so did my horse.' We came in through Rabun Gap."

Jim Roberts remembered a song that has been sung,

by merely substituting the new name, about all the mountain passes through which the restless seekers pushed in the years when the war of the Revolution seemed not to have settled things the way it was hoped it would, a way all wars have of doing. He sang it for us:

> Let's lay down, boys, and catch a nap,
> We got to rest up to make the Rabun Gap.

> The first white man to cross the Gap
> Was a Indian tradin' chap.

> Cherokee's hidin' behind every rock
> And the flint lost off his old flintstock.

> Know a Indian girl in the Rabun Gap
> She's got chillun as calls me "Pap."

> So, let's lay down, boys, and catch that nap.
> It's goin' to be fun when we're through the Gap.

"There was a feller back in the old days my Daddy told about," said Jim Roberts, "that said, when he had got through the gap to Nacoochee Valley, that he reckoned the only reason the Lord made all them piled-up mountains between here and North Carolina was to hide Hell." He chuckled. "Now we know better," he said. "We know it's to attract the tourist folks."

It is from these Georgia slopes of the Blue Ridge that the tributary streams come pouring down, converging finally to become the Chattahoochee. The young river flows, clear and chattering, possessing all the life and beauty that the poet Sidney Lanier saw in it, as it weaves across the bench of the Dahlonega plateau, the only true piedmont country in Georgia.

Near it, we sat on a porch and talked with Amicus Abernathy, who was born on a mountain farm up near the farthest headwaters.

"Son," he said, "don't be fooled by her beauty. She looks pretty and she is. She babbles like gossip and giggles like a girl. If you didn't care for beauty, looking at her way up here, you might be callin' her a piddlin' river. But, son, she ain't. I've seen her come out of the mountains like a wild stallion with logs in his mane. I've seen her take gristmills and grind them up in their own stones. I've seen her tear up bridges and twist steel until it looked like bands for hogsheads.

"I worked as a boy helping to build the splash dams up there in the mountains when they began to cut the timber. I remember the men standing there with shinin' eyes saying it would take twenty years to cut what they wanted. It took nineteen. The river had more water then, before they cut the logs. Son, she was something to see when the logs were leaping in the white roar of her.

"You don't see trees like we had then. My granddaddy was here in the Indian times and he said I saw it as a boy the way he first saw it, except, of course, for the clearings for the cabins and the farms in the little valleys up there.

"They timbered her off greedy-like. They didn't bother with a tree unless it was a big one. I've seen them go through the woods callin' and markin': 'I'll give you a dollar for this one . . . that one seventy-five cents . . . there's one worth two dollars.' Once I saw a tree sold for two dollars saw up into five thousand feet, and many is the dollar and the dollar-fifty trees I've seen saw up into three thousand and four thousand feet. During the Second World War, I saw them cut trees that wouldn't make more than a two-by-four, and they have been sellin' the hardwood at two hundred dollars a thousand. Well, you just don't see trees like that any more. The second growth is back good, but the ridges don't hold water the way they did — not any more — not any more. When you think about it, most of our liabilities here in the South are man-made. We've wasted so much — so much of everything.

"I remember a Boston company . . . seems to me like it

was the Dutton Lumber Company . . . was one of the first ones. I recall the 'river driver,' too. His name was Bill Cornell. We built splash dams, and when the rains came we floated the logs on down through the valleys to Gainesville and a mill there. You couldn't get it out of here any other way. We haven't had roads very long even now. . . ."

We went to see Uncle Ed Westmoreland. He was pushing one hundred years, and he lived the first sixty of them up there in the climbing ridges. His valley house faces them and we found him in a hickory split-bottom straight chair, his still-sharp blue eyes resting on the haze of the ridges he had known all his life.

"Uncle Ed," we said, when he had seen us and asked us in and told us to sit, "we want to know what it was like in the old days up there in the mountains where the Chattahoochee's creeks begin."

He tapped his worn, peeled hickory stick on the porch floor. The corners of his mouth turned in a quiet grin.

"It was like a lot of hard work," he said. "When you think of the mountains in the old days, don't you go thinkin' about them in terms of picnics and these little walks you call hikes. I remember the ox-carts strainin' and creakin' and complainin' along the ridges. I think of men walking a hundred and sixty miles to Augusta — walked it myself a few times — and fetching back things they needed on their backs, or maybe packin' it in on a horse. Some drove oxen there. It took a couple of months to come and go. A wheel might break or an ox might get sick or break a leg. A man's folks didn't begin to fret about him until nine or ten weeks had passed. It was long, hard work. I think about it a lot, now I got time to think. I made my last crop down here in the valley when I was eighty-four. I just rest now, and think about things. It was hard, but we made out. The wood was always cut on Saturday for Sunday. The Presbyterians wouldn't cook on Sunday. They called them 'bluestockings,' even though they didn't wear none. Sunday was a day of rest. Today, I don't know. What with all the radios a-squallin' and all the useless goin' and comin' on the blacktop roads, I sometimes sit here and say to myself that maybe the oxen were the best after all. A feller sure didn't hitch up and go some place unless he needed to, or wanted to mighty bad.

"When the new settlers came in, we had the house-raisin', and when they was ready to clear land, we had a 'workin'.' There was always plenty to eat and for them what wanted it a jug behind a bush.

"Some of the ox drivers were good at it. Amicus was good. He learned from his daddy. I remember once Amicus drove a team of eight oxen hitched to a dray and took thirty-two children to a Sunday School meetin'. It was seven miles there. Amicus's daddy had the first water-saw here in the mountains. After they found gold, of course, things changed. That work was too hard, but they all had the fever and the folks began to come here from everywhere — from England and Spain and France and New England. But you asked about the old days when I was up there where the headwaters rise. The river was a part of our life. We folks up there didn't have it like they did down here along the river. We were mountain men and we liked it better. A feller that come back from Augusta could get a lot of folks to listen to his tales, but we stayed at home. I saw people have to haul out of here with oxen as late as 1910. They were hard years, but like I say, I get to wondering now and then. They make mighty poor use of the roads, seems to me. . . ."

In the late afternoon we came to Grady's Place, and sat on the front porch and looked down at Little Tesnatee, red with the last rays of the sun. Pop Lacey came out and passed us tall, cold glasses, with the moisture trickling down their sides.

"I spent my life here, most of it," he said, "and I can tell you about the mountain water. It's fine water for making whiskey. I never made none, but I heard so all my life. It's good, clean, sweet water, and it suits the making of sour-mash whiskey like a warm hearth suits a cricket. There are trout in the streams, brown and speckled. Not like the old days. But they are there, as you know. They and the mountains are good to look at. I never have tired of them in nearly seventy years. And for me," he said, "this is Georgia. You can have the rest if it."

I told them then about the bookstore in Rome and the old man who had wanted to know about Georgia and the South.

"There are two Georgias, and many Souths," said Pop Lacey. "You told him right. People in the cotton South had slaves and didn't learn how to work. Ever since they have been complaining about things and figuring life's been hard because their granddaddies lost a war. I didn't know Italy was like that, too."

The sun dropped behind the slopes and the cool air began to run down the valleys, smelling of ferns, rhododendron, and deep damp ravines. The dusk lasted for only a short while and then darkness was on us, and we sat there listening to the Little Tesnatee chuckling down below.

"Just fit for poets, trout, whiskey and lookin'!" said Pop Lacey. "Dinner will be ready soon. And if it tastes like squirrel stew, don't ast me if it is. The season ain't in yet."

As we began to eat each man had in his mind the image of his own particular South. For none was it the same. The South I knew was not the one I had known as a boy. It assuredly was not the South my father had known. And each of us knew that all our Souths had changed since we heard the news on December 7, 1941.

Grady's Place is one of the many valleys of the Blue Ridge Mountains. The men and women who peopled them had entertained little feeling of kinship, if any, with the people of the Piedmont and the coastal areas of cotton, rice and slaves. The legends, myths, songs, culture and folklore of the

Appalachian South were unrelated to those of the plantation South. And somehow it was this latter South which, as the Second World War ended, seemed farther away in time and space than it was.

Once, on a visit to Warm Springs, I'd heard Franklin D. Roosevelt say that Georgia was an unfinished state and the South was an unfinished region. He explained, saying the development of the Southern states had been halted by the Civil War and that postwar recovery had been tortuous and slow because of the corrosive poverty and the pressures of politics, prejudice, and economic exploitation which had developed after the reconstruction years.

There must be a beginning again, and perhaps, he said, it will come out of this depression. He was right about it. There was a beginning again. It did grow out of the heartbreak of the depression years. Volunteer pines began to grow in many fields where the old cotton terraces could still be traced. Sharecropper and tenant cabins were emptied as the tractors began to come. Men talked of cattle, of broilers and of dairying. The pace was slow, but the South changed as industry and the machines began to replace muscle and inevitably the white man's image of the Negro began to change. But even more important was the fact that the Negro's image of himself was changing.

There was change everywhere. In the South of the Appalachians I remembered some lines from Stephen Vincent Benét's *John Brown's Body*:

> A pioneer island in a world that has
> No use for pioneers . . .
> One need not weep romantic tears for them,
> But when the last moonshiner buys his radio,
> And the last, lost wild-rabbit of a girl
> Is civilized with a mail order dress,
> Something will pass that was American
> And the movies will not bring it back. . . .

There are factories in the valleys now, and television aerials above the roofs of old log cabins. The hard-topped roads lead to town and there are motels, jukeboxes, neon-lit dine-and-dance places. But the old clan virtues endure. And so do the independent spirit and the feeling that the people of the plantation areas are somewhat alien and soft and that they somehow took advantage in putting their stamp on the South.

Changes came fast at the war's end. Even in 1945 Southerners in cities had ceased to be startled by Negroes appearing on juries. Voting rights, still crudely, often viciously, denied in rural areas, were increasingly granted in the cities. Politicians were seeking those votes and there began to be a more equitable justice in the courts. Police brutalities grew fewer.

By 1950 the people of the rural South were moving into urban communities, large and small. The really rural counties were everywhere losing population. It was plain that the future of the South, whatever it was to be, would be worked out in the urban areas.

By 1960 there was at least a beginning of school desegregation in twelve of sixteen Southern states, including Delaware and Maryland. In 1961 two Negro students were accepted at the University of Georgia, the first break in the heatedly and repeatedly pledged defiance of "never" by the tier of Deep South cotton states. To one who had been a part of it for a lifetime the changes were dramatic.

The sit-ins were, without question, productive of the most change. Whatever the lawyers may say of them, they have an honored place in history and literature. Shadrach, Meshach and Abed-nego refused to obey the laws of Nebuchadnezzar because a higher moral law was involved. Henry Thoreau wrote civil disobedience into literature. Gandhi used it as a lever to win independence for India. It was morally wrong, and it was preposterous, that a customer in a store was not merely permitted but invited to buy anything on sale, but if he was a colored customer he could not buy food or drink. No argument in a court of law could have dramatized the immorality and the irrationality of such a custom as did the sit-ins. No force brought change as quickly as they.

They did more than this. The sit-ins reached far out into the back country. They inspired adult men and women, fathers, mothers, grandmothers, aunts and uncles, to support the young students in the cities. Not even the Supreme Court decision on the schools in 1954 had done this. But the students picketing the lunchrooms and the department stores — this was something they could see and understand. From the day of the first sit-in the students brought a stronger front to contest against discrimination than could have been created by any other course. The sit-ins did a third thing: they demonstrated the Negro's economic strength. And, fourthly, they brought white students to protest with the Negro students.

One remembered Gunnar Myrdal, who had written in *The American Dilemma* that the central problem was neither the exploitation of the Negro people nor the various effects of this exploitation on the American society, "but rather the moral conflict in the heart of white Americans."

This was true. And what the school decision had not done to make sensitive Southerners aware of this fact, the sit-ins did. The central moral problem was enlarged. It could be seen impairing the efforts of our diplomats abroad, harassing United States representatives in the United Nations, embarrassing our friends, comforting our enemies, eroding education, harming the economy.

It was less and less easy for Southerners to argue the very material progress that had been made. One could understand how the White Citizens Councils came into being. But it was no longer possible to be patient with them.

It also was no longer logical to rationalize the failure of senators, congressmen, governors, mayors, editors, clergymen, businessmen and publishers who in 1954 had let the golden moment slip and failed in leadership by silence or, worse, by inciting mobs and defiance.

But, still, the American dream held true. The phrase ceased to be a cliché as the words of the Bill of Rights stood up from the printed page and became living symbols in the presence of the first Negro students to pass through the barriers of state laws and screaming pickets into the classrooms of schools and universities.

The dream of those who made the American Revolution was that this country would, through the years, give to all the world its own freedom and its own faith. By the time the twentieth century was half over we learned that failure to do that for about twenty million of our own citizens had blurred the image of liberty and faith so that the totalitarian areas of the world could scoff at it and deny its validity. We learned that to export our revolution of freedom we had to live it.

There was a beginning again.

One day, before the Supreme Court school decision, a Negro schoolteacher boarded a plane at Knoxville, Tennessee, and was seated beside me. She was, it turned out, on her way to Chicago to visit her parents. She taught in a rural Southern town. We talked.

"You know," she said, "I can't stay up there. Down in the South I feel I am a part of all that is going on. That means something to me."

To have been, and to be, a Southerner in all these years is the finest sort of luck. But I know from being with them that to be young Southerners is the most delightful, mystical and wonderful agony of all.

II

A Long Night in London

AT ABOUT 11 P.M., May 17, 1954, in the telephone booth of a small hotel near the Marble Arch, London, I learned that the United States Supreme Court unanimously had decreed racial segregation in the nation's public schools to be unconstitutional.

Having, on impulse, quit Manchester two days before to go to London to witness the triumphant return of Her Majesty Queen Elizabeth from a round-the-world tour, which demonstrated that though the empire was diminished the sun still did not set on it, I found the city crowded with others of like mind. An obscure hotel on a side street at last provided a room. It was, I learned some hours later, an inn frequented by refugees, mostly brooding Poles. Up one flight of stairs there was a small private club to which one could purchase membership for two shillings. Around midnight it was a wonderously unreal place to be. There was always a sad Pole who played Chopin's nocturnes at a shabby piano. Others sat, steeped in melancholy, beer and spirits, on stools before the small bistrolike bar. Still others silently played dominoes or talked moodily at the half dozen tables. There was nothing of a mazurka in them or the room. On first entry one had the uneasy feeling of having stepped into a set of some as-yet-unproduced play by the late Eugene O'Neill. On this evening, having gone there for a nightcap, one of the men on one of the stools raised his head and looked at me sadly, slowly turning his glass in his hands.

"You like Poland?" he asked.

"I like it fine," I said. "I liked it from the first time I heard Paderewski play the piano when I was a boy."

This story has no relevancy to the court's decision save that it was precisely at this moment of answer to the melancholy Pole that a young man from the desk came to the club and said I was wanted on the phone in the small lobby. Gene Patterson, then of the London desk of the United Press, was on the wire.

"We'd like some comment from you on the Supreme Court decision banning segregation on the basis of color," he said. "It was a unanimous decision."

I was tempted to go back and brood late and deep with the Poles. Instead I went to my bleak room, retired and lay long in the dark and in excited thinking and remembering.

It had been a long, wearying time on the way — that decision. It had not come precipitately, nor on little cat feet, like Carl Sandburg's fog. The Supreme Court for some years had been ringing the warning bell and blowing the heralding whistle. The Plessy *v.* Ferguson "separate but equal" decision had been handed down before our war with Spain. It involved a railroad transportation case but was given almost immediate application in schools and all other aspects of public life — save, of course, in the spending of hard-earned dimes and dollars for merchandise in retail stores. They could be spent on an integrated basis. Nor was there ever anything equal about the separateness. It was callously inferior and inadequate. And quite often it was so separate as to be invisible and never to be found — such as in parks, high schools, hospitals or justice. In the "separate but equal" formula a neat legalism had been found by a Supreme Court composed largely of corporate lawyers bemused by the racial problem which was troubling the great industrial surge of the late nineteenth century. If the court had any idea of responsibility for keeping a judicial eye on the effect of the ruling through a word to the lower courts, it never so indicated. There was never anywhere an effort to make the separateness equal.

It was almost as if the court and the nation had given a deep sigh of relief as the last word of the Plessy decision was read, and had then forgot all about it.

They had postponed it for other generations, and little attention was paid an eloquent, prophetic, indignant dissent by Associate Justice John M. Harlan.

By the time the nation had survived the depression-tossed seas of the 1930's, all but the never-knowing knew that Plessy was constitutionally old hat. In those years of national self-examination, the Negro had come to recognize himself as an essential ingredient of the intense political force which had been gathered together by the political genius of Franklin D. Roosevelt to win elections and provide legislative legs for the imaginative policies of the New Deal. In the middle and late thirties the great court itself gave plain indication it, too, was not of the same mind as the majority of associate justices who had written the Plessy decision. Harlan's dissent had, through the years, taken on more and more meaning. The hypocrisy and inequity (and, too often, the inhumanity) of the "separate but equal" law were a heavy weight on the nation's conscience. Two federal court decisions in the field of graduate study made it plain that the new path even then was being cleared.

But the Second World War came on. About ten years were to pass before the U. S. Supreme Court considered other cases and rendered decisions which plainly were notice that the separate-but-equal contention was no longer regarded as constitutionally sound.

Perhaps the greatest change was in the national mind. Well before the German and Japanese surrenders, millions of persons who never before had faced a decision about the problem of the Negro citizen knew it would not again be possible officially to have one sort of America for most citizens and a second America with less freedom, opportunity and justice for others.

Lying there in the darkened room in a corner of London, I knew that for many the decision had come like a thunderclap because almost none of those whose duty it was to cope with the effect of it had done any preparatory educating or planning. In the thoughts that came and went was memory of a column I had written a year before titled "One of These Days It Will Be Monday." It had to do with the fact that the Supreme Court customarily hands down decisions on Mondays, and that one day the school case would be one of them. It was then coming closer and closer — right down the middle of the big wide road of history. And almost nothing had been done to prepare the people for it. The column attracted only a few letters of abuse. For two years the more violent voices, including those of political leaders, had been proclaiming that the court would not dare reverse the ruling of 1896. Few heard those who were declaring that in the last half of the twentieth century the justices couldn't do anything else.

But there was no escaping the fact that even in the Deep South the politicians knew the truth. They had hoped against hope. But they knew. They had understood the real meanings of earlier decisions which had opened the graduate schools of law and medicine in universities in Texas, Oklahoma, and Arkansas to Negroes. That they fully realized what the courts meant was revealed by the galvanic action which followed. It was, in essence, a most expansive confession and privately they so admitted it to be.

About two years before the 1954 decree, the Deep South, with almost frantic urgency, began to do something about the much relied-on, much ignored Plessy decision. To the sound of hammer and saw, and to the Wagnerian bellow of oratory in their legislative halls in behalf of emergency bond issues, the South began to build modern schools for Negroes. Bond issues and building authorities mushroomed. It was an almost compulsive confession that the schools had not been equal and that there had been no previous will or intent to make them so. Privately, too, there was considerable self-accusation. "We should have done this years ago," they said. "Then maybe we could have prevented all these court cases."

Tremendous progress could be made, and was. But the gulf was too wide to bridge. And since there had never been equal facilities in schools, transportation, hospitalization, or public facilities in general, it was not possible for a sudden effort, however determined, to succeed. Yet the hurried activity went on.

Tempers wore thin in those days. It was difficult to make orations about the sacredness of the Constitution, to stand on the Plessy decision, and at the same time be confessing, by the accelerated construction of schools, that the Plessy provisions had been cynically ignored.

Millions were spent in the span of two years, and some magnificent schools were built to replace shacks or ancient, toiletless, brick and wooden buildings. This was progress. But while the Negro teachers, pupils and parents welcomed them, the shining new buildings were a reminder of long years of injustice and a rebuke to the leadership which had not ameliorated it. Everyone knew, and none better than the Negro, that the cases before the Supreme Court were the architects and builders of the new schools — not the political leaders or the legislatures.

No Southerner, knowing the path his people have come through these generations and what they have met with along the way, can condemn them wholly. He can be against their prejudices and he can disagree. He has contempt for the hypocrisy and the falsehoods. But knowing how, and across how many harsh years, the twig was bent, he feels a compassion even for those whose meanness and abuses he most detests.

I remember the late novelist Jimmy Street saying one night, as we talked of a Southern article he was writing, that those who truly love the South, love her as parents love a crippled child. They love her the more fiercely and defensively because they hate that which had crippled the child and which had, therefore, made her weaker and less capable of full participation in life than other children. This simple analogy explains much of "the South."

Lying there in the dark of the small hotel room in London, I could hear again the torrent of sweaty oratory to which I had listened across the years, all of it seeking to justify the past to the present. I could smile at some of the memories because one of the charms of the more preposterous Southern demagogues had been the utter irrelevancy of much of their shouting. It came to me also that almost without comment the professional Southerner had all but disappeared and that I had really not noted his going.

He was a pleasant fellow, or lady, who cultivated a drawl and emphasized good manners. These Southerners made really superior weekend guests in the twenties. In the roof gardens, and, later, the nightclubs, they could be very picturesque by covertly requesting the band to play "Dixie" and then giving the rebel yell when the gallopy swing of it began. At college they were more often viewed as charming, rather than bores. These professional Southerners passed with the depression, and it was a pity, really, because they worked very hard at learning the role they played. But, of a sudden, there was no more demand for it. The same thing was beginning to happen to the old stereotype of the Southern statesman.

It was during the period of depressed, desperate economic reality that the South's aura of "charm" and "quaintness" disappeared, never to return again. In their deep and secret heart all save the insensitive knew in those years a deeper sense of the wrongness of things. Only a few of these had ever heard of Plessy *v.* Ferguson, but they could see with a great and terrible starkness, as the economy crashed about them, that there was a vast separateness, but nothing was equal — not even the suffering caused by the depression. It could be seen, too, that we were all caught in it, white and colored, the haves and the have-nots.

When the collapse of the 1930's came, the cotton South was just emerging from the ruins wrought by the boll weevil of the 1919-1922 period. This had brought on a great crash of banks, the emptying of tenant and cropper cabins, the abandonment of land, the bankruptcy of thousands. In many counties in the Deep South the insurance and mortgage companies owned eighty per cent of the arable land by the time of the mid-twenties. Some of that land never went back to cotton. It reverted to pine trees and, coming today on old cotton terraces in the depths of pine lands, it is difficult to believe that once cotton grew there and hands called to the patient mules or sang to them through the long hot days of plowing and hoeing. I remember walking over pine-grown fields and hearing from the man who owned them how, in 1919, they had produced over a thousand bales of cotton and, in 1921, with the same seed and effort, less than two hundred.

Well before the stock-market crash of 1929 there were empty cabins in the land of cotton, their doors swinging drunkenly or fallen on the ground. Grass grew in the once clean-swept yards and weeds were high about the well. Before them men had cursed in bitterness and had wondered what in God's name a man could do, with things going from bad to worse. Before those fireplaces defeated families had decided to pack up and go — to Dee-troit, where there were jobs in the tire and automobile factories . . . to Chicago, where men could work in steel . . . to Pittsburgh, where the big mills were. Some went secretly by night, leaving their debts behind. Some signed with the labor recruiters by day. But something went with each of them — something silent and unseen. The South was never again to be, seem, or look the same.

This was in the twenties in Dixie.

The boll weevil and the depression, just about ten years apart at the peak of disaster, were a one-two punch in the economic solar plexus of the South.

It was a jarring blow, too, to something else. . . .

There had always been those who justified the inequities of the "separate but equal" legalism, so entirely honored in the breach, with a fine and honest paternalism, a genuine sense of *noblesse oblige*. Some who felt this were conscious of the sophistry. Others believed the *status quo* to be quite proper, but felt it imposed upon them and their code a strict duty to protect and "look after." There flowered in this relationship many real and enduring friendships, a mutual understanding of the separateness of things which was often touching in its deep sincerity. There were affection and compassion which were heartfelt and undenied.

More often than the white friend knew, the Negro would say, going back to his home and his family: "He knows it's wrong. He knows it's hard to be a nigger. I can feel his heart reaching out to me, wanting to say it. But he can't do anything about it except be my friend. And he's that. He'll take care of me if I'm sick, or my family. He'll take care of me and mine.

"If one of my boys gets in trouble he'll hire a lawyer and see the judge and get him out. He or his folks, if I pass on, will see I get a Christian burial. They will be at my funeral and will weep for me. They will stand and say I was a good man and that the Lord and His angels have welcomed me. They will speak of the goodness of God and the mercy of Jesus and all over the church my folks and friends will say 'Amen.' I'd do the same for him. He knows I will be there weeping in the church if he goes first. He knows he can call and I'll come. I know I can call and he'll come."

And what the Negro may never have known is how often the white man would turn away from the faithful tenant, or helper at the store, and shake his head, putting away the accusation which seemed always to come knocking, in those moments, at the door of his heart. Or how often that man went to the back pantry and poured himself a stiff drink and took it, saying in a half whisper, "Damn the first man to bring slaves here. Damn every man that ever enslaved another and did this thing to them and to me. Damn them all, and damn me for being soft about a thing that is too big for me. . . ."

There was this — and variations and degrees of it. But the depression began to winnow it out. Men had to tell their tenants, who had lived on the "place" for generations, there wouldn't be another crop. The boll weevil had come. The bank had failed. Some wept, some cursed. But they had to see their tenants pick up and go, hunting a job for hands that had never known anything save the handles of a plow or a hoe. After the depression and the New Deal there was not much left of the old paternalism or the old feelings. There was social security, and old-age pensions. The government. The government would do the "looking after." Something kind and compassionate died with *noblesse oblige.*

But before the weevil and depression, there always had been, too, the other side of the coin — cold-eyed, cruel, calculated, rapacious exploitation. And this was everywhere and there was no kindness or friendship in it. And no compassion. It was in the towns and cities, on the farms and plantations, in the old convict lease systems, in the turpentine and sawmill camps, at the commissary and general store. There was no humanity in it, but a wringing out of profit. It brutalized those of both races. It created hate and crime. It made semi-animals of white and colored. It corrupted and depressed. It worsened with the depression.

"No goddamned pencil and paper nigger can work on my place, coming to me to figure out what he has coming and what he owes. . . ." I heard a man say that once. His face was red and his eyes were evil. He knew he had cheated and swindled every man who had worked for him. It was hard for him to get hands, and when he had taken on this one who came to him to figure out the arrangements, he had cursed him off the place. He had done this out of meanness and guilt. He could do it because, even as old Booker T. Washington had said, to hold the Negro down in the ditch he had had to get down there himself.

"Make the mark-up high and the credit easy," I once heard an old man say, with a cackling laugh, as he sat in the small office of his general store. It was in a small cotton town, where the Negroes and the small white farmers came on Saturday afternoons to buy and to walk around the town and see the train and the buses come and go. He had robbed others and made himself wealthy, but he was chained to the wretched crossroads town and was as naked of any appreciation of sky or cloud, of flower or landscape, as were his account books. He, too, was brutalized, though he was a pillar in his church. He could take away a man's mule or his cow, his crop or his wagon, with never a twinge of remorse or regret.

"I don't have no damn trouble keeping hands on my place," he said, as I talked with him one day in deep south Georgia. "I treat 'em good. Nearly anything they want, they get . . . just so they sign. They talk about leaving and I say, 'You leave here without paying what you owe and I'll have the sheriff bring you back.' "

I remembered all these things that night in the London room, as old memories came back like waves.

Anyhow, I thought, it has come . . . a sort of second emancipation proclamation. And not merely for the Negro, but for the white man, too . . . maybe more for him than the Negro . . . and an emancipation for that intangible thing the orators call the American dream.

Henry Adams, and his father, old Charles Francis, came into the night's mixed train of thought. I imagined them waiting and walking and worrying in London while the Civil War was being fought out, with slavery as the oversimplified symbol of what the war was all about. They seemed very far back in the past, and yet, that night as I lay sleepless, London's news sources were alerted and excited by a new chapter out of the long aftermath of that conflict the Adamses, father and son, had watched at such a distance so long ago.

So, the incidents, recollections of people and old conversations, laughter, tears, joys, fears, sorrows, and excitements poured in and out of the mind like the changing color patterns of one of those kaleidoscopes which children hold to the eye and turn slowly with their hands.

Bilbo's face came to mind and I laughed out loud.

In 1940 Mississippi's Senator Theodore Bilbo, leader of the racist stereotypes even then dying out, had done me the honor of denouncing me for an editorial critical of his verbal excesses. He had referred to me as a limicolous person. I looked up the word and found it to refer to shore-dwelling birds. I assumed he meant I was throwing mud at him.

A short time later I was in Washington waiting outside the Senate Chamber for a member to whom I had sent in my card. As I waited Senator Bilbo came out. I walked up to him, and, smiling, introduced myself. He was a small man, who looked like the cartoons of him. He stepped back and half raised his hands.

"Senator," I said, "all I want to ask is where you learned the word."

He smiled back and said, "I learned it as a boy," and moved on.

Neither of us knew that even then he did not have long to live. He was the last of his kind. Other demagogues were to come, but they would never try to match Bilbo's crassness and insults. I laughed because it was so odd to have his intense little face peer in the windows of memory just before dawn in London, England. I almost wished for him to be still around so as to have heard his furious cursing of the court.

I remembered my own boyhood, and the stern Welsh-Scottish Calvinism of it, on a farm along the Tennessee River in the foothills of East Tennessee. A town called Soddy, a farm trading center turned into a small mining center by the discovery of coal, was ten miles away. Some of my family drove there once or twice a week for mail and supplies. It was there I first saw a train and a Negro. I was used to seeing miners about the steps of the general store and at the small station, their faces streaked black with coal dust and sweat. But this man was different. I was five or six years old then and I asked, somewhat in the words of Chad Buford in John Fox's mountain romance *The Little Shepherd of Kingdom Come*, "What's *that* man got on his face?"

That seemed incredibly long ago — that night in London.

We are all bent twigs — persons, states, regions, nations. And the South is much, and agonizingly, bent. Once slavery was near to abandonment because it was economically unsound. But Eli Whitney came. Then there was a span of years from the 1820's well into the 1830's, which heard mounting criticism of slavery as a moral and social wrong. In almost every state, particularly in Virginia, Georgia, and North Carolina, the attack on the "peculiar institution" had been strong and consistent. There were a few congressmen who spoke up for an end to it. Few newspapers of any standing then defended the principle of it. The Southern scholars, which was the word of that time most comparable with "liberals" today, included many voices raised against the enslavement of man.

Then had come the cry from the planters, "Let us and our property alone." They organized. They raised money. They lobbied. They hired writers to produce pamphlets. Richard Furman, South Carolina's Baptist leader of the 1820's, had the state church convention address the governor declaring the holding of slaves to be sustained by Holy Writ. He was one of the first major voices to so speak.

The twig began to be bent back again . . . stronger and stronger, farther and farther.

"It's my property," they said, clutching their slaves to their breast, "it's mine. The Constitution guarantees it to me and you can't take away my property from me."

Legislatures were goaded into action. Business and land owners cried out that to end slavery would bankrupt the state and its business and agriculture. More and more of the clergy found themselves forced to the rationalization that God himself had ordained slavery for some, freedom for others. Those scholars and clerics who did not join the chorus, departed or maintained an unhappy, consuming silence.

There was a hard core of men and women who sought to stem this tide of extremist reaction. They were to oppose fanaticism and the theory of secession until the first guns were fired at Fort Sumter.

Sleep came when, in the early hours of the morning, I was thinking of how odd it was that in 1954 the Ku Klux preachers, the states' rights fanatics and the extremists, confronted with the issue of full citizenship for all Americans, were repeating the words of their counterparts from about 1830 until Edmund Ruffin pulled the lanyard of the first gun to fire at the fort in Charleston's harbor.

III

My Parents

I HAVE SAID that there are many Souths, and I have briefly reviewed the changes that came with gathering speed after the Second World War and were given final acceleration by the momentous Supreme Court decision of May 17, 1954. Now I want to turn the clock back to the South of which I have my first impressions.

One of my earliest pictures of my parents was when I was about four years old, before we had moved from the old farm on the Tennessee River. My mother, dark-haired and gay, my father and I were in a small skiff. I remember the yellow water and some new, hand-riven oak shingles that floated by, a few of which my father took from the river. My memory is of the deeper, contrasting shades of the wet, golden oak shingles, and I have liked that color ever since. A cloudburst the night before had washed a great stack of lumber and shingles into a creek which flowed into the river some miles above our place. I recall, very vividly, the sight of the golden yellow parallelograms in the muddy red of the Tennessee River, the youthful faces of my parents and my father reaching out and catching two or three shingles as they floated by.

Another early memory is of my mother, whose face always reflected her moods, my grandmother and an aunt weeping over a letter which brought news of the death of a young uncle of mine in the Philippines in the so-called insurrection that followed the Spanish-American War. I must have been a trial to them, because I remember asking three or four times to be told the strange place where he had been killed — and then of going about the house saying it out loud, "Philippines . . . Philippines . . . Philippines."

There was a fairy ring out in the pasture before our house. A child's memory says it was a perfect circle, but whether perfect or not, it was a circle and a delight. All about it the grass grew tall. But inside the magic ring the growth was short. A boy could lie there on his back, himself hidden from sight. All he could see would be the sky and clouds, and the waving edges of the tall grasses and weeds about him. A fairy ring was a fine place to dream.

There was also the Watkins Products man who came in a sort of gypsy van cart. From him we farm people bought spices and flavors, liniments and remedies. My grandmother always got from him a supply of maple-sugar syrup. Saturday night was a time for either flannel cakes, or fried mush. Maple syrup was my first sweet taste thrill. Molasses and sorghum, which were produced on our farm, were a poor second choice.

I recall, too, the buggy rides to Sunday services, the steamboats stopping at the landing on our place, the Bible readings each night, the coming of the threshing machine, the wide fields of green corn, the big barn and the pond in which ducks and geese reveled. (We grew no cotton in East Tennessee.) Uninterrupted memory began with our removal to Chattanooga when I was about six and a half years old. This may be because the events and experiences from that time on were new, while the ones left behind were familiar. But that is when it began, with the talk of moving, the excitement of it, and our trip down by train with our small supply of furniture following in two farm wagons.

The reasons for moving were commonplace. My paternal grandfather had died some years before. The six-hundred-acre farm was left to the mother and children. Had it been evenly divided, there would not really have been enough for anyone, so it was decided that the sisters would stay on until they married and then the farm would be sold. My father and a brother of about the same age sold their shares to brothers and moved to Chattanooga. Both wanted to be near schools. Many Southerners of that generation, which had so little chance for schooling, had almost an obsession about educating their children. The economic pressure grew worse a few years after Grandfather's death. Father and the others who left the farms in that time were, in a sense, like many of their counterparts of today who are pushed off the land by the coming of machines. He was not trained for urban employment. But before moving, he had found a job with a small heating and roofing company. He became a good salesman, winning an occasional prize from the manufacturers of heaters, and gave all his working life to the company.

Ours was a happy family, largely because of the spirit and faith of my mother. There was never any extra money to spare, but we were quickly established at the Central Presbyterian Church, and made friends in Chattanooga. There were relatives about, on both sides of the family, and I recall no loneliness growing out of lack of neighbors or friends. There was, of course, that inexplicable plague of personal loneliness. All my life I have had recurring moods of sadness growing out of it. My mother used to say it was the Welsh strain in me. But I never then, nor thereafter, was aware of any feelings of hostility or resentment toward either of my parents. It never occurred to me to wonder whether I was loved or wanted. I was. So were my three sisters. And we all knew it.

It is really remarkable that my sisters and I got along so well. I, as an only son and the eldest of the children, was the favorite. My mother tried valiantly not to show it, but she did in little ways which the girls recognized and teased her about, to her confusion. I think it was because there had been a son born two years before me, who had lived only a few weeks.

My mother, I was told, sorrowed deeply. I suppose some of the attention shown me was because of memories of that infant son, her first child and first intense grief.

One spring I came home from the school with a burning fever. The doctor sadly informed my mother it was scarlet fever. Those were the days when scarlet fever, diphtheria, and measles brought out a man from the city health department who tacked up quarantine signs. One soon appeared on our house with *Scarlet Fever* printed on it in large red letters. My father was permitted to go to work, and my mother could go out in emergencies. We children were under house confinement. The inevitable happened. About the time I was recovering, my eldest sister came down with it, and a week later the second sister was ill. It was seven long weeks before the quarantine was lifted.

In those weeks I learned to play the game of jacks and became quite expert. This innocent game, greatly fancied by my sisters and their friends, is still familiar today. It involved a small rubber ball and an uneven number of jacks, seven, nine or for the experts, eleven. The jacks were small, triangular shaped bits of metal. The ball was bounced and one had to "pick up jacks" between each bounce.

I helped Mother enthusiastically with the cooking, learning how to make and bake a cake and biscuits, to concoct soups and do a fairly good job of general cooking. The enthusiasm for this stayed with me for years, and I still like, now and then, to cook a meal.

It was not possible to go to the library for books. In desperation I learned to knit and crochet, my mother and eldest sister Bessie instructing. Before the quarantine was lifted I had knitted several inches on a scarf. The three of us managed to finish out the weeks without any serious rows, and I don't recall that we were weary of one another, although we must have been.

In family talks, my mother recalls the weeks of scarlet fever as a time of grave concern. My sister Bessie and I were seriously ill, and each had several days of delirium. "I never let anyone see me," my mother said, "but several times each day during the crisis period, I would go from the bedroom to the kitchen, close the door and have a cry and then pray. It was such an alone feeling to be shut off from all the world by that dreadful quarantine. I appreciate all the advances in science, but to me the most wonderful thing is the conquering of scarlet fever, typhoid, tuberculosis and diphtheria."

My mother had, as a child and a young girl, encountered worry and a grief which she still could not quite understand; yet she never showed me the face of discouragement. Her mother had married, against the family wishes, one of those restless, charming men, who could never find a place which would hold him. Anderson Skillern was a newspaperman with a talent, as I was to learn years later, for writing in the flowery journalistic style of the day. By all accounts, he was a man of laughter, with a personality which all found winning. He married Nancy Isabel Clift and a few years later, when the restlessness was on him, took her away to Texas, where there was, he said, greater opportunity. In those days there was a vast migration to Texas. Tennesseans felt perhaps a stronger urge to go because of Sam Houston and Davy Crockett.

My great-great-uncle, Colonel William Clift, who had come from Wales with some of his family and sent back for others later, had become a prosperous developer of coal mines and farmlands. He prophesied the marriage would come to no good end and he was right. Anderson Skillern left his wife and two children — my mother Mary Lou and my Uncle Fred — in Bell County, Texas, with a promise to send for them. But he disappeared without trace, and so Colonel Clift went to Texas and brought the abandoned family back to Tennessee and home to Soddy, some twenty miles north of Chattanooga, on the Cumberland chain of the Appalachians where he had recently opened a coal mine. He was, legend has it, a decent, generous man and never once said to my grandmother, "I told you so." So my mother and her mother lived on with relatives who were all so glad to have them there was never any doubt of their welcome. But the hurt was there. I never knew this grandmother, for she died when my mother was a young woman. No word ever came from Anderson Skillern, save an unconfirmed rumor he had died of fever.

None of the Clifts mentioned him to me until my Aunt Molly Clift Walker did so in 1948. She was then ninety years old. Her memory was such that the Library of Congress sent a man down to record her singing some of the old Welsh and English ballads that one could hear from old people years ago in the Appalachians. She lived to be ninety-two, worked her garden every summer, and was lively as a cricket all winter. On the occasion of this visit with her, she abruptly broke off talk about her garden and the questions about the family, and said:

"You knew your grandfather was a newspaper writer?"

I nodded, too surprised to answer.

"Would you like to hear something he wrote?" she asked.

I said I certainly would, and could I go fetch it for her from wherever she kept the copy or clipping.

"You can't," she said, "because it's in my head. I memorized it about the time he married your mother. It's called 'A Welcome to Spring,' " she said.

With that she recited a flowery tribute to spring such as editors write in our time when they are stirred by the first robins, the new buds, or maybe an early blossoming of forsythia, though, I must admit, the modern form is more subdued.

It ran to about two hundred words, and I had her say it again. I was of a mind to take it down, but on second hearing, I decided not. It was meaningless and brought no understand-

ing of the man who had written it. I had never heard a word
of criticism or malice from my mother. There was a resentment I could never really bring to focus; so it was not possible
to become emotionally upset about a grandfather I'd never
seen and about whom I had heard so little.

"He was not a bad man," said my Aunt Molly. "Weak and
selfish, I guess, but his trouble was that the horizon always
lured him on. I always meant to tell you this, and now, at
ninety, I decided not to wait."

My mother was glad when we moved to Chattanooga. She
wanted a place that was her own. She was popular and liked
by all the kin, but she wanted my father out on his own. So,
quietly, she encouraged him in his talk of it, without ever asking him to move, so that when he did, he thought the decision
wholly his own.

It was my father who early encouraged me to read. Books
were few at the farm. Most of them were religious in theme,
including collections of Presbyterian sermons. I could read
well before I entered the first grade, an event delayed by an
illness that came on me just after we moved. My father had
taught me. It was he who, on reading a life of Benjamin
Franklin, lent to him by one of the teachers who came to in-
struct all grades at the four-month school session each winter,
promptly informed one and all that he had changed his
name from Benjamin Wallace to Benjamin Franklin McGill.
He did, too. And in time, it seems, everyone forgot it had ever
been anything else. He was a hard-working, kindly man. There
was a streak of stubbornness in him, as well as brooding, but
these moods were always short. He was pretty much the Calvinist Puritan and was inclined to be dogmatic in his views.
If he ever took a drink I never knew it, and if he ever used
profanity I never heard it. Yet I never had even a light spank-
ing from him, though I deserved many.

In an old family Bible it is written that my father's great-

great-grandfather had been born on one of two sailing vessels which left North Ireland in 1753. The ships were separated in a storm and never sighted one another again. Most of those with whom my father's people were associated moved on down from Philadelphia into North Carolina, from whose territory Tennessee later was to be created. They took up land along the Tennessee River and began to produce farmers, Presbyterian preachers and an occasional teacher.

After the move to Chattanooga we placed our letter with the Central Presbyterian Church. The pastor, Dr. Thomas H. McCallie, had two brothers, James and Spencer, who were headmasters of McCallie Preparatory School, on nearby Missionary Ridge. The McCallies all attended the Central Church. They took an interest in me, and my father in them and in the school. He later sent me there, borrowing the money for my tuition each year, and somehow managing to pay it back.

I never knew of my father's dreams, hopes and disappointments. I was, I guess, too much occupied with my own, though I believe that children generally and understandably do not give much mind to parental hopes and ambitions. At about twelve years I was convinced that at the rather elderly age of twenty-one I would, of course, be settled down at whatever I was to do.

When I did learn of at least one of my father's defeated dreams, it was a sad thing. He died when he was seventy-two after two successive attacks of double pneumonia. I was there to see him before he sank into a long coma. My Aunt Gertrude and I were with him in the last long watch. She had married my Uncle Paul, the youngest of the brothers, and is, like my mother, one of those great rocks in a weary land.

The day after the funeral, at my mother's request, I went through a large, beautiful old wooden chest which some cabinetmaker friend had given my father thirty-odd years before. In it, along with other things he had put there, including his watch, which was for me, were two old copies of

Blackstone's *Commentaries* on the law. I opened them and there on the flyleaf of each was my father's signature, obviously written many years before. I took them to my mother.

"What about these?"

"Your father bought them with the first money he earned," she said, "long before we were married. His great boyhood dream was to be a lawyer. He told me he had read them there at the farm, but it was no use. One had to be in a lawyer's office for some instruction. He brought them to Chattanooga and I tried to persuade him to find some attorney who would give him some help, but he shook his head and put them away. He would not discuss them again."

We both wept.

Chattanooga was a good place for a boy to grow up in. It lies in the foothills of East Tennessee and is not, and never was, a Southern city of the fly-caught-in-amber sort. The river and the railroads and industry early made it an industrial and distribution center. The city is literally surrounded by mountains and ridges and all of them are crowned with history. It begins with the Indians and the long rifles of John Sevier's time and with the flatboats coming into it from the Ohio.

There was history in the very names of these ranges — Signal Mountain, Lookout Mountain, Missionary Ridge.

The city is located in a spectacular, beautiful, unique and abrupt conjunction of mountains and deep valleys where the Tennessee cut its winding path in the early geologic ages.

There were stories to hear and read — about Indians and the Civil War. There were old men and women who remembered the battles, the all-day roar of cannon, the wagonloads of wounded coming into the city.

General Braxton Bragg, a timorous man at best, and to Tennesseans who had ridden with Nathan Bedford Forrest an incompetent and a coward, was uneasy there in that mountain-girded city in command of Confederate forces in the autumn of 1863.

"It is said to be easy to defend a mountainous country," Braxton Bragg said to General D. H. Hill, "but mountains hide your foe from you, while they are full of gaps through which he can pounce on you. A mountain is like the wall of a house that is full of rat holes."

The anxious general paused, as General Hill remembered it, and then said, pointing toward Walden's Ridge, "Who can tell what lies hidden behind that wall?"

What even then was behind that wall was General W. S. Rosecrans and an army moving in to drive General Bragg from Chattanooga on September 9.

There followed the tremendous battle of Chickamauga, just south of Chattanooga. The widespread force fought for two days through woods, small fields and clearings. It was short-range work with cannon, hand-to-hand fighting and many bloody charges.

"Never in any battle I had witnessed," wrote Charles A. Dana, Assistant Secretary of War, who was on the field, "was there such a discharge of cannon and musketry."

Here George Thomas held on to become the Union's "Rock of Chickamauga." Half the Union army had fled in a rout into Chattanooga. In the night Thomas led his men there.

At dawn "old Bedford and his Critter Company" were atop Missionary Ridge looking into Chattanooga. He could see the chaos of the Federal retreat. He sent back a note suggesting the army press forward as rapidly as possible.

He held the ridge all day. Nothing happened. As dusk fell and "the day was lost," Forrest said bitterly, "What does he fight battles for?"

Nearly sixteen thousand Confederates were dead or wounded. More than eleven thousand Union troops were casualties and over five thousand were captured. Infuriated,

General Forrest went to General Bragg's tent and stuck a lean left forefinger in his commander's face as he tongue-lashed him for cowardice, pettiness, and rascality. There too, came Confederate President Jefferson Davis to interview the higher command. In the presence of General Bragg the four active commanders present, James Longstreet, D. H. Hill, Simon Bolivar Buckner, and Frank Cheatham, said they believed their commander's usefulness lay elsewhere.

Forrest refused to serve further under Bragg. He was sent to Mississippi — without any army. He went — and created one.

To Chattanooga came Ulysses S. Grant, on crutches from a fall at New Orleans. William Tecumseh Sherman came. In November the massive Union push began.

Bragg retreated to Dalton, Georgia.

It would be spring before General Sherman would say "Forward" and drive that army, then under the skillful command of Joe Johnston, on to Atlanta.

A boy in Chattanooga could go to Orchard Knob and stand where Grant was on November 25, at the center of his long line. He could look to the right, as Grant did, and see Lookout Mountain captured; watch Thomas's men keep going up Missionary Ridge when the enemy broke before them, rather than halt where ordered by the battle plan; see Sherman's men held by Confederate gunners who, unable to deflect the barrels of their cannon low enough, lit the fuses and rolled the shells down the ridge.

I lived in history. On Saturdays and Sundays boys in our neighborhood formed groups to find Minié balls, pieces of shells (sometimes whole ones), rusted pieces of bayonets, and an occasional belt buckle washed clean by rain.

We fished for perch, trout and channel cat in Chickamauga Creek, shivering a bit as we recalled stories of how once it had been choked with bodies and had run red with blood.

We rode the St. Elmo trolley out to Lookout Mountain and

climbed about the steep cliffs where Joe Hooker's men had won the battle above the clouds.

When I was about ten years old, a family moved near us in which there was a grandfather who had ridden with Forrest. I hung on his words. He was a lonely old man whose stories had begun to bore his family. But not me. He and I roamed Missionary Ridge and once went to Chickamauga. There he showed me where Forrest and his men had fought as dismounted troops — from tree to tree, like Indians. We went, too, to where Forrest's men had made two gallant, effective charges.

Once I overheard his daughter say to my mother, "They are like two children together." I puzzled over that then, because Old Man Bean certainly was no boy.

I soaked up Civil War history. It was all around me, in monuments, memorials, markers and old veterans. It was biased history, but I heard it from both sides and this more or less evened it out. I could never get enough of it. My family had the usual history of Tennesseans — some in both armies. Generals Robert E. Lee, Stonewall Jackson, Nathan B. Forrest, U. S. Grant and "Old Cump" Sherman were early in my pantheon of military gods — but never Braxton Bragg or Jefferson Davis.

There were days when we went to the fields about the old mounds at nearby Citico, hard by the river, to hunt, and find, Indian arrow points and pieces of pottery. My father took much interest in these findings and once came home in triumph with a whole Indian clay pot, gashed only slightly on one side where a plow point had struck it, to add to my collection (I still have it). One of the men at the shop had uncovered it in plowing his spring garden, and my father bought it for a half dollar.

Chattanooga took, even then, a pride in its school system. I went first to the Fourth District School, a large, ugly, square two-story brick building with gravel-covered playgrounds.

I early learned about politics and came to know about the two-party system. In election years, local and national, there were furious juvenile arguments, in which we sought to repeat what we had heard at home, between the Republicans and Democrats. Often there were fights. Tennessee had sent about as many men to the Union Army as to the Confederate, and while the Democrats usually carried the state, there were exceptions. East Tennessee was Republican country and my father was of that political faith. My mother, in those pre-women's suffrage years, said she would be a Democrat if she could vote. It pleased me then that she wanted to vote.

One year we had a new principal, Professor John Counts. Early in the year, he appeared and announced that for every class from the fifth grade on, the final period on each Thursday afternoon would be given to reading. Children ought to read more, he said. It could be, he announced, exciting. So, then and there, he read us a chapter from *She*, by H. Rider Haggard. It was exciting, as millions of readers already knew. I was then in the fifth grade, so our class had three years of this. Under his stimulation we read *Treasure Island* and a number of the Henty books. Now and then Professor Counts would drop by to read us a page or so, or listen to one of us — or he would ask questions. Looking back, I cannot be sure that all of us enjoyed the reading. But there were enough of us who did to create excitement. And if there were some who didn't care for it, we did not notice. The Henty books gave me my first interest in foreign history and I shall always remember them, and Professor Counts, with gratitude. The effect of his plan was marked, although I do not know if the school authorities so recognized it. They did not use the idea at any other school. But three years later, when that fifth grade graduated as the eighth, we were pointed out as an exceptional class. Three or four of us were trying to write stories and poems.

At home, my mother was the guiding force, but so quietly

that it was years before I realized it. It was she who soon persuaded my father to buy a home, a very modest one, from which a Presbyterian preacher was moving to accept a call from a nearby town. She had a remarkable ability to stretch the salary which my father made. It was meager in those early years, and at no time large, but she made it do. She sewed, cooked, and kept the house neat. She encouraged and inspired. She was always a believing person. She had a personal faith which sustained her and others. For some years she laundered all our clothes, and somehow it seemed a natural thing for me to help her.

Soon after we had been settled in the new home, she learned that a lady one street over from us gave piano lessons. I really do not know how she possibly managed it, but one day a piano appeared in our front parlor and I was told that lessons had been arranged. For two years I went dutifully for one lesson a week, with my music properly in a leather roll, and all the neighborhood boys making fun. I was the only boy in the class. There were a dozen or more little girls. The biannual recitals were agony. There would be all the starched and ribbon-sashed girls and I — the lone male — sitting straight and still in the two rows of chairs. The teacher, a kindly lady named Mrs. Thomas D. Buford, would have us play our recital pieces in turn. My mother was very proud and derived, I think, great pleasure from my four appearances. But the pressure of play, of Civil War Minié ball hunts, of neighborhood jeers, and a mysterious illness which frequently recurred, with fever and nausea, and kept me thin and weak, were too much. I am sure my mother was pained, but she allowed me to stop the lessons, saying, quietly, I would likely regret it later on. I did.

My mother had been, according to my Aunt Molly, a popular girl, a fine square-dancer and a person of sweet spirit and a zest for life. She is, as I write, eighty-four, and likes to make journeys by aircraft. She reminds my son, who in his teens is among other things a guitar player and a square-dancer, to be sure and invite her to the next dance. I have always been glad that I can remember her as a pretty young woman in the small boat in the river with my father and me.

IV

Ralph Waldo

I was once introduced to an audience in St. Paul, Minnesota, by Pierce Butler, a grand person, a lawyer of considerable renown, and a Republican who had been one of the eager amateurs in the Wendell Willkie presidential campaign in 1940.

"I don't know how this Tennessee-born Georgia editor comes out of the South with the New England transcendentalist name of Ralph Waldo Emerson," he said. "But he does."

When I was a child I knew the name was different. Indeed, one of the earliest memories I have is a consciousness of its uniqueness in our somewhat isolated Calvinist farm community located some twenty miles upriver from Chattanooga. People in our village almost all had first names from the Bible — James, John, Abel, Joseph, Isaac, Matthew, Mark, Luke, Mary, Ruth, Martha. There was, of course, an occasional William to commemorate William of Orange. But the Book was the proper source of names.

My father had only the inadequate schooling offered in those foothills of the Appalachians, but he had a liking for books and a grief because he had not been able to have more education. Old Dr. Dick Walker, who served the community from his home and office in Soddy, and who was related to many of its members, was greatly beloved. His son Richard, graduate of the University of Tennessee Medical School, had begun practice a year before. Young Walker brought medicine and literature to the community. He was, by accounts, a gay and gallant young man with a gift for conversation and reading aloud. And Ralph Waldo Emerson was his favorite writer and philosopher. Had it not been for his father, things might have gone unpleasantly for him. Some of the elders, and the stern bluestocking Presbyterian preachers who came there for services, denounced Emerson's Unitarianism and transcendentalism as heresy and worse. All the faithful were warned against the seductions of Emerson and his New England associates. But young Dick Walker was a rebel and made a point of bringing Emerson into discussions.

My father saw in the young college graduate all he had wanted to be. They became close friends. Young Walker lent his books and there was, as I was to hear so often in the years ahead, a mighty shaking of heads and special prayers. But my father persisted. When the time came for my being born, old Dr. Walker was sick and sent his son. Both my parents were pleased. He was about their age and they loved him.

My father was so warmed by the whole prospect that he gave over responsibility for my name if, confidently expected, a boy arrived.

"Splendid," said Dr. Walker. "We'll call him Ralph Waldo Emerson."

They say that for months the minister found ways to avoid christening me with so dangerous a name. But at last, with obvious reluctance, it was done. Somehow along the way the Waldo was dropped, by something like mutual consent. But I can remember the Pauls, Johns and Davids shouting, "Waldo! Waldo!" at me. So it was that, quite early, I knew I had a meaningful name.

My own passion for books did not have an opportunity to develop until the family left the farm for Chattanooga and sent me to public school. I could not bear not sharing the wonder of books and developed the habit of following parents or guests about, reading aloud to them. My Aunt Grace became my very favorite relative because she never wearied of hearing me read the pages I was so sure were too good to keep from others.

Chattanooga was, after our farm community, a fabulous, magic place. All of it seemed to challenge me. I was a thin, scrawny youth, but I tried hard to play baseball and football with the sandlot teams which we formed in the absence of any organized sports in the elementary school. Yet it was the Carnegie Library that drew me most strongly. In those early summers I would ride my bike two miles every morning to check out a new book. I read so much that in the second summer in Chattanooga it was necessary to send me back to the farm upriver to stay with my grandmother. I was "not strong," as the saying went, and the doctor prescribed more out-of-doors. In the succeeding summers I managed to read books found on the farmhouse shelves, mostly on religious subjects, and learned to pitch hay and wheat, and handle a double-shovel plow in the job of "plowing around" corn. I can yet remember the mystery of being lost in the long rows of corn, the stalks taller than I.

They were long, lazy summers, and without any notice of it from me, my health came slowly back. Now and then I would be sent three miles to the gristmill, the half-filled sack of shelled corn balanced across a fat old plow horse's withers. The dirt road wound through forests, and I imagined myself an early settler with Indians lurking in the dark depths of trees. There was a general store close by the mill. Sometimes I had business there. Two or three times my Aunt Grace or my grandmother would entrust me, once safely on the horse, with a basket of eggs to be swapped, as we called it, for Arbuckle's coffee, thread or needles and pins. Or, if I had no eggs, I would go there anyhow, since usually there would be one or two persons ahead of me at the mill. The store smelled of calico, in bolts on the shelves; of kerosene; of the big wheel of yellow cheese from which generous wedges were cut, costing five cents each; of new shoe leather and, most wonderful of all, of bananas. Sometimes I went with an uncle and learned to feel very grown-up sitting on the store steps with other farmers, eating Maine sardines, packed in cottonseed oil, fishing them from the can with the blade of a pocketknife.

The mill, too, was good. There was mystery in holding one's hand under the meal falling from the grinding stones, feeling it warm to the touch, and smelling the released nutty smell one somehow never imagined was locked in the grains. And there was wonder, too, in climbing to where the water spilled on the wheel from the swift-flowing race and feeling the hypnotic spell of the slow turning of it as the compartments filled and spilled with an even, unaltered rhythm.

My first two summer trips to the old home place were made on the steamboat *Joe Wheeler*. It was named for the Confederate cavalry commander who had devoted much of his postwar career to conciliation between the North and the South. The *Joe Wheeler* then plied the long river winter and summer. The steamer left the wharf at Chattanooga in late afternoon and did not make the landing at our farm place until well after dark. Of all the journeys I've made, none had the flavor of those on the *Joe Wheeler*. A boy's imagination flavored them, but I can yet remember with etched clarity the shouts and cries, the bellowing whistle and the goodbye calls, as we moved out into the wide stream and the huge paddles began to push us upward against the current.

The roustabouts stretched out to rest or sleep on the high-piled sacks of corn and wheat. The night came on and the boat's searchlight swept the river as the mate moved it, picking out the channel to watch for floating logs and landmarks along the banks.

Supper was excitement. The heavy bowls of sugar and the pitchers of syrup shook with the vibration of the straining engines. There were heavy platters of thick-sliced country ham with red gravy, and of fried, tough round steak. There were bowls of stewed corn, string beans, boiled potatoes, and huge plates of soda biscuits and square-cut pieces of cornbread. There were always fresh round "pounds" of butter, soon gashed and reduced by the reaching knives. Strong coffee was poured from graniteware coffee pots into heavy, handleless cups. And always everything shook with the laboring of the wide paddle wheel as the heavy-loaded boat moved upstream.

I remember standing a long time watching it as the churned yellow water frothed and foamed about it. There was a large acetylene light above it, and one could see the silt-stained water pour off the strong, many-bolted oak paddles, and the water boil a creamy white in the wake.

The landings were drama to a watching boy. Bells would ring. The boat would edge toward a cleared spot on the bank where men waited with lanterns. The boat's searchlights would focus on it, bringing the shadowy figures to life as men and women with expectant faces. The paddle wheel would still slowly move. There would be more bells, shouts from the pilot-captain, and the curses of the mates. Ropes would be flung and caught. And as the bow of the cumbersome boat touched the bank, the gangplank would be run out, deck hands would leap ashore, and the *Joe Wheeler* would be secured.

Then, hied on by the cursing mates, the Negro deck hands would spring into action. Heavy barrels would be rolled ashore, sacks of flour and grain toted, and other freight laboriously inched ashore with pinch bars. Passengers, cords of wood, crates of chickens, and other crated things would come aboard. Messages were shouted to the captain to take to men at other landings upriver. Then came the leaving, the bells in the engine room, the churning of the wheel, as the *Joe Wheeler* backed into the stream.

At our landing there would be some of the family among those waiting and as the boat moved in I could hear them calling to me. We would always wait until the gangplank was in, and the *Joe Wheeler* moved out, her whistle hoarse on the river, her lights and the sparks from her stack making her seem like a majestic, beautiful thing as she moved out of sight around a bend, leaving the water still stirring and lapping against the eroded banks, and the dark hills still echoing with the hoarse bellow of her steam whistle.

We went from the farm to Soddy by horse and buggy once or twice a week. In the summers when I was nine or ten years old, I was taken along by my grandmother on her shopping trips, when she would tell me tales of the early days and of her mother, who "had the Gaelic," and of how some big pewter platters brought from the old country had been lost in a fire that had burned the original farmhouse. I liked these trips, but best of all were those on Saturdays. The small, coal-dust-dingy town was crowded with farm people on Saturdays. Everyone waited for the local train which came up from Chattanooga with the mail at about 7 P.M. There were coke ovens across the tracks. The mountain range rose close behind them. As night came on the red flare of the ovens was frightening to a small boy reared on stories and sermons of John Calvin's everlasting hell with its lakes of fire.

Was hell like that, I wondered. How awful it would be to be thrust into flame much hotter than that which burned with such a red-and-white heat in the ovens across the tracks from where we waited. They had a gassy smell and surely that was the way hell smelled. Every Saturday night I resolved anew to be good.

The Soddy mine drew on the young farmers in the winter when there was little work that could be done at home. This was especially true in years of poor crops. The pay was scant and the danger ever-present. There were few safety standards in those days. A man who was hurt received no compensation and the families of those who were killed had no recourse to law. Some perished in falls of slate and coal. Others died because they were not skilled in handling the blasting powder used to dislodge coal.

One winter my father tried working in the mines. I can remember his coming in at night, his face and hands still stained with the black dust. There had been a bad year for corn and wheat. And, with a new baby, there was need for cash. My mother stopped him before spring came. There was too much torture in the waiting.

Years later I interviewed John L. Lewis in the period when his United Mine Workers were powerful and influential. I described my boyhood memories of Soddy, the coke ovens, and the mines, and he went on to tell me what I had long suspected — that the Soddy mines had been, from the miner's viewpoint, one of the worst of employers. It was so bad, he said, that local No. 1 of the U. M. W. had been formed there.

Rainy days were fine for talk, as were the long, lazy Sunday afternoons. And, of course, in those days there was much talk of the Civil War. My grandfathers took opposite sides in that bloody dispute, my mother's people going with the Confederacy, and my father's with the Union. Legend has it, as I heard it from my grandmother, that there had been a McGill at King's Mountain. It may be. There are enough McGills in that area to have a reunion each year. Whatever the validity of the legend, it is true that for most of the mountain men the Union and the flag were revered. I recall hearing a schoolteacher quote Andrew Jackson's toast, "The Union — it must be preserved."

East Tennessee had been strongly Union, and nowhere were there more savage feuds. Bushwhackers were lawless and cruel; homes and barns were burned by both Confederate and Union bands. In our community there were old soldiers from both armies and I drank in their stories. I heard guerrilla, or bushwhacker, stories to curl the hair. I learned, too, to think upon Robert E. Lee, Nathan Bedford Forrest, Joe Johnston and Stonewall Jackson with reverence and awe, but to have a great distaste for Jefferson Davis and Braxton Bragg. Since I liked all the old men, I also acquired early a high respect and admiration for U. S. Grant, "Cump" Sherman and Old Abe Lincoln. I do not recall ever hearing the latter referred to save as "Old Abe."

East Tennessee had never been a slave section and from these veterans, Unionists and Confederates alike, I early acquired a poor opinion of slaveholding people. In the plantation regions the preachers had rationalized slavery as Christian and ordained by God himself. But they did not do so in my part of the country. I never heard a defense of slavery even from men who had worn the gray.

From the elementary school in Chattanooga I moved up to the McCallie Preparatory School where I managed to make the football squad, was accepted for the drama and literary clubs, but was hastily removed from among the glee club hopefuls after my first audition. I was like an untrained bird dog puppy, running happily about scaring up coveys. For me, McCallie, on the slopes of Missionary Ridge, was the equivalent of stout Cortez's peak in Darien. I remember no frustrations in all the four pleasant years, save in Dr. James Park McCallie's math classes.

In our school plays and literary club discussions we enlisted the cooperation of the young ladies from the downtown girls preparatory school.

One of the GPS girls was Rebecca Mathis. Through her a new sort of world opened up for one but lately come from an upriver farm. For all my enthusiasm, I was painfully shy. The Mathis family saw this, and when I came calling on their daughter, which was as often as I could, they took me in and made me welcome. Thereby was I introduced to music, paintings, books and a culture older than mine. More, even than that, I was a part of conversations about issues, international and domestic. They listened to me and did not smile at my naïveté or the immaturity of my conclusions. The Mathis family gave me something I would not have found anywhere else in Chattanooga — an awareness of international events and of forces which were involved in them. Well before the First World War was declared I knew it might come. They were a very real inspiration to me, broadening the horizons of my mind and making me see and understand beyond the provincialism of Chattanooga.

Adolph Mathis, an orphan boy, had been brought to America at the age of twelve by an aunt and uncle from Königsberg, Germany, home of the famed philosopher Kant. His was an American story in the Horatio Alger tradition. His wife, Hanna Simpson Mathis, had been born in Chattanooga. Her father, Joseph Simpson, had fought there with U. S. Grant's troops in the capture of the city. He liked the city and when the war ended he brought his younger brothers there and went into business. Their forebears had come originally from Bohemia, but had spent a generation in England before coming to the United States in 1842. Mrs. Mathis was, I believe, the most regally handsome woman I have ever seen. It was a wonderful family and I loved them all.

In my first autumn at McCallie I made the football team, playing at tackle. I was much too light. We had few veterans, and we learned that season the bitter lessons of defeats.

In the next summer events moved to a bridge at Sarajevo. This dominated conversation. At the Mathis home I learned much German history and the feelings of people who cherished the Germany of literature and of music, but had hated its militarism from which their forebears had fled. Woodrow Wilson became my hero. I read all of his writings I could find. Football went better, and that winter I won the gold medal in the oratorical contest, giving an original paper with the imposing title "America's Position Untenable." I was heartened by the presence of the Mathis family, smiling encouragingly from the second row. I was trying to write short stories for the literary quarterly *The Pennant*, had memorized a dozen or so poems, mostly Kipling's, for reciting at the weekly sessions of the Daniel Webster literary club, and had discovered the Waverley novels. Somehow I never had any direction in my reading. I read hungrily, with darts here and dashes there. It was an odd mixture, including, for example, Wilson on government, O. Henry's stories and poems, Opie Reed, Lafcadio Hearn, Whitman, Shakespeare, Frank Norris, Ralph Henry Barbour, Owen Johnson, Robert W. Service, and of course, Emerson's essays and poems. The novel which made the greatest impression on me in those days was Norris's *McTeague*. I can still see, in my mind's eye, the gross Dr. McTeague, torpid with steam beer, asleep in his chair in his dental parlor; Maria Macapa, searching for the mythical dishes of gold which rang sweeter than church bells, and the final scene in Death Valley. There was not then so much talk of symbolism, but none could miss the many symbols which Norris gave. But somehow, more's the pity, I never had an English teacher in prep school who gave either inspiration or direction. The result was, and is, that my reading has large gaps in it. Professor Spencer McCallie made ancient history come alive for us. He would, on occasion, act out the parts of both the heroes of Greek and Roman history and the gods on Mount Olympus. The professor was tall, quite bald and thin, but strong, and possessed of great endurance. Once, in a lecture on the philosophy of the Greeks, he delivered a profound conclusion and then paused.

"I wish," he said sadly, "I had that engraved on a mallet so that I might hit each of you on the head with it."

Years later, when he was an old man, I learned he was dying of leukemia and went to see him. It was summer, and he was on a bed on a screened sleeping porch. We talked and laughed of the old school days. And then he said, "I'm not worried about death. I have my faith and I learned how to die from the old Greeks and Romans." Two days later he was gone.

The annual school play was for me a profitable educational course. A young Chattanoogan, Robert Straus, had had a few small comedy roles on Broadway, but he was not a great success, and for three springs he coached our drama club. In my last two years he gave me the lead role. The senior year it was in *What Happened to Jones,* and we took it on the road to two small nearby Tennessee towns. The role required me to kiss one of the young ladies. We were, in our town at least, an unsophisticated generation, and for me, with my preposterous shyness, the awkward kiss at each performance was agony.

I saw every play I could and there was then a good road season even in cities as small as Chattanooga. I saw some of the celebrated actors, John Drew, David Warfield and Robert Mantell are the three I remember best.

Bobby Straus later caught on with Fritz Leiber, a really competent Shakespearian actor, who had been Robert Mantell's fine young star before forming his own successful company. After the First World War, when I was at Vanderbilt University and working part-time on the *Nashville Banner,* Leiber's troupe came often to Nashville. Straus was playing the lead comedy roles. I carried spears, was a messenger in *Macbeth,* and in *Hamlet* once filled in as the second gravedigger. I was wild to be taken on. Straus arranged a talk with Leiber.

"First, let me tell you," he said, "that I'll take you. But, second, let me tell you, in all kindness, you do not have the voice for it. You can never play the really big parts."

We looked each other in the eye for a moment, and then I thanked him, and went out, blinking back tears. It had been a great dream.

That night I was the messenger who brought word that Birnam Wood had, indeed, been seen on the move. There seemed an even greater rejection in Macbeth's lines, delivered by Leiber: "Get thee hence."

But that, of course, is a story of a later time.

My years at McCallie closed out wonderfully in June, 1917. I had been captain of the football team, won the city declamation medal, but missed the senior medal because of the frustration in Dr. James Park McCallie's math classes. President Wilson was urging all secondary-school graduates to go on to college until their draft boards called them. I wanted college with a deep, indescribable yearning. But boys I knew who were a year or two older were beginning to enlist, and I knew that, soon or late, I would follow. I had learned not to hate a people, and some of the excesses of anti-German feeling against the music and the language sickened me. But I had learned to hate the philosophy symbolized by Kaiser Bill. And I knew some of the meanings of the international power struggle. I had become aware, too, of some of the things which made the South different, though my thinking was far from being in focus. My Calvinist conscience was stirred by some of the race prejudice I saw. I had learned none at home and brought none with me from the old place up the river.

All in all, it had been a grand four years. I couldn't decide whether I'd learned more in class or out. But I knew that one complemented the other, and that, I guess, was the beginning of wisdom.

V

The Summers

IN MY BOYHOOD CIRCLE in Highland Park, the suburb of Chattanooga where we lived, vacations were the time when a boy got a job to earn spending money and help out with his clothes. Vacations — Christmas and summer — found us hunting down jobs. One Christmas I earned enough to buy a fine edition of Kipling's poems and a pair of shoes. While in successive summers I worked as a back flagman on a surveying crew, a collector of "small, mean bills" for a wholesale drug company, and as a salesman in a haberdashery store. I liked them all.

The survey job was like a frontier adventure. We ran the line which later became the Suck Creek Road up Signal Mountain. Now and then, on visits there, I travel the curving asphalted road. There is a certain pride in it, but remembering the wild beauty of the wilderness through which we surveyed, I am sometimes sorry it could not have been left as it was.

The Tennessee (before the TVA dams) came out of East Tennessee like a wild horse of a river. In its upper stretches it receives the waters of three great rivers: the French Broad, the Little Tennessee, and the Hiwassee. From Knoxville to Chattanooga, the Tennessee follows a southwestward line. But just below Lookout Mountain the river turns northwest and cuts a deep, curving, tortuous path through Walden's Ridge. Into this constructed channel poured the mighty forces of the vastly augmented waters. This stretch was a terror for navigators. The first obstacle in it was the Suck. Legend made this whirlpool more fearsome than it was, but it was a dangerous problem to the old flatboats of the first settlers.

Suck Creek, which, of course, was so named because it flowed into the Suck, rose deep in the Appalachians. Our survey line ran along its valley. Every day was exciting. There was still game to be seen. Once we saw a black bear with a cub. We walked up occasional wild turkeys, woodcock, and quail. The valleys of Signal Mountain, one of the many folds of the Appalachians, are thick with huge stones. We felt like pioneers in the new world. About halfway in we came upon an ancient log cabin in a clearing of small fields. An old man was on the porch. His daughter-in-law came out as we stopped. She made us coffee to go with our lunch and reluctantly accepted the half dollar the chief surveyor insisted on paying. The son, they said, was away on "a job." We imagined a still or perhaps a prison term for moonshining. The old man told us his name was Hesse. He had always "heared," he said, that his great-great-granddaddy had been a Hessian soldier who had been captured in the war of the Revolution. When it was ended he had made his way down into Tennessee and taken up land. The old fellow had no papers. His name was a story handed down.

The Suck Creek survey took up much of the summer. The job of rear, or back flagman is a lonely one, but I enjoyed every hour of it.

The summer of collecting "small, mean bills, some of them damned old and mean," was a fascinating one. Fritz and Wiehl was an old, highly respected company, selling the usual line of drugstore supplies, from drugs to artificial legs and arms. It also offered patent medicines such as cough and cold remedies, aids for "female complaints," liniments for man and beast, tonics for chill and so on.

It was this range of latter items which provided me with a

job. Small slum grocery stores always had a shelf full of them. Since they frequently went out of business or changed hands, it was necessary to keep a close check on them by frequent duns. That is where I came in. I was fourteen and a half years old and not, certainly, a commanding figure. But they did not need one. All they wanted was someone to present the bill as a reminder and argue for payment.

On my first day the head bookkeeper, who looked like a character out of Dickens, gave me what now has come to be called an indoctrination. The accounts were all bad, he said. "In fact," he said, "they are bad and mean, some of them damn mean. They are not worth the trouble they make, but we are an old Chattanooga company and do not like to refuse small transactions." So he gave me fifty cents for carfare and I started to work.

The characters I met that summer were weird and wonderful. The rough ones couldn't really get too angry with a boy. "Why in the hell is Fritz and Wiehl sending a boy to torment me?" angrily demanded one tall, malarial-looking man who had a small shack of a store. "Business is bad enough without them acting up about what I owe."

His small store buzzed with flies. Our remedies had been so long on his shelf the labels on the bottles looked faded. I heard him out and suggested he pay something on account. Any amount would do. I collected payments as small as twenty-five cents. Only rarely did I receive the full amount. I would write out receipts with an indelible pencil.

That summer I learned all the mean streets and slum neighborhoods in collecting mean accounts. It was shoe-leather-punishing work. I rode the trolley to the street nearest a neighborhood which harbored two or three businesses in arrears, and then trudged about to find them. The poverty and squalor about some of the mills and ironworks were a shock. I had seen coal-miners' poverty in Soddy, Tennessee, but this was worse. From one of my old accounts I learned a new word — incest. If there were customers, or just neighbors in talking, I usually sat and listened until there was a lull and I could lure my man to a quiet corner to present the bill. Also, I liked to listen. I remember once hearing a group damning some man in the neighborhood who had had a child by his daughter. Someone knew the word incest. He said he had once served on a jury which heard a like case. The story and the word depressed me all that summer.

It was a hot, sweaty, lonely summer. My legs and health improved. I had met all manner of defeated, shiftless, shifty, pathetic, and interesting good people. Fritz and Wiehl professed to be pleased with my results and the manner in which I kept my own accounts. That fall my legs were so good I made the all-city football team as a tackle.

The summers as a salesman in a haberdashery store were interesting and easy. The owners were amiable young men and left things pretty much to the two salesmen, an older, experienced man, and me. I learned the peculiarities of tastes in ties, shirts, and underwear. I also became acquainted with the vanity of the male animal.

My summer job in 1918 was at Parris Island, S. C., as a Marine Corps recruit. The disciplines of that summer are with me yet. The best and most rewarding summer job, and my first real boss, came the summer after I was mustered out of the Marine Corps. Early in 1919 the Corps notified its "duration" enlisted men that those who planned to return to school could apply for discharge on that basis. Certain papers of recommendation and, I believe, an oath of intent had to be provided. Mine was filed, declaring a purpose to return to Vanderbilt University at Nashville, Tennessee, where I had been a freshman at the time of enlistment, and I was discharged about mid-March.

It was too late to enter spring term, but I went to Nashville and arranged to be on hand in September. I also applied for a student loan and put my name on the list of those who would need part-time jobs. After a brief visit with former classmates, I went on to my home at Chattanooga.

Through my father's assistance, I got a job. It was one about which I often find myself thinking today, as the Deep South racial tensions, fanned by unreasoning fanaticism and exploited recklessly and cynically by politicians, take on preposterous proportions. I was the only white member of the working crew with which I had a job, and the foreman was, of course, a Negro. I worked with him from late March through August, and it was a pleasant and rewarding summer.

My father was now a minor officer and sales manager of the small heating and roofing company in Chattanooga. The approaching recession of 1920 was beginning to be felt, and there were not many summer jobs. I wanted one which would be out-of-doors hard work, as in the fall I intended to try for the football team. After three days of job hunting my father looked at my discouraged face and said, "One of the roofing crews is short a man."

"Could I have it?" I asked.

"It's Charlie's," he said. "You mind working under him?"

"No," I said, "Charlie's fine."

The real rough work of roofing was done by Negroes, with white sheet metal workers doing the flashing, gutter, and ventilating jobs. Charlie I knew rather well. He had been with the company a long time, and I had been seeing him around for years when I would go by to see my father. In elementary and secondary school years I frequently rode the two miles from our suburb to the Chattanooga Carnegie Library for books, and I'd always drop by the company office before the journey home.

Charlie White was a humpbacked man, quite black, of indeterminate age. He must have been in his early sixties. His arms, I suppose, were no longer than average, but because of his hump, which caused him to seem to be thrown forward in posture, the arms dangled and appeared, at least to my boy's

eyes, abnormally long. Despite his deformity they were powerful and he was as agile as anyone else. He had a deeply
lined face and an almost aquiline nose. His bright, quizzical
eyes gave him a quaint, almost elfin look. I remembered that
the first time I saw him, years before, I was startled by a sort of
coincidence. I had just finished reading *The Hunchback of
Notre Dame*, and when I walked to the back of the shop and
saw Charlie, I was, for a moment, almost afraid. But then he
came over and asked me who I was, and I saw he was just a
kind man with a humped back. On days of heavy rain the
roofing crews would come into the shop, and Charlie, when he
saw me there, would always have some pleasant word with
me. So, when my father said it would be Charlie's crew, I told
him it would be fine. He nodded and added, "You'll come in
with me early tomorrow."

In these last several years of tensions I have tried hard to
recollect any rationalization I may have gone through about
working with a Negro roofing crew. I have been unable to recall any. Now and then, in the weeks that followed my going
on the job, the president and chief owner of the company, a
smug sort of man who wore a collar later to be made famous
by Herbert Hoover, would see us come in from an early finish
on a job. Two or three times he stopped me and said, "How
are you and Charlie getting on?" "Fine," I'd say. I recall he
had a somewhat questioning look on his face. It never occurred
to me that he was probing for some answer about how it felt to
be working with, and under the direction of, a Negro.

Certainly I was asking myself no questions on that first morning when I went down to begin the job. We — my parents and
I — were from East Tennessee farm backgrounds and Scottish and Welsh ancestry. We were strict Presbyterians, with
prayers at meals and Bible reading at night. On the farm,
prior to our move to Chattanooga, any house help we had was
from the white tenants on the place. I did not see a Negro until I was six years old. I was never taught any prejudice about

them since that was not according to Scripture. I knew in school, of course, that many boys thought otherwise, but somehow it always seemed some problem of their own. So I wasn't bothered when I went to work. Nor was I troubled during that pleasant summer, though the work was dirty and hard and often exhausting.

Charlie was waiting by the old Ford truck, and three Negro men, all older than I, were standing nearby talking. The truck was loaded with shingle-width bales of composition roofing, ladders, sections of gutters, sheets of galvanized iron, and two fire pots of the kind used by sheet metal workers to heat their soldering irons. The talk was desultory. Charlie teased me a bit, saying that he doubted if a college boy could do the work without "white-eying," a phrase used to describe being overcome by heat. I told him that once, when I was about thirteen and was spending the summer back on my grandmother's farm, I had white-eyed pitching hay into a loft on a very hot afternoon. My uncle had told me the phrase had come into use because when a person collapsed from the heat the eyes rolled back until only the whites showed. Charlie asked me a few questions, and I told him I wanted to get my legs and back in shape for football. He chuckled and said, "Imagine that." I went on to tell him I had played guard as a freshman and explained how important it was for a lineman to have good legs. He found this amusing, chuckling over it. And I guess, in retrospect, he had a right to be amused.

The first job was to roof a new house, a single-story one and not too large. Charlie backed the truck up close by the house. Then he and two of the other Negroes put up two ladders, tied on carpenters' aprons with pockets for the roofing nails, filled them about half full, took their hammers and heavy scissors, and went up to the roof. The third Negro, the youngest, and I were to carry the baled shingles up the ladders to the roof as they were needed. It looked simple. One balanced a bundle on a shoulder and, holding it lightly with the fingertips, climbed on up with it. One of the men had such a fine sense of balance he could go right up without putting a hand to the load until he was at the top and had to put it on the roof. But for me, it was difficult. The bundle bit into my shoulder, and the roughness of the edges chafed my neck and cheek. On the first trip up I almost fell backward with it. But I persevered. I knew they, especially Charlie, were watching me.

They may have had some questions about my willingness to do a full share of work. And Charlie, though he never said so, must have thought I was a fool talking about working to strengthen my legs. Late that day he said to me, as I started to climb, "This sorta thing will help yo' legs." I looked down at him, but his face was impassive. That night when we came in, Charlie walked over with me toward my father, who was looking at us inquiringly. "This young man," he said, "he is goin' to be a *good* helper, yes sir, a good one."

I think I was. I began to look forward to the days and my ride out to the jobs beside Charlie. We talked endlessly. At noon we ate our packages of lunch together. He talked to me about the trade of roofing as if he believed I would follow it. He had a strong, honest pride in his work because he was expert at it.

The worst part of the work for me was the tar and gravel roofs. They meant pulling up huge buckets of gravel and smaller ones of pitch with block and rope. The "cooker," a dirty monster coated with glistening tar spilled on it from past jobs, had to be set up, fired, and filled with lumps of tar cut from their containers.

The roof first had to be covered with a composition material which had a feltlike texture and smelled of tar. It came in rolls. Once it was down, the whole thing was covered with hot pitch, spread with mops. In the worst rags of old work shoes to be found, our feet wrapped in sacking, we toiled like demons in the smoke and heat, spreading the hot pitch. There could be no delay. Nor could the pitch be too thin or too thick. Charlie, a hunched, black Mephistopheles with his own mop, tarred and sticky, was everywhere, directing here, giving a spot there a needed touch. The gravel had to be spread into the first coating of still soft tar. And that, too, was fast and demanding. And then came another pouring and spreading of tar. It was furious, backbreaking, arm-wearing work, and the heat was sometimes dreadful. But none of us white-eyed, not even in August when the thermometer was around ninety-five in the shade.

By midsummer I realized I had become very fond of Charlie and he of me. Neither of us expressed it, but each knew that the other understood. Two or three times when we were too late getting in from some distant job to go into the shop, which would be closed, Charlie took me to his house. His wife was a large, motherly woman who always had a pitcher of iced tea and graham crackers waiting. They had no children. We'd sit on Charlie's small front porch, with the summer dusk about us, and drink the tea, grateful for the end of the day and the departure of the sun. There were houses crowded close on either side, and their occupants, too, were on the porches seeking coolness. It always seemed to me that Charlie talked a little louder than usual, to be sure they would hear. He would talk of the job, and he never failed to brag mightily about me, declaring I was the best helper a man could have. I had caught on quick, he vowed, and could make a good roofer if I wanted to. He never mentioned my legs, after the first day, and I was grateful for that.

In my last week on the job we both began to talk sadly of my quitting to go off to school at Nashville. I, of course, was eager but felt a real regret at parting with him. He knew I had to have a job there and that I would borrow some money. I had explained the student loan system. He worried, as did I, that I hadn't saved more out of my pay. He was inclined to blame my spending habits on my having been in the Marines.

There were to be two or three days between my quitting and my departure on the Dixie Flyer. It came through around midnight, and Charlie insisted he would bring the old truck out and take me and my trunk down to the station. He came about ten-thirty. My parents and I were sitting on the front porch, waiting. Charlie was wearing a neat, dark suit of what certainly was not summer material. He spoke to my mother in an old-fashioned Chesterfieldian manner, and then he and I carried the trunk out and into the truck. He waited there while I went back and bade my parents goodbye.

I climbed into the familiar front seat, with the old smell of tarred composition roofing about it, and we went to the station, saying little. We checked the trunk and then stood outside talking, since the waiting rooms were segregated. Mostly we recollected amusing things about some of the jobs and some of the near-accidents.

The train came, backing in as it did at Chattanooga's old Union Station, and it was time to go. We walked over by the gates. I looked at him and he at me. Suddenly he moved up and put his arms around me and I put mine about him, feeling, with a sort of shock, the hard thrust of the hump on his back. "Don't forget me," he said. "I'll never forget you, Charlie," I said. "You are one of the finest men I've ever known."

He stepped back, reached in his inside coat pocket, and took out an envelope.

"Don't you open this till you get on the train," he said, "and it's out of the station."

We shook hands, with the people who were waiting for arrivals looking on curiously, and I turned so he wouldn't see my eyes and walked hurriedly up the train to my car.

When the train was out of the station, I opened the envelope. There was a folded five-dollar bill and a scrawled note. "For my helper to spend at school," it read. It was then I wept.

I wrote Charlie and thanked him, and later I wrote him about making the first football squad. I told him the legs were strong from climbing ladders. My father wrote me that Charlie read the letters to his crew and made his new helper, a young Negro, unhappy with stories of his college helper.

During the Christmas holidays I went to see him, disturbed to hear he had been sick during November with pneumonia but had gone to work. He was bright and gay and pleased with the present I had brought. His wife had baked a chocolate cake for me.

In January I had a letter from my father. Charlie had gone home ill again and had died two days later of a second attack of pneumonia. I sat there in the fraternity house room, remembering him with his arms tight about me at the station and hearing him say, "Don't forget me."

VI

Formaldehyde and Poetry

VANDERBILT University was, for me, a sort of Tibet, high above all other plateaus I had known. The air was heady with excitement. I would not have traded my dark, bleak room in shabby old Kissam Hall dormitory for a castle in Camelot.

The hall had been designed by the New York architect Stanford White, at the outset of his career. It was a large, four-storied, U-shaped structure. Yet all the baths and toilet facilities were in one wing of the basement. No student above the first floor entertained any save the most hostile feelings toward the memory of the playboy architect. Indeed, a legend grew, after he had been gunned to death by Harry K. Thaw, that the killer had, under another name, spent a winter as a freshman in a fourth-floor room at Kissam Hall and had then and there taken a blood oath to liquidate Mr. White. Evelyn Nesbit, so the legend went, merely put the finger on him. Indeed, I am sure Vanderbilt is the only university in America where toasts were drunk to Harry K. Thaw. Once in my time, during a particularly severe winter, a handsome, hand-painted poster was put up in the facilities quarter. It read: "In grateful tribute to Harry K. Thaw, who rid the world of a damned bad architect."

But Kissam Hall was glamorous to me. To be in a college dormitory, to walk the campus from class to class, and to stroll about it at night, were sheer excitement.

Hero worship for an older cousin who had graduated from

Vanderbilt Medical School had persuaded me to register in the pre-medical department. No one counseled me. I registered and found myself with biology, math and chemistry classes. Oddly enough, I took to biology with enthusiasm. It and English were my favorite courses. The teachers made them so. Edwin E. Reinke, Princeton-trained, who taught biology, and Edwin Mims, in English, are the only two teachers I had at Vanderbilt who have in any degree remained with me. They communicated. Reinke and I became close friends. He invited me often to his apartment and I came to know his quiet, nice wife and children. He was a philosopher. We talked of Darwin, then acutely controversial in the South. (The Scopes trial at Dayton, Tennessee, was just ahead of us.) He set me to reading selected writings on evolution. He talked of the disciplines of science, and the need of having always a doubting, inquiring mind, which distrusted the glib and the dogmatic. He insisted on a search for values, and decision about them. In his class I happily dissected earthworms (they have the equivalent of five kidneys) and rabbits. To this day the smell of formaldehyde brings to the nose of memory the reek of the mangled cadaver of my rabbit when it was removed from the cooler and the loathsome rag of a cover taken off. I learned to identify muscles at a glance and to be able to call off the names of the various nerves when Reinke would pick them up with a pair of tweezers. On a test I named them without a miss and was charmed when Reinke, always a bit taciturn in class, said, "I'll be damned," and moved on. When mid-term examinations came I wrote most of my answers in rhyme. This delighted him and he chuckled about it for days. By then we both knew I would never take another year of biology, but I stayed with it dutifully and looked forward to each class because I was learning. I had a respectable passing final grade in biology, but well before the year's end I had stopped thinking about it as a subject. It was just a mechanism to learn from Reinke.

Freshman English meant Edwin Mims and poetry, mostly

Tennyson and Milton. Keats, Shelley and Browning ran a sort of dead-heat second. Other poets received what might be called honorable mention. We memorized and we read aloud. Professor Mims enjoyed reading to the class. As he read his eyes moved back and forth, like a man watching a tennis match on a miniature court, seeking to find a nonattentive face. Once I recall, as he read "The Charge of the Heavy Brigade," as a counter to the "Charge of the Light Brigade," he decided the face of a freshman named Matt Wiggington lacked luster. Wiggington's hair had been clipped in some initiation ceremony. Professor Mims shouted at him, "Wiggington, you look like a bald-headed oyster. No oyster can hear the thud of horses' feet at the gallop; no oyster can hear the rattle of the scabbards, the creak of leather. But it's all here in this poem."

It was, all in all, a good class for stimulating one to read poetry and to memorize it. The very first day's assignment was to learn the part of Tennyson's "Ulysses," beginning, "Come my friends, 'tis not too late to seek a newer world." I can say them yet. But we heard almost nothing of contemporary poetry. (Revolt against Dr. Mims was to be one of the motivating forces that led to the founding of the Fugitive Group in 1919-1920.) He was an earnest man, with an earnest passion to teach, and if he excluded everything since Browning, he nonetheless made a generation of freshmen classes aware of poetry. He wrestled mightily with young minds out of the small towns of Tennessee and adjoining states, seeking to make them "see" and "feel."

It saddens me to think that save for Reinke and Mims I do not even recall the name of another freshman-class teacher who sparked my mind to read or think.

In the fall of 1917 a good many of the senior and junior football players had gone off to officers' training camps. Thus bereft, it was possible for a one-hundred-fifty-two-pound prep-school tackle to make the varsity as a guard. It was a wonderful, magnificent adventure. Dan McGugin, a kindly gentleman and a former member on Michigan's famous "point-a-minute" teams, was our coach. He took time out from a substantial law practice to teach football each fall for almost thirty years. Alonzo Stagg's Chicago team was on our schedule and as that game approached, excitement mounted. Freshmen made up a good half of the squad. Few had ever been in a Pullman sleeper and not one of us had ever been to Chicago. We arrived on a Friday morning, and some of us rode the elevated in from the Midway hotel where we were housed, and walked along by Lake Michigan, thrilled by its beauty, awed by its size. At one point we came to reproductions of Christopher Columbus's three ships, the *Santa Maria,* and the smaller *Pinta* and *Niña,* left over from a world's fair. These I remember as plainly as if seen yesterday.

Coaches Stagg and McGugin were friends. They arranged for the two teams to have dinner together on Friday evening. We from Tennessee were somewhat self-conscious and when, dinner done, the Chicago squad began to sing some of their university songs and one or two made popular by vaudeville, we were tremendously impressed. When they were done their captain said that perhaps we would like to sing some Vanderbilt songs. Sing? We were struck dumb with an agony of fear! Sing? We had never sung. At Vanderbilt singing was done by the glee club. We had never thought of singing together. So, we sat there, dry of lips, tongues cloven to the roofs of our mouths. Dan McGugin, God bless him, stood. Surely he would rescue us. But no. Though neither he nor we could carry a tune, he would not have us fail to respond. We would, he said, have a try at our Alma Mater. And so, with our tuneless coach leading us we lifted up our voices and sang, thinly and awkwardly, the one song whose words we knew. Its tune and its words, like so many, many Alma Maters of secondary schools and colleges over the land, revealed a liberal borrowing from Cornell. The urbane Chicago squad sat without smiling. They even gave us a nice round of applause, though I am sure they all howled when we were gone. The next afternoon they ran us into the ground, 42 to 0.

That night, our train being late, we walked around the old La Salle Street Station, wide-eyed at the many saloons and the crowds. That was "life" such as none of us had seen.

It was a good year. There was much talk at Kissam Hall and at the Sigma Chi House. Many a night at the old hall we talked and read poetry until dawn. I had almost no money and my wardrobe was meager. I had bought needles and thread and some yarn and I darned my own socks and occasionally did minor repairs on my coat and trousers.

Dan McGugin had put me on the list of student waiters and I worked all year at that in the large common dining room. The head chef was Robert Wingfield. He was a tall, dignified, elderly Negro who had been in the university kitchen for some thirty years. He was a devout Christian, and he felt a responsibility for his boys — the student waiters. It was his custom, since the dining room did not serve a Sunday night meal, to invite, about once a month, two or three of us to his house on Sunday afternoons for coffee, sandwiches and cake. We would be served at a small table in the living room by his wife, a quiet, matronly woman, who had little to say. Robert wanted to ask us about ourselves, what we thought about things, how we were doing in class, and to admonish us against the lures of the devil, who was rather active in Nashville. There was always a prayer before we left. These sessions and some firm admonitions and advice I had from Boland Fitzgerald, Negro trainer for the football team and head janitor at Kissam Hall, were, as best I can recall, the only university counseling I had that freshman year from anyone connected with Vanderbilt.

It was a fast-moving year. The war was in our ears, and in the spring a good many of us left. It was those months at Vanderbilt which kept me out of France. One day on Parris Island, as a harsh Marine Corps boot-training period neared an end, the drill instructor ordered all those who had a high-school education or better to step forward. The others were dismissed. We were ordered to non-com school.

In the fall of 1919 with a loan of $125 in Chattanooga and another from the university loan fund, I was back at Vanderbilt. Then began two more fast-moving years. The football squad was heavy with returned veterans and stars of other years. I played at least part of all the games and won a letter. But already there were other interests. The campus was in a ferment of talk and new ideas about books and poetry. Some of us felt we were of the lost generation and if we could not be expatriates in Paris we would make do with what we had in Nashville and at Vanderbilt.

John Crowe Ransom, one of the younger members of the English faculty, whose poems had already been published in a number of magazines, began to attract about him students and teachers who were interested in poetry. Allen Tate, who was in my class, turned to poetry with an enthusiasm and a dedication rare and exciting. He always seemed to be writing poetry, or talking about it.

One evening as a group of us from the sophomore literary fraternity walked across the campus to a sorority house where poems were to be read and coffee served, Tate was reciting as he went. I recall the closing line of the poem, which was heavy with symbolism to have been: "They bore on high the phallic symbol bold."

One of the group protested. "Gee, Allen," he said, "don't you think you might embarrass them?"

"No," said Tate, "all these girls come from Middle Tennessee high schools. They won't have the vaguest idea what a phallic symbol is."

As far as one could tell, none did. Tate read the poem with fine dramatic effect. Even the housemother showed no sign of shock. It was a fine, exciting evening in the best sophomoric tradition with Tate's comment and poem symbolizing it perfectly.

There were at least a half dozen students whose pockets, like Tate's, were filled with copies of poems. Others were writing novels. Merrill Moore, later to become a distinguished psychiatrist in Brookline, Massachusetts, was even then producing sonnets at an unbelievable rate. It was a facility he never lost. My own energies, after bitter frustration with verse, turned to the weekly student newspaper, the *Hustler*. A column idea was submitted and accepted. It ran column one on page one and quickly involved me in discussion and controversy. Some of the latter led to blows, but it was fun. There was an excitement in getting the four pages ready for the paper. We made an all-night job of it, talking and arguing on a variety of unrelated subjects.

Two of the fraternity chapter alumni worked on the *Nashville Banner*. By spring I had begun to visit them in the city room when the late afternoon street edition was waiting on the baseball detail to conclude. One day, arriving earlier than usual, I found there was a great to-do because the young man who usually took the play-by-play as telephoned in from the park, had quit. I filled in. The detail came in slowly — "Smith struck out. Jones flied to right. Johnson singled to left," etc. A stranger to a typewriter could make out. This was my first newspaper job, and it was agreed it would be a regular one. I reported at 2 P.M. each day the ball club was in town, and worked from 3 P.M. to 3:30 A.M. on other days. On Saturdays I worked from noon until 2:30 Sunday morning. That summer I was also a part-time police reporter, and held minor assignments. The pay was seventeen dollars per week. I can still recall the intense excitement and the pleasure of those days. I knew then I had found what I wanted to do.

At Vanderbilt in the year of 1920-1921 the group which later called themselves "The Fugitives" was already the talk of the campus. Two of them, Merrill Moore and Stanley Johnson, were my close and valued friends. Johnson was in the English Department, and his wife, Will Ella, was university librarian.

Their apartment in the old theological school dormitory attracted three or four of us almost nightly. Contemporary poetry was read aloud. I can yet remember the pleasure we had in Edwin Arlington Robinson. Johnson was writing a novel, later published and titled *Professor*.

Merrill Moore learned shorthand. He needed it for his notes and it was helpful, too, for writing sonnets. Frequently, Moore, at a party or dinner, not wishing to attract attention, would quietly write a sonnet in shorthand on his left shirt cuff.

John Crowe Ransom and Walter Clyde Curry, who taught courses in Shakespeare and Chaucer, were telegraphing sonnets by night letter to a young lady in Murfreesboro, Tennessee, forty miles away. The idea caught on and each Saturday evening at least a half dozen other poets began to telegraph sonnets to young ladies in distant cities. I know of one such custom which was halted abruptly. One tearful damsel telephoned to say that her father had said if he were awakened one more Sunday morning by Western Union he would take a cane to his daughter and also make the journey to Nashville to cane the idiot who was sending the poetic telegrams.

On the *Banner* four of us found an evening or so each week on which to read plays out loud, with the parts assigned. We discovered Eugene O'Neill. We read Russian plays, all of Ibsen's, and mixed in Broadway plays whose long runs had interested publishers in putting them in book form. The new novels were devoured and discussed. I can yet remember the impact of *Jurgen, Main Street* and *Babbitt*. Most of us on the *Banner* and at Vanderbilt were from small towns or cities and though Gopher Prairie was in the Midwest, we were enchanted to find something of our own Tennessee home towns in *Main Street*, and were sure Lewis must, at one time or another, have seen our local Rotarians. Henry Mencken, of course, was our knight in shining armor who each month slew the dragons of dullness in the pulpits in Washington, the governor's office, the legislature and in the seats of the mighty generally. Who else could have written of President Warren Harding's prose: "It reminds me of a string of wet sponges."

Ellen Glasgow was a welcome relief in the flood of novelists. I read her slowly, not swiftly as with most of the new novelists, recognizing her for a pioneer and a writer with something to say. I still remember Judge Bland in *The Romantic Comedians*. Time has not used her well. Her novels are, in my opinion, quite the equal of Willa Cather's. Scott Fitzgerald's *This Side of Paradise* moved conversation to a higher pitch. The twenties were the American Renaissance — not, perhaps, in the classic sense of the word, but a renaissance just the same.

Years later Willa Cather was to say that the world broke in two in 1922, or thereabouts. In retrospect — it did. But those who lived it did not note it. There are many who have diagnosed the 1920's, and most of them have been close to the mark. Students and young reporters had a vast contempt for Warren Harding, and, later, for Calvin Coolidge. They came along when the nation's elders, the voters, in substantial majority, wanted normalcy. But those who believed in the League of Nations, and those who saw in the corruption of Harding's years and the crass commercialism of Coolidge's a symbol of what it was they were in rebellion against, did not feel that normalcy was the answer. The young rebels were, perhaps, as charged, guilty of "Byronic self-consciousness" and of occasional posturing and excessive self-confidence. Even so, it was a mood more honest and nearer the verities than that provided and propagandized by the spokesmen for all that was represented by Harding and Coolidge. It is unrewarding to speculate on what direction the country might have taken, and what it and the world might have avoided, had James M. Cox and Franklin D. Roosevelt been elected in 1920. Cox was pledged to the League. He was a proved progressive.

We never thought deeply about these things on the campus at Vanderbilt, or in the city room at the *Banner* or the rival *Tennessean*. It was exciting to be alive. So we were stirred by the new ideas, the new poets and novelists. T. S. Eliot, Archibald MacLeish, Elinor Wylie, E. E. Cummings, Stephen Vincent and William Rose Benét, each had their acolytes.

Countee Cullen was the first Negro poet I remember reading and discussing.

Dorothy Parker was, we all agreed, a healthy influence, debunking much of the pretense of the time. The twenties could laugh when she wrote:

> Authors and actors and artists and such
> Never know nothing, and never know much,
> Sculptors and singers and those of their kidney
> Tell their affairs from Seattle to Sydney.
> Playwrights and poets and such horse's necks,
> Start off from anywhere, end up at sex.
> Diarists, critics and similar roe
> Never say nothing and never say no.
> People Who Do Things exceed my endurance;
> God, for a man that solicits insurance!

We in Nashville were, of course, provincial innocents. The Marxist worm, for example, never bored into our lovely apple. We read the New Masses and the hastily put-together proletarian novels — they came late in the twenties — along with the others and never felt a taint. They were all a part of the new freedom. As Miniver Cheevy yearned for the grace of iron clothing, we yearned for the garrets and fleshpots of Greenwich Village. Occasionally, by dint of saving, one or two of us would go to New York. Once I sold a story, based on an experience as police reporter, to one of the confession magazines and made it to New York for a weekend. Lonely and lacking any acquaintance in the Village, I wandered there two afternoons and evenings, a naïve small-city reporter seeking some contact with the gods. Nor was the journey a failure. I met no writer of note; saw the shabby and the faking, but excused it utterly. Merely to walk there, and to eat in one of the small candle-lit restaurants and see the tables of arguing, eccentrically clad guests, was to touch, for a moment, the hem of the garment of the goddess of Bohemia.

Vanderbilt's poets gave us a feeling of being in the main current by publishing, in April, 1922, the first edition of the magazine *The Fugitive*. They had, of course, been meeting to read and criticize each other's poems for about two years. Noms de plume were used and the campus buzzed with speculation for days while those in the know smiled smugly. John Crowe Ransom, whose volume, *Poems about God*, had already been published, was the shepherd of the Fugitives. (His poems had been soundly attacked in some pulpits as expressions of a man opposed to God.) Henry Mencken rallied to the Fugitives, making them few friends in other Tennessee cities and colleges, by writing that the first issue "constitutes, at one moment, the entire literature of Tennessee." This brought forth cries of rage and protest from a number of papers and critics outside Nashville, but Vanderbilt and the Fugitives loved it, and wrote letters of appreciation to the sage at Baltimore. The Fugitives purchased post cards and had an ad printed on the message side. It was headed "The Fugitive in the 'Sahara of Bozart.'" These appealed for circulation. *The Fugitive* was published from April, 1922, to December, 1925. Faculty members were John Crowe Ransom, Donald Davidson, Walter Clyde Curry, Stanley Johnson, and William Y. Elliot. Students were Merrill Moore, Allen Tate, Robert Penn Warren, Jesse Wills and Ridley Wills. Nashvillians, of whom Sidney Hirsch — at whose home the group met — was the patron, completed the list. Most of the latter were Vanderbilt alumni.

Because the South for so long had been, in truth, a Sahara of the beaux arts, the Fugitives deserved, and had, national recognition. Louis Untermeyer, Christopher Morley, Robert Graves, and others contributed to, and hailed *The Fugitive* with generous praise.

After 1925 the university-connected Fugitives began to disperse. But their influence did not. For the next quarter century three of them, Ransom, Warren and Tate, profoundly influenced, if indeed they did not dominate, American literary criticism. John Crowe Ransom left Vanderbilt for Kenyon College. He made the *Kenyon Review* a respected, and accepted, voice of criticism. Allen Tate, easily the most energetic, ambitious and least disciplined of the talented Fugitives, produced a steady procession of competent critical essays. The phrase "The New Criticism" began to be widely used. Only three or four of Tate's poems gained any recognition. One of these, "Ode to the Confederate Dead," is a favorite of editors of anthologies. But Tate was a tireless correspondent, lecturer and propagandist without equal. He taught, moving restlessly from job to job. He took a nondescript *Sewanee Review* and with an eye on Kenyon made it into one which rivaled the masters'. But he never really seemed to come to grips with himself or his work.

The "New Criticism" mothered, in the manner of a hen with new chicks, a closely knit group of poets. They indulged, perhaps, in too much praise of one another, but after all, the outlets for their criticism were few. They also began to strain after esoteric symbolism and learned metaphysical exercises. There were those critics who insisted that too many of their poems were written in a sort of Esperanto for which only the members of the club had a pony. The New Criticism mocked at Stephen Vincent Benét's *John Brown's Body,* for example, as third-rate stuff. There were a few hesitant moves toward putting Robert Frost in his place, but resolution was lacking.

Robert Penn Warren was, and is, the colossus of the Fugitives. A winner of a Pulitzer Prize for poetry and a novel, he continues to teach and produce first-rate novels and poems. As a young reporter I lived one summer in Vanderbilt's old West Side Row dormitories with Warren as a next-door neighbor. His light always was burning, no matter how late the hour. I marveled then at his disciplines and have never ceased to do so.

In 1930 some of the Fugitives, with new recruits called to the colors, made an error which all but one or two die-hards regret.

Proclaiming themselves Agrarians, they published a collection of essays titled *I'll Take My Stand*. It was a composite, posturing plea for a return to the economy and the culture of the plantation. *I'll Take My Stand* did not quite advocate slavery. It did, however, most earnestly recommend a return to a paternalistic system in which civilized planters would halt the writing of a poem to turn smiling faces to Uncle Tom, who, hat in hand, had a request to make. One essay began, "The Southern white man wishes the Negro well — he wishes to see crime, genial irresponsibility and oppression replaced by an informed, productive Negro community." Tate seemed to apologize for any past criticism of a perfect culture and announced he would never criticize the South again. The year 1930 was to see the beginning of the end for what was left of the "Old South," the myth of which so gently drew the suddenly sentimental Agrarians. By 1933 the idle hookworm-and-pellagra-sick cotton sharecroppers, and the bankrupt "Big Houses" all testified eloquently that the one-crop economy was finished.

There was a determined effort to forget *I'll Take My Stand*. Only Donald Davidson stood on the burned-out deck.

Merrill Moore, youngest of the Fugitives, was in many respects unique in the group. He was the real individualist. He had no unusual eccentricities of manner or dress. He did not drink to excess. He was a quiet, wonderfully stubborn young man, with much courage and compassion in his make-up. He was a few years younger than I but we were close and enduring friends. The Moores lived a few miles out from Nashville in a large, two-story white clapboard house. The father, John Trotwood Moore, was a novelist of the old school, and a poet. The mother was a sweet, gracious, patient lady, who served, later, as state librarian. She had a wide knowledge of books and poems. There were, in those days, two pretty, very young sisters, twins.

John Trotwood Moore was a born talker and storyteller. There usually was a crowd at the Moores' on Saturday nights and Sunday afternoons. We went on possum hunts, and talked books and poems. John Trotwood would read some of his, or perhaps an excerpt from a story or a novel on which he was at work. This tall, kindly man was in demand throughout the South as a friend and speaker. He kept writing almost to the day he died.

Merrill Moore went serenely on through the academic years, and four more in medicine. It seemed odd to us that he wanted to be a doctor, but he did. As a medical student, he wrote sonnets about the cadavers, the professors, and diseased livers and hearts found in post-mortems. He early knew that he wanted to specialize in neurology and psychiatry. He did so at Boston City Hospital and the Boston Psychopathic Hospital. Merrill Moore possessed an unusually brilliant mind. Dr. T. L. Wells, assistant professor of psychology at Harvard Medical School, published an article about him in 1939 titled *The Mental Measure of Merrill Moore — a Psychometric Study of the Author of M, One Thousand Autobiographical Sonnets.*

Moore, Dr. Wells wrote, had scored astonishingly high in various tests of intelligence and various psychiatric experiments with language or non-language symbols. Merrill had, too, an uncanny intuitive grasp of things. He was, I am sure, seldom depressed, rarely melancholy. He was sentimental, but never gushing. He was a disciplined man. After he went to Boston, we kept in touch by mail and telephone. During the Second World War he did magnificent things in setting up an army hospital in China. He sent poems and rhymes, some bawdy, as an army is, from New Zealand, where he was before going to China. No mention of loneliness, unhappiness, weariness or boredom ever crept into his letters. I doubt if he felt any of these emotions. I long have believed that he wanted to be a priest or minister, but somehow could not, and so went into medicine. He quickly saw that the really troubled persons were those who were mentally disturbed. This drew him. At least a hundred exceptional acts of kindness to disturbed persons, young and old, are known to me. Two classmates were saved from suicide by him — one a narcotics addict and the other an alcoholic. Both were fully restored to mental health and productive work.

His intuition often was a sudden thing. A friend in Boston recalled that one night after a dinner — which he and Robert Frost had attended together — Merrill said that something had just occurred to him. Would he, Frost, ride a few miles out in the country? They drove, with no explanation from Merrill, turning, at last, into the huge-pillared entrance of a large estate, and along a curving drive to a darkened house. Merrill went confidently to the door, a curious Frost by his side, and made the heavy knocker boom. After a bit lights came on, and a robed, slippered figure (the butler as it turned out) turned on an outside light and cracked the door.

"Why, Dr. Moore," he exclaimed.

"Come in, Robert," said Moore.

Frost, according to the narrator of the story, later said that in the big, deeply carpeted entryway he could see two or three faces looking over the upstairs railing where the stairway led.

Merrill inquired if a young lady, whom we here shall call Mary Anne, was in. She was. She was one of those peering down from above.

Merrill, familiar with the house, walked through an entry into the library. The young lady, about twenty, came hesitatingly in.

"This is Mr. Robert Frost, Mary Anne," said Merrill. He added they had been driving by and had decided to stop and talk for a while. The young lady, Merrill informed Robert Frost, was a poet.

So they talked. The enchanted girl, soon over her initial nervousness, was asking questions and talking of her favorite poems by Frost. After about a half hour Merrill said they would be going. Driving out, said the teller of this story, Merrill replied, in answer to Frost's demand for a postponed explanation,

"Therapy, Robert, therapy. You are her hero. She has been wanting to meet you but was too frightened to try. It suddenly occurred to me tonight that if we came in as we did she would be in your presence before she knew who you were, and talking with you before she had time to become disturbed. It worked admirably, Robert, and I am greatly obliged."

Merrill Moore died of cancer in 1957. Until a few days before his death he was writing sonnets. His practice, which was large, did not halt publication, at frequent intervals, of the volumes called *Clinical Sonnets*. In them his compassion for troubled humanity, and his deep insight into its weaknesses and strength, come through.

One of his psychiatrically based sonnets will illustrate:

> Mrs. Broderick was a very unusual woman,
> But she was different from what most people thought.
> They called her a hard woman, sinister,
> But she was neither sinister nor hard;
> That was a grotesque reputation nearly
> Forgotten now by those who crossed her yard.
>
> Actually she was extremely sympathetic.
> Once when two Italian laborers were correcting
> A leak in her cesspool she had a pitcher of lemonade
> Sent out from her kitchen. They were not expecting
> Such thoughtfulness; their gratitude was pathetic.
>
> And another time she got up in the middle of the night
> To pour ice water over some lobsters that
> Were waiting in a sack to be boiled (alive) the next day;
> She was a very unusual woman that way.

Looking back from the sixties to the twenties, the Fugitives are seen as the best symbol of the South's campus response to the many motivations of rebellion, or flight, from the tyranny of the Southern Brahmin. Poems were written in class, pages from proposed new novels were read along the paths between classes. They were fine sunlit days. The cup of life seemed always running over. A poem by Richard Eberhart, titled "If I Could Only Live at the Pitch That Is near Madness," reminds me of those years. It begins:

> If I could only live at the pitch that is near madness
> When everything is as it was in my childhood
> Violent, vivid, and of infinite possibility:
> That the sun and the moon broke over my head.

Looking back, the temptation is to say that Vanderbilt, per se, did not contribute much to me in those days. Yet, this would not be strictly true. I do not remember much from classes. But there were other stimulations in them. Dr. George Pullen Jackson, who taught me German, was, for example, the man who led in establishing a symphony which Nashville supported for a few years. I learned too little German, but a considerable amount about symphony instruments and a working knowledge of the more familiar composers.

Many students were trying to write, and those who weren't talked of it. Yet, Vanderbilt had no course in writing novels, poems or plays. For me, the nights with Merrill Moore and Stanley Johnson provided the most stimulation to read and think.

Newspaper work thrilled and held me. I got to know, and claim distant kin with, a young congressman named Cordell Hull. Politicians at all levels fascinated me. I came to know speakeasy keepers who were ward or precinct bosses. It was good to know gutter politics, and to understand and have a sort of affection for the rascals in it because of their being so much alive and a part of things. One of the finest classrooms I ever attended was an upstairs suite of bedroom and sitting room over Foutch's all-night drugstore. The prescription counter sold clear corn whiskey in ten-ounce bottles labeled witch hazel. All the young political and police reporters, seeking to be sophisticated cynics, made of Foutch's a sort of late-night-clubhouse. In the upstairs room mayors were made and unmade, as were city councilmen. Once I hid under the bed and heard a decision I could not print because I could not prove it and it was, when I reported it, regarded as preposterous. But it came off.

Nashville had a theatrical road. I reviewed plays (always with enthusiasm if with little acquaintance with critical values). David Warfield, Anna Pavlova, Robert Mantell (who had a McGill among his distant forebears), Fritz Leiber, Mantell's brilliant leading man, and later had his own company, and a young actor playing in stock named Ralph Bellamy, all became inspirations. Once Anna Pavlova, apparently contrite over a brusque refusal for an interview, asked me to dine with her after a performance. We did. I have never forgotten her face and the tenseness of her personality. She set me to reading about ballet. Years later I dropped in on rehearsals of the Ballet Russe de Monte Carlo when assignments took me to New York during the season. Thus I came to know Alexandra Danilova, Maria Tallchief, Ruthanna Boris, and to interview and talk with others.

The *Banner* city desk, thanking heaven for an eager beaver who asked for them, loaded all possible night and early morning assignments on me. I thanked them for it — and still do.

Who else has ever met the famed tenor Beniamino Gigli as he got off a sleeper at 6:30 A.M. in Nashville's smoky old Union Station and, climbing the grimy old iron steps up to the taxicabs, heard him break into "It's Three O'clock in the Morning" to the sparkling delight of porters and other early workers? Will Rogers, Geraldine Farrar, William Jennings Bryan, Clarence Darrow, the Four Horsemen of Notre Dame, Bill Tilden, Rudolph Valentino in an exhibition dance, with the women shrieking to touch him — all these, and others, came and went.

Edna St. Vincent Millay came to lecture — and wanted gin for orange blossoms. It was simple. At Foutch's the prescriptionist mixed alcohol, oil of juniper and glycerin, shook it, labeled it witch hazel, and I hurried with it to her suite in the

Hermitage Hotel. She wore the first shimmering gold-metal cloth dress I'd ever seen and she was, to me, one of the most fey and beautiful persons I've ever met.

And the wrestlers and fighters —

Tommy Gibbons liked ice cream and one night, after an exhibition, he and I ate a full quart each as we talked. And Dempsey, Firpo, Sharkey, Battling Siki, and the Frenchman Carpentier —

There was love and laughter . . . and songs: "Tea for Two," "The Man I Love," "Ol' Man River," "My Blue Heaven," "Stardust" —

And death. . . .

One night, on a death watch at the state penitentiary, a man waiting to be electrocuted just after dawn, sat and stood, sleepless, while his companion somehow slept.

"You can't sleep like your friend," said a callous reporter.

"Where I am going I'll have a long time to sleep," he said, simply, and without emotion. . . .

And the man in a small hotel room in the Maxwell House, with bottles littered about, a shotgun on the bed by him, and a huge hole blown in his stomach, grinning a foolish grin as shock masked the death that reached for him as we stood there. . . .

And the girl from Ruth Ray's house who had swallowed carbolic acid and smelled so antiseptically but moaned so piteously as she died in the patrol wagon on the way to the city hospital. . . .

And the frail, slim body dead on a bed in one of two cheap rooms over a grocery store — a note on the table by her saying the son of the jewelry store owner where she cleaned silver had got her pregnant on a promise to marry her — and wouldn't. She had found death by knowing her job. The silver polish used by commercial firms in those days contained cyanides. She had forced herself to eat half a can of it. As long as I live I will remember that slender form on the shabby bed, the pregnancy obvious beneath the clinging gown, and the old woman weeping.

It was not always great to be young and eager in the twenties —

In the spring of 1922 a combination of a column in the *Hustler*, which the chancellor did not like, and a bit of by-play in inter-fraternity rivalry, caused the chancellor to suspend three of us. I went to work full-time at the *Banner*.

VII

Boss Crump's Town

WHENEVER I hear the phrase "personal journalism" I think of Major Edward Bushrod Stahlman, and of the time I was fired from my job as a cub political writer on the *Nashville Banner*.

When he died in August, 1930, Major Stahlman had been owner and publisher of the *Banner* since 1885. In all those years the paper mirrored not so much the news as it did his personality and convictions. Always on the attack, he gloated in victory and never asked quarter or whined in defeat. Politics was his passion, but he was always an independent, never affiliated with party or faction, but fierce in his support of a candidate. He was ruthless and merciless in his opposition. Both affection for him and distaste of him were intense. He was picturesque in appearance, his thick, long, silver-gray hair combed gracefully and neatly back to his shoulders. He walked with a sort of rolling gait, employing an unusually heavy stick with a curved handle, because of a crippled foot suffered as a boy.

It was his custom to pick a young reporter from the staff and make a political writer of him as a backstop for the veteran who ordinarily covered the state house. The managing editor, Marmaduke Beckwith Morton, informed me that I had been so selected, and I went to the Major's office in the Stahlman Building, two blocks from the newspaper office, for my first instructions.

The year was 1922, and a great political feud was raging between the Major and Colonel Luke Lea, owner of the morning paper, *The Tennessean.* The Colonel housed his paper in a building formerly occupied by a gambling house known as the Southern Turf. (Nashville, in that period, was a city with gambling houses, a sprawling red-light district back of the capital, and a Western spirit somewhat like that of Chicago.) The dislike between Colonel Lea and Major Stahlman had been so intense when World War I began that the Colonel, recalling that his political foe had been born in Germany, attempted to have him interned as an enemy alien. It was a petty and unworthily bombastic try, employed chiefly for local headlines, but it made the feud between the two publishers a bitter one.

The *Banner* was printed in those days in a three-story structure that once had been a furniture store. The city room was on the second floor, up one flight. All but the more timorous reporters kept loaded pistols in their scarred old desks, along with a bottle of bourbon whiskey. Nashville was legally dry, but there was a plentiful supply of red liquor brought in by bootleggers from neighboring Kentucky. Legend had it that one day the Leas would come surging up the stairway with revolvers drawn and the shooting would begin. All this was very thrilling to a cub reporter just out of Vanderbilt University. In a way, I guess, we lived our own TV Western stories.

Old Man Marmaduke Morton, a tall, thin martinet, was a Kentuckian who had worked under "Marse Henry" Waterson on the *Courier-Journal.* He was rarely seen without a cane-stemmed corncob pipe in his mouth. The three drawers of his desk contained loose, dark-leaf twist tobacco cut for his half dozen or more pipes and a pair of .32 Smith and Wesson revolvers, which he kept as secretly as possible, apparently not knowing that most of the staff was armed.

Major Stahlman spoke every election year in the city primary campaign. The meetings were held at night, and the speaker's stand was a mobile pickup truck with holders on each side for two kerosene flares. I was assigned to cover the Major. Before I left the office Old Man Morton always called me aside and handed me one of the pistols, which I stuck inside my pants at the waist so that the summer seersucker coat would button over it.

I can still smell the stink of hot kerosene. The moths and a peculiarly offensive hard-shelled beetle would circle the flames in great swarms. The red shadows would flicker on the faces of the crowd with an effect both weird and exciting. It never occurred to me, standing there making notes on a wad of copy paper, that I was both bodyguard and reporter, but I guess I was. There were always policemen about. They knew that the reporters carried revolvers, and one of them, Sergeant Ed Wright, would walk up to me and ask, "What's that bulge there at your waist?" "An extra pencil, Sergeant," I'd reply. "Be careful and don't let it shoot you in the foot," he'd say and go away laughing loudly. At the end of the speaking, when the Major was safely gone, Ed Wright would hunt me up and say, "Get that thing back to the office." He didn't laugh then.

We reporters all loved the Major because he was such a reckless and courageous fighter. Life was on a higher, exhilarating plateau when he was carrying the fight to the opposition. He wanted to be quoted exactly, with none of the brimstone omitted. If he identified an opponent as a scoundrel fitted more for a penitentiary cell than public office, he wanted it printed that way. There must have been libel laws in those days, but politicians never invoked them. There was a legend in Tennessee, coming down from Andrew Jackson's time, that a gentleman didn't sue.

After a few weeks, Major Stahlman sent me on the road with a Luke Lea-supported Memphis attorney, Gus Fitzhugh, who was contesting for the Democratic nomination to the U. S. Senate seat held by Kenneth D. ("Kaydee") McKellar, also of Memphis. McKellar had blocked the Lea efforts to have Major

Stahlman declared an enemy alien. Thus, the lines were drawn in bitterness and revenge.

Before sending me to join Fitzhugh, the Major told me to count every crowd and report its exact number. He also wanted me to note every catcall and the response to each point. In brief, I was to do a hatchet job on Mr. Fitzhugh, although the language was not then enriched with that phrase. I went at it with great enthusiasm and succeeded rather well. I recall that in Tullahoma a delegation visited my hotel room after the speech and tried to send me out of town on the midnight train. The sheriff, summoned by the hotel manager, stopped us in the lobby and restored me to my room. The feeling grew so intense that the paper's business suffered. The circulation and business managers suggested to the Major that he might ease up.

"Young men," said the Major, "this is my newspaper. If I want to float it down the Cumberland River on a raft, I will do so." That ended that.

The campaign traveled mostly on day trains and stopped at small country hotels. Often I found myself seated just across the aisle on the train from Mr. Fitzhugh or at the same breakfast table with him at about 5:30 or 6:00 A.M., with a sleepy waitress trying to serve us before the early train left. Fitzhugh used to lash out at the Major and me in his speeches. He had to do that. But I learned to honor him for never making a personal issue of it off the platform. My schedule was a strain, broken by occasional open dates in speeches and a return to Nashville and the *Banner*.

Filing copy was not easy in those days. The Western Union offices in the small towns usually closed at 6 P.M. Rare were those open as late as 8 o'clock. My first job, on arriving at the town where the night meeting would be held, was to look up the Western Union operator. Most of them were middle-aged or older women. If we arrived but a half hour or so before the speaking, it was still necessary to learn the identity of the operator and her place of residence. Then, fortified with a box of candy and my best manner, I would call and ask if the lady would do me the great favor to open the office after the speaking and send my copy. Before the lady could answer I would say that if she were interested in attending the rally I would be honored to escort her there. At this moment I would present the box of candy as a token of my appreciation for considering my problem of late copy. I do not recall a single turndown. I was not, however, under any illusions about my charms. In a small country town the appearance of a candidate for governor or the United States Senate was one of the year's big events. And to be escorted there by a reporter from the state capital was an added attraction.

It was not always smooth sailing. Now and then I encountered an operator who thought Mr. Fitzhugh was just grand. One lady stopped midway in sending my copy. I sighed and said I would dislike to report it to the Nashville office. She finished, but would not permit me to escort her home.

In the really small towns the railroad telegrapher doubled as the Western Union man. Many a night I have written in small depots and seen the story go out between stops to send or receive messages concerning late trains or lost freight.

Covering the state was not easy. The local or "accommodation" trains were all day coaches. It often was necessary to take one after a night rally and arrive at the next town at 3 or 4 P.M., in order to be there for a morning engagement. There were places which could be reached only by car. The roads were mostly dirt. Late one afternoon as we went down a very long, steep road to a ferry across a river, en route to Smithville, the brakes failed on our Ford touring car. The local county manager was driving and Fitzhugh was in front with him. A reporter from the *Memphis Commercial Appeal* and I were in the back seat.

The driver ran the car up on the side of a bank, away from the deep ravine which yawned on our left. It almost turned over. He yanked it back into the road. Candidate Fitzhugh wisely jumped. The momentum flung him forward so violently that he fell sprawling. I was on the side next to the ravine and had to wait on the Memphis reporter's exit. I encouraged him loudly and at last he made it with me at his heels. We, too, sprawled. The driver headed the car into a tree at the ravine's edge. That stopped it. He escaped with a bruised forehead, but the car was done for until a mechanic could attend it. We walked half a mile down the hill, dusty, bedraggled, and shaken, carrying our bags.

The ferry was across the river. We rang and rang the bell, and finally the attendant came. He had been home to supper, he said. We had no transportation, but he told us of a farmer, "up the road a piece" who had a pickup truck. Being the youngest of the four, I volunteered. The farmer wanted ten dollars to take us in. We paid it gladly.

It was court week in Smithville and the two small hotels, which were two-story clapboard houses converted into inns, were jammed. There was a room for the candidate. The local manager stayed with a relative. Memphis and I slept in a hallway on an old opened-out sofa. It had a heavy musty smell and the old springs gouged and squeaked with each movement. People came and went through the darkened hall. There was not much sleep.

Next morning at breakfast, I saw Fitzhugh at a neighboring table. He was having a cup of coffee, waiting for the local committee, which was to dine with him and discuss plans. He was lost in his thoughts. A man's face is naked in those moments. His looked sad and forlorn, defeated and weary. One knew that he was wondering why he was there in that wretched hotel, sleepy and bruised, when he might be in his commodious office in Memphis, where life was ordered, comfortable and rewarding. One of my knees was cut and raw from gravel on the road. My pants also had been torn by them, and I was thinking that Mr. Morton would never okay a repair bill unless

I took the trousers in and showed him the rent. But, even so, my heart went out to Gus Fitzhugh. I resolved not to be quite so caustic with him.

My stories were satisfactory, the Major said. They were top play on page one every day. They reported that local leaders everywhere predicted Fitzhugh's defeat, that he frequently had been jeered, and that his speeches were flat.

This was all true, especially the latter charge. Fitzhugh was a very successful corporation lawyer and a man of some wealth. He was heavy-set, of average height, with a nice face, but he could never really break out of his shell of dignity and reserve. The more he tried, the more apparent it was that he was trying — and failing. He had no gift for small talk, and he was not at ease before the shirt-sleeved farmers and their families who filled the sultry courtrooms or gathered in some grove around a platform of new-sawed lumber to hear political candidates. Such ease is acquired only through experience, and it is not even distantly related to the confident mien which an attorney may assume arguing a case before a jury or a judge.

Invective at that time was even more an effective weapon than now. Fitzhugh didn't know how to use this sort of firepower, and his instincts were against it. One week, he began to charge that McKellar was nothing more than a messenger boy in the Senate and declared that the great state of Tennessee needed a man who could provide some leadership and stature. "Tennessee," he would cry, waving his right arm in an old-fashioned flailing gesture, "deserves more than a messenger boy."

There was some truth in this. McKellar paid great attention to letters from constituents. He was forever badgering the various departments with petty requests and complaints received in letters. Whatever legislation he introduced was worked out with Ed Crump and his associates. McKellar almost literally was a messenger boy for Crump and the voters. This was, of course, his political strength.

It was not my opinion that the Fitzhugh charge was in any degree effective. If anything, it made Fitzhugh seem a little pompous to be suggesting that he, an awkward, unentertaining speaker, was really a great statesman. But it seemed to sting McKellar. He bided his time until a Saturday when he spoke at the Middle Tennessee rural town of Sparta. The courtroom was packed with farmers and their wives. McKellar was an old pro. He had been schooled in Crump's Memphis classes for years before being promoted to the Senate. A medium-tall, square-faced man, with modest paunch adding senatorial dignity to his silhouette, he was afflicted with a heavily veined, enlarged nose which suggested drink. Actually, he was a teetotaler and rarely failed to tell the rural audiences that he had promised his mother never to drink and had kept his word. Cynics, looking at the nose, sat always in the seat of the scornful.

He was, all in all, a true politician and knew all the old tricks of the campaign trade. He employed one at Sparta to disembowel the already feeble Fitzhugh. In Sparta there lived a gentle old couple who, when their son had been reported missing in the first action by United States troops in the great war against the Kaiser, had wired Senator McKellar for assistance.

After the usual ritual of introduction and remarks was out of the way, the senator, who but for the nose would have resembled a pious deacon, reduced his voice to a sort of confidential whinny.

"I see," he said, "two old friends of mine in the front row." He pointed and named them. He asked them to stand, and they did, and the crowd applauded. "You all know them," he said. "Now my opponent has called me a messenger boy, and I want to confess it. During the great war to make the world safe for democracy, their fine son was reported missing. His sorrowing parents wired me. Ladies and gentlemen, when I received that wire in Washington I did not telephone the

War Department. I did not send my clerk. I did not wait and order a cab. I put my hat on my head and walked over there and I said to the Secretary of War, 'I want to learn the fate of this fine Tennessee boy, and I want it quick.' I went back again and again until they let me know he was wounded but would live, and then I wired them he was safe and would come back to their arms." He paused, his hand held high, so that the sound of weeping could be heard, and then he brought his hand down sharply as he said, in a great, shouting voice, "If that is being a messenger boy, I thank God for the title!"

The roar that followed was mighty and long. The Sparta courthouse box was safe.

Toward the end of the campaign a great McKellar rally was held in Memphis. It followed by a night or so the one for Fitzhugh, and I stayed over for it. Fitzhugh had a good crowd, which filled a large downtown theater. The rally was a dignified success, although there was an uneasy sense of futility about it. But the Crump machine turned out a torrent of people and sound for "Kaydee."

Ed Crump, a tall, thin man of velvet-covered arrogance, had created a sort of oligarchy as a front for the more sordid operations of his organization. He attracted some good names and reputations for his major candidates. He saw to it that the tax rate was low, that government was efficient, and that patronage went to the faithful. A card-index file of every citizen, his job, family, church, probable income, and credit status, was in his offices. Ward and precinct meetings were held regularly. Newcomers to Shelby County or Memphis, the county seat, had a prompt call from one of the precinct workers, who arranged for the water and gas connections to be made quickly and for an invitation to be issued to a "neighborhood party." At most of these, sandwiches and coffee were served, although in some wards liquor flowed. The organization made sure that eligible voters were registered and, more important, that they voted. In Mr. Crump's Memphis, the Negro was a Democrat, and he voted. There was never any restriction against Negroes' voting so long as they voted right. I never believed the Crump machine stuffed boxes. It didn't need to be so crude. It got out the vote.

Crump, when I first met him and saw him operate in my cub days, had an aura of romance about him. He was the first political boss I ever knew. He always took care to see that the "newspaper boys" arriving with candidates were "looked after." A justice of the peace, whom we all knew as Louie, usually was assigned to us. We'd go late, after rallies, to the Silver Slipper or another night place for dinner and the floor show. It was during Prohibition, but liquor and gambling flourished.

No bills were rendered.

The romantic idea of Ed Crump lasted maybe a month or two, though, actually, there wasn't much choice. Fitzhugh and McKellar had no real issue between them save that one was anti-Crump. There was an idea abroad that McKellar might be defeated by the upstate vote. Well before the summer was over I would have preferred Fitzhugh, for all his fatuousness, but for my loyalty to and delight in the feud.

It was just after the big Memphis rally that I got fired. Marmaduke B. Morton was an inflexible sort of man. He had a rule that every reporter had to be at his desk at 7 A.M. After one warning, a second offense meant firing. I managed a second one during one of the breaks in the campaign and was fired. I had no excuse and no defense. I checked out, drew my pay, and went up to tell Major Stahlman goodbye. I told him it had been fun and that I was sure McKellar was safe. He heard me out. He said never a word, but stood and took his hat and cane from a hall tree rack.

"Come with me," he said.

I followed him out. We took the elevator down to the street floor. We walked down Third Avenue to the *Banner* and climbed the stairs to the city room. Neither he nor I had spoken since we left his office. He walked to where Old Man Morton sat wreathed in acrid smoke.

"Morton," he said, in a voice which crackled, "I want you to know this boy is working for me. He will come and go as he pleases, and he will be responsible only to me. Is that understood?"

Old Man Morton nodded.

The Major turned and went out.

I returned to the road. McKellar won the nomination by almost ninety thousand votes. I was glad for the Major, but I had learned that McKellar was a machine-made mossback and that Boss Ed Crump was, after all, not really a romantic figure, as he had seemed, but a corrupt and corrupting boss. The feud had lost its savor, and I left Nashville not long thereafter with the hurt between Marmaduke B. Morton and me entirely healed.

I had made a step in coming of age. Looking back, I realize there is something of the Major in me. I do not hold with his extreme, almost compulsive partisanship. But I believe in being strongly partisan on issues which require a choice. That guarantee of freedom of the press is in the Constitution for just one reason — to enable newspapers to speak out. Also, it seems important that newspapers should have, as the Major had, an acute sense of right and wrong. There are some newspapers which are mute and others which carefully engage only editors with chronic laryngitis. But there comes a time in all controversies when one must hit the issue right on the nose or turn tail and die a little. The Major's style was to walk right out of his corner when the bell rang and throw his Sunday punch. This, I learned, often leaves a man vulnerable to a hard counter. Sometimes it is better to spar for a while or back away for a good look. But finally the issue must be hit hard. In the Major's day it was easier. The owners of papers were themselves vigorously partisan. The people didn't get much news. The facts and issues were beclouded. But the people did know there was a fight.

VIII

Uncle Alf Taylor

MY FIRST BLACK EYE was received in a fist-swinging political controversy between supporters of the Republican
and Democratic parties. It took place on the old gravel-covered
grounds of the Fourth District School at Chattanooga, Tennessee. I was ten years old, and was then fighting under the
flag of the GOP, a fact which in later years was a source of
considerable amusement to my friends who know the story.
My family was divided politically, as were so many in East
Tennessee. My mother was a Democrat. But women at that
time were not permitted to vote. My father as I have said, was
a faithful Republican whose hero was Teddy Roosevelt, and I
had taken up his cause. He could vote and did without fail.
Not only that, but he took me with him.

I have only episodic memories of baseball, the Methodist
and Baptist revivals to which I went for excitement, of circuses,
and other entertainment. From those years I recall a fat, chunky
catcher on the Chattanooga Sally League team, called "Buttermilk" Meek. He was a home-run hitter. But I recall him chiefly,
I think, because my mother was about that time trying to
persuade me to drink buttermilk on the grounds it was health-
giving. Mr. Meek reportedly drank great amounts of it and
could hit home runs.

But politics I do remember. My father took me along to the
polls. After he voted he always stood around for a while and

talked over the outlook for the Republican candidates. Since he went to work early he could not vote until evening. This made it more fascinating for me. In our precinct the election was held at No. 5 firehouse. The huge, wonderful horses would be there in their stalls, their heavy harness suspended above them ready to drop at the clang of a bell. Close beside the engine was the shining brass pole down which the firemen could slide from their sleeping quarters up above. Even a small boy could pat the horses on the neck and twine himself about the pole, imagining the swift descent amid the clamor of bells.

The hall was lit with electricity, but the bulbs were few and small. There were always a few kerosene lamps about on the tables. One of my sharpest memories is of the heavy aroma of cigars. They were passed out on election days by emissaries of the major local candidates, and most of the inveterate pipe smokers would thereby be persuaded, so that there was much cigar smoking.

One of the proud days of my life came on an election day. It was on a school holiday and I had gone early to the fire station on my own. A small crisis arose. A fringed surrey had been hired by the Republican ward organization to fetch elderly and crippled persons to the polls and return them home. The Negro driver didn't know the streets in our suburban area. A friend of my father saw me and asked me to accompany and direct the driver. I was given a sheet of paper with names and addresses. I recall trying to be calm about it, but when I had climbed up in the high seat by the driver and we drove off for our first voter I was hugely excited and thrilled. I would have changed places with only a few persons on that day. I labored lovingly for the GOP, going to the doors, ringing the bells, and then assisting the elderly or infirm residents out to the surrey and into a seat. We could carry nine in our three wide seats and we must have made quite a sight going and coming all that day. I know I was the envy of all my schoolmates, and I yet recall the casual, man-of-the-world gesture of greeting I cultivated during that magnificent day. It was years later I realized that for my passengers, too, it was a fine moment. Most of them were from homes in poorer, white-collar neighborhoods. Their lives must have been barren of such transportation. For them, riding in a grand surrey behind two high-stepping horses, must have been a highlight. Also they enjoyed their status. They were needed. The Republican party wanted them.

Best of all, though, were election nights. After the polls closed we had a late supper at home. My father and I would take a trolley down to the *Chattanooga Times*, founded by Adolph Ochs, of the *New York Times*. Election returns were thrown from a window in the *Times* office onto a large screen across the street. After almost half a century, I can still feel the pulsing of excitement within me when the bright shaft of the magic lantern cut through the night to light the screen, and the murmurs and laughter of the crowd hushed so that full attention could be given the figures that appeared there. The cheers and groans that went up from the partisans were wonderful to hear and I joined in with a will. If the contests were close we stayed late, taking the last streetcar, called "The Owl." I saw the returns in 1908 when William Howard Taft beat William Jennings Bryan. I was too young for the result to mean anything to me save to share in my father's partisan joy.

But in 1912 when Woodrow Wilson won I was already secretly a Wilson man from much reading of his speeches and newspaper accounts of him. In 1916 I was strongly and openly for him. My father took it well, but was, I think, a little hurt. He rather thought, he said, that I had been over-persuaded by some of the Presbyterian teachers I had at McCallie Preparatory School. I reminded him that he was a stanch Presbyterian himself and that perhaps it was predestined I would become a Wilson man. He laughed and did not mention it again until years later during the depression of the 1930's. He heard my enthusiasm for Franklin Roosevelt with quiet approval. He never told me, and I did not know until after his death, that in 1936 he had voted for F.D.R. An old GOP friend of his told me my father had told him of it, but had asked him not to reveal his desertion of the party to which he had given so much loyalty.

At any rate, whether it was predestination or not, I was a Wilson Democrat before I could vote.

The fascination of politics, of partisanship, has endured through the years. When I became a reporter there was the same stabbing thrill, waiting for a wire service Morse "bug" to start its chattering dots and dashes and the Morse operator to tap out the message, as when as a small boy I had seen the shaft of light burst from the *Times* window and reveal the results on the screen. I suffer with the candidates to whom I have given belief and endorsement, and the night of the returns is agony for me unless, of course, a lead builds up quickly.

For a number of years writing politics was my trade. I think the finest time I had as a young reporter was traveling one summer with Uncle Alf Taylor, of Happy Valley, Carter County, Tennessee. Uncle Alf was even then a legend, living in the shadow of the greater one of his brother Bob. The Taylors were early settlers in a corner of East Tennessee which was then almost inaccessible to the state governments in North Carolina and Virginia. The settlements along the Watauga, Holston and Tennessee Rivers organized the first white society west of the Appalachian peaks. The district in which the Coopers lived was that of John Sevier, William Blount and Andrew Jackson.

My own people had settled south of there in East Tennessee, and I heard of the Taylors at about the same time I learned of John Sevier. The story of the Taylor brothers and "the War of the Roses" was one I must have heard talked about a hundred times before I learned to read.

In 1886 Robert Love Taylor was the Democratic nominee for governor of Tennessee, and his brother Alfred A. Taylor, was the Republican choice. Mountain men are individualists, and none thought it odd that their father, Nathaniel Green Taylor, a graduate of the College of New Jersey, later Princeton, was that same year the prohibition candidate for governor. The old gentleman made no speeches and asked for no votes. He was so dead set against whiskey in any form he believed the prohibition cause should have a candidate. When none offered, he did, as a matter of principle.

The two brothers campaigned together. On the way from Chattanooga to the capital at Nashville at the outset of the contest, they were in a train wreck at Bridgeport, Alabama. They spent the night at a small hotel there. The next morning the lady who ran it went into her garden and cut two roses. As her guests departed she pinned a white rose on Bob and a red one on Alf. "I want you to accept these flowers, gentlemen, for the sake of your mother. I know she must be proud of boys who can be politicians and still be brothers." A newspaper correspondent wrote a story of it, calling Bob "Knight of the White Rose," and Alf "Knight of the Red Rose." The campaign soon became known as "the War of the Roses."

There is no end to stories of this brotherly contest. My favorite is that of their stay with a mountaineer. The rivals were traveling in a buggy. The roads were bad, and along the way some spokes were broken when the lurching buggy scraped a wheel against a rock. A crossroads blacksmith repaired it, but night caught them miles short of their destination.

A mountaineer and his wife put them up, retiring, themselves, to a bed in the log cabin's attic. The ebullient, fun-loving Bob slipped out of bed while it was yet dark, made a fire in the kitchen stove and put a kettle of water on for coffee. At first dawn he went to the barn and milked the cow. When he returned, the somewhat embarrassed mountain farmer and his wife were in the kitchen, the latter frying ham and eggs.

"I always get up at this time," explained Bob, who was really a lazy, easygoing man, "but I will appreciate it if you will be quiet and not wake my brother. He likes to sleep late and have breakfast in bed. I'll take a tray in to him later."

The three ate in near-silence, the mountaineer lost in thought. Like most mountain men, he was a Republican. At last he could stand it no more.

"You say your brother eats breakfast in bed?"

"That's right."

There was another interval of silence. Finally, he spoke again.

"Well," he said. "I never thought I'd vote for no Democrat! But I'm damned if I'll vote for a man who eats in bed."

A sleepy-eyed Alf came in soon thereafter and never understood the coolness of his host until they were a safe distance from the house and he heard the story from his hilarious brother.

Bob died in 1912, having been three times governor and a United States senator. When I first met Uncle Alf on assignment to cover his campaign he was the incumbent governor and was running for re-election against Austin Peay, of Clarkesville. It was 1923. Uncle Alf was seventy-five years old.

The Taylor brothers had been fiddle players, fox hunters, and tellers of tales. But Uncle Alf was more of the hunting squire than brother Bob. At seventy-five he looked the part. Short, stout, he dressed neatly but plainly. His face was red from wind and sun because all his days he had been, in truth, a mighty hunter of foxes. His pack of Walker hounds was famous throughout all East Tennessee. And at three score years and fifteen he rode to hounds.

Fox hunting is the great democracy. Lawyers, doctors, businessmen, and an occasional minister joined with small farmers out of the coves to follow hounds on day hunts. Many of them liked, also, to go at night, riding roads and trails, and listening to "the music." They had an unerring ear and could identify the hound which was leading and those which were well-up. The most famous hound in Uncle Alf's pack was an aging veteran of the trail, and also a noted sire, "Old Limber."

The campaign was a delight. Uncle Alf traveled with a mountain quartet, three members of which were his sons. Old Limber also went along. He dozed on the floor each night by the speaker's table, and at afternoon rallies, peered at the crowd with the dignity and calm of the serenely old. He accepted pats on the head and the stroking of his back as his due.

There were occasional off-days during the campaign which we spent at Happy Valley. It was pleasant to sit in one of the numerous deep rocking chairs, with feet on the long rail atop the balustrade, listening to the conversation of neighbors and visitors in the other chairs. I liked to look down the row at the mountain faces, noting the different look of the townsmen and those from the small valley farms. Tobacco was in unanimous use. Pipes and cigars gave off a fog and there was much expert spitting over the rail by those addicted to chewing plug or twist. The talk was chiefly of politics, and foxhounds, past and present.

But the great Republican tide of 1920, upon which Uncle Alf had been swept to the governorship, had ebbed. And in November, 1923, when I split the Democratic ticket to vote for Uncle Alf, I knew he couldn't be re-elected. He went back to Happy Valley, untouched by bitterness or regret.

On his eightieth birthday I went back for a huge celebration that had been arranged. At dawn all the best hounds of East Tennessee, young and old, would be cast and there would be a barbecue, fiddling contests, and fun.

It was a magnificent day. I will never forget the more than two hundred eager hounds — Walkers, July, Red Bones, and Triggs, held by handlers in one vast semicircle on a high bald dome some eight miles up from Happy Valley. They were released when the red ball of the morning sun rose over the highest peak. They went away like a torrent to a spine-tingling blast of fox horns, and I recall the look on Uncle Alf's face. No fox hunter had ever had such a birthday.

Asked for an explanation of the success which had come to him and his even more famous brother, and of the many loyal friends, he said, "We played the fiddle, were fond of dogs and loved our fellow men." He died three years later after that massive cast of foxhounds, content and unafraid.

The years passed, and in May, 1954, the U. S. Supreme Court ruled that Negro children could not be denied entry to any public school because of race. The first test case came out of Clinton, Tennessee. A name leaped out of the news dispatch as I read. The federal judge who would hear the case was Robert Love Taylor, son of Alfred A. Taylor. This was Uncle Alf's son who had sung in the quartet in the old campaign. He was named, of course, for his Democratic uncle, Bob, who had been the rival in "the War of the Roses."

I grinned to myself, and felt a surge of relief. I knew that a Taylor would never permit any prejudice, pressure, tradition or caprice to prevent him from ruling according to the law as interpreted by the highest court of his country. I also knew he would not seek any loophole to avoid or delay a ruling. And so it was. Judge Robert Love Taylor bore the brunt of all the early fanaticism against the school ruling. Before him also came the cases of those who agitated and created mob violence. Precisely, with quiet, unruffled dignity, he handed down decisions which, by their force and clarity, helped calm the troubled days. All those preaching defiance of law knew that law prevailed, and would continue to do so.

I was more innocent in those early years of political reporting, but I do not recall any of the preposterous or vicious racist demagoguery met with in later years. It could be heard in states to the south of us but we largely escaped it.

It would not be honest to be smug about this. There were few Negroes in East Tennessee. Middle Tennessee had no history of racial agitation of politics. West Tennessee was a rural economy save for urban Memphis. And there Mr. Crump ruled. The Negro voters were a part of his organization.

I was not then experienced enough to discern that even though the Memphis Negroes were a cog in a most efficient machine, the very fact they voted gave them a status above that enjoyed by Negroes in Southern cities where few voted. They had communication with those who governed. It was a paternalistic system, but they were recognized as voters.

Even a ballot controlled by an organization has value. It did not surprise me when, in 1948, the Negroes of Memphis broke with the old organization to go for Senator Estes Kefauver. I recalled the days when I, the young reporter, knew Beale Street was the symbol of Negro life in Memphis. Even then it had moved far from the days of 1909 when a young Negro band leader wrote a campaign lyric on the cigar counter in Pee Wee's Beale Street Saloon. He titled it "Mr. Crump," and it read:

> Mr. Crump won't 'low no easy riders here,
> Mr. Crump won't 'low no easy riders here;
> We don't care what Mr. Crump won't 'low
> We gon' to bar'l house anyhow,
> Mr. Crump can go catch his self some air . . .

Memphis politics of that day are a grotesque caricature compared with the procedures of the 1960's. There are times when, looking back at the changes I have seen come to the South, it seems incredible, not so much that they have occurred, but that the conditions requiring so much reform should have existed at all. That White Citizens Councils still oppose voting rights and defend injustices and inequities of citizenship as being a part of these things "we hold most dear" is the most incredible fact, and commentary, of all.

But in those early days of reporting politics and foxhounds,

I did not consider how a moral force could be tied down like Gulliver by so many strings of tradition, custom, greed, apathy, and fear as to require more than a quarter of a century to begin to break the cords and struggle free.

IX

The Twig Is Bent

IN MORE THAN a quarter century of giving ear to Southern politicians, Klan speakers and preachers — and in more recent years the White Citizens Councils, mob members such as those of Little Rock, New Orleans and, later, by the Snopeses at "Ole Miss" in Oxford, Mississippi, and the interpositionists — I came to believe in something of reincarnation, or the more likely fact of numbing unoriginality of minds prejudiced by race.

Now and then someone came along like Uncle Earl Long, or the late Cotton Ed Smith, who raised the art of irrelevance, vulgar invective, and demagoguery to preposterous heights of entertainment. But even they were playing their own arrangements of original composers.

One summer vacation I used up some of the leisure hours culling the benders of regional twigs until I had four whose ideas, blasphemies, prejudices, sophistries, syllogisms, phrases of invective, and theories have been, and yet are, repeated most often since the Supreme Court decision of 1954. It is unlikely those who use them most are aware they are repeating. The words and phrases have for years been floating in the South's political air, like motes in sunlight, to be breathed in and expelled.

The twig benders left after culling were: Thomas Roderick Dew, 1802-1846; Benjamin Ryan Tillman, 1847-1918; James

Kimble Vardaman, 1861-1930; Thomas Edward Watson, 1856-1922.

In reading of the early turbulent, reasonless days when sectionalism grew in the South and the region began to think on how different it was, I was struck with how often both politicians and demagogues of that early day had to turn to their scholars to provide substance for poor arguments.

In 1831 it still was the custom of the Virginia legislature to look to the college of William and Mary for guidance. In that year the Assembly made a request of Professor Thomas Roderick Dew that he produce for them a summary of the long controversy on the abolition of slavery.

There is no intent to injure the feelings of the professor's ghost, but it is nonetheless true the authors of the request knew that whereas his predecessors in the chair of "History, Metaphysics, Natural and National Law, Government and Political Economy," George Wythe and St. George Tucker, had been antislavery men, as were others on the faculty, Professor Dew was an ardent slavery man. He comes through very plainly to us from the records of his time. He was a self-satisfied little man who yearned for the limelight. He was the favorite son of a Virginia planter. His father, Thomas Dew, was of an old Maryland family. When a young man, he had moved to King and Queen County, Virginia, where, by successful farming and judicious moneylending, he came to own slaves and a plantation which he named Dewsville. He married Lucy E. Gatewood, a native of the county. One of their ten children was Thomas, who entered the College of William and Mary in the grammar school department and progressed to graduation with an A.B. degree in 1820. His indulgent father sent him to Europe for two years of travel. In 1827 he was appointed to one of the six faculty positions at the college where he did much to make the subject of political economy a major one.

The request from the Virginia legislature pleased him and he eagerly responded. Professor Dew added no new knowledge to the assigned subject. But he did something which made the politicians more effective. He took all the arguments which had been made for slavery and gave them organization and a smooth, scholarly persuasiveness. There were no qualifications or doubts in his conclusions. His reasoning had a quality of polished, genteel finality.

He was most persuasive to those eager and waiting to be persuaded. The professor began by casting his eyes back through history. Where were the great civilizations? He saw them in Greece, in Rome, along the Nile. Captives, instead of being put to death, were put to work. The arts, architecture, freedom, private property, leisure — in fact the true civilizations — flourished only where there was slavery.

This was Dew's preamble. He proceeded then to prove that slavery benefited the Negro. Unfitted for freedom by nature, slavery gave him protection, care and security. His lot was much more desirable, the professor found, than that of the miserable free worker who was exploited and meagerly paid in the North where materialistic clamor and vulgar commercialism made civilization impossible.

Nor did the Scriptures condemn slavery or in any manner suggest the slave owner had committed any offense against God or man. New England traders had bought them — English regulations and, later, the laws of the new Republic, required their retention. Let those responsible for this look to their consciences. The slave owner need not feel any twinges. God approved. It was foreordained to be.

As for freeing them, or sending them to Liberia, that would be worse than slavery. As free men they would be exploited as wretched wage slaves. They would lack all protection, care and security. In Liberia quick death awaited them.

Professor Dew looked with benign eyes upon the slave owners of the South and saw them as characterized by "noble and elevated sentiments, by humane and virtuous feelings." "Selfishness might exist elsewhere, but was nowhere to be found among Southern slave holders." It was "Christian" to care for inferior people, unfitted by intellect to be free. This was a harsh repudiation of Thomas Jefferson who had, of course, been mistaken.

All the sentiments so carefully collected and unchallenged in the seclusion of his academic cloister carefully were marshaled forth. He closed by asserting to his own and the legislature's satisfaction, and proving, that slavery, far from interfering with the democratic form of government, made true democracy possible by bringing all white men to "one common level."

"We believe," Professor Dew wrote, "that slavery in the United States has accomplished this, in regard to the whites, as nearly as can be expected, or even desired in this world. The menial and low offices are being performed by the blacks, there is at once taken away the greatest cause of distinction and separation of the ranks of society."

Thus, in so gentle and scholarly a manner, was white supremacy defined.

There was no bitterness in Professor Dew. Out of his background of birth, and out of his seclusion with books, he believed even the more preposterous of his arguments. He delivered his lecture to the Virginia Assembly as if it had been one of his classes, savoring its applause.

So well pleased were its members that, at their suggestion, he had his paper published in Richmond, titled *Review of the Debate* [on the abolition of slavery] *in the Virginia Legislature of 1831-1832*. So popular was it that a second edition was required. Soon other legislatures were repeating it. Pulpits rang with it. Newspapers printed large excerpts with extravagant endorsement.

The more vocal Southern Nationalists praised it — without stint. *De Bow's Review,* which had a large part in the emotional factors which brought on the Civil War, declared the South would forever be indebted to Professor Dew. Already the various state and local political arrangers of Professor Dew's composition were beginning to repeat it with their own variations and embellished interpretations. They still are.

Happily for Professor Dew, he did not live to have his and similar verdicts disproved.

In 1845, when the dialogue had become much more angry, but while he was still acclaimed as the great defender of civilization, this amiable, angular professor, innocent of most of the world outside books and theaters, then forty-three, fell in love. He married Natilia Hay, the young daughter of a Clark County physician. They went to Paris on their honeymoon and there he died, of pleurisy or pneumonia.

By the time he died there were voices rising in the land which were angry, defiant, demanding, pleading. South Carolina's Robert Barnwell Rhett, son of New England forebears; Alabama's William Lowndes Yancey, graduate of Williams College; Virginia's agronomist Edmund Ruffin, and William Gregg, Virginia-born but long a South Carolina manufacturer; full of sound and fury, were already moving to occupy the stage — which they were to hold all through the 1850's. But Dew's "classic statement" still served as the model. In all their Wagnerian thunders his theme could be heard. One feels that if the spirit of Professor Dew was around it did not approve of the clamor. It wasn't good manners and it did not jibe with his picture of a perfect, Greeklike civilization and the assured, poised culture which could flower only out of slavery. But the theme was his.

J. D. B. De Bow's *Review* already was saying: "The South's cup of endurance is full." (This exact sentence was often heard in Southern legislatures after the 1954 school decision.)

Ben Tillman of South Carolina was a second mover and shaker, a bender of twigs. He, unlike Professor Dew, had a youthful environment which was emotionally violent. He grew up a favorite of his widowed mother. Two brothers were killed in war. Another died of fever. When Ben was nine, an older brother, George, killed a man in a gambling feud and served two years in jail. In his ears were the frequent sound of sobs and his mother's resentful protests against such heavy blows from fate.

The young Ben was his mother's constant companion in managing the plantation and the many slaves. She had him tutored at home and later sent him to a private school. He became apt at English and Latin.

In 1861 he left home to join the Confederate Army but soon came down with a never fully diagnosed illness which made him a semi-invalid for two years and cost him the sight of one eye. Resentment and a sense of injustice became a part of his personality.

In 1868 he married Sallie Starke of Elbert County, Georgia. His mother helped him to four hundred acres adjoining her holdings. It was land leached poor by many years of cotton cropping and the returns from it were meager.

He was an intense man, bitterly inhibited, spurred always by the feeling that life and fate had treated him shabbily. He was unattractive in appearance, quick-tempered, irascible and unpopular with his neighbors. For a time he dabbled ineffectively in county politics.

By 1885, discontent lay on all the farmlands of America. The fever of Populism ran hotly in all the agricultural arteries and the emotions of it brought the Southeast and Midwest close to class warfare. Its yeasty ferment caused men long inarticulate to have the gift of tongues. In August of that year, near bankruptcy like most of his neighbors, Ben Tillman made a speech which caused men to talk. Their interests, he shouted at a meeting of farmers, were being betrayed by the merchants and lawyers, who fed on them and their poverty.

From that day on he harried the farmers to organize. In every conversation or speech, he indicted the merchant and lawyer class with angry and violent charges of exploitation. Many of them were basically true, and not too greatly exaggerated.

He somehow hated the Negro. No one knew exactly why. It seemingly irritated him that Negroes were free. But whatever the reason, his hate was irrational and vindictive. The Negro, he declared, was not a man but an animal and savage. He was, perhaps, the missing link. Negroes, he argued, had produced no civilization of their own; they were best off as slaves.

Education of the Negro was a subject which excited him to near hysteria. Education of people not suited for it, he shouted to his crowds of landless and discontented, to the hot-eyed small farmers with mortgages and crop liens on their depressed acres and crops, would bring on a bloody war between the races. His preachments were incredibly wild incitements to violence and restriction. The Negro became the scapegoat for all the resentments of small farmers and plantation owners caught in an economic and political squeeze.

Nor did he restrict his tirades to his own county. By 1892 he was absolute master of South Carolina politics.

At his fiery command distinguished men who had served their state nobly — eminent Confederate War hero and aristocrat Wade Hampton among them — were voted out of office and replaced by men who faithfully imitated their master.

He had himself elected to the United States Senate. He took to the Chautauqua circuit and went all over the nation picturing the Negro to be a beast and a person unfit for citizenship or education. He sought to arouse sentiment in the Congress to abolish the Fourteenth Amendment and urged force to nullify the Fifteenth.

A bitter foe of Grover Cleveland, Tillman had urged his followers in 1894 to "Send me to Washington so I can stick my pitchfork in his [Cleveland's] old ribs."

His mobs loved it — and called him thereafter "Pitchfork Ben."

In 1896, hoping for the Democratic Presidential nomination, he addressed the party convention. His dark features, his savagely snapping jaws, his masklike face twisted with hate, made him a fearsome figure. He lashed out as if one of his mobs were before him. Many approved. But he was too extreme for a candidate. They nominated William Jennings Bryan. The defeated man went back South where crowds were more approving.

Tillman fought President Teddy Roosevelt, charging him with hypocrisy in dealing with trusts. The President produced documents indicating fraud by Senator Tillman in the purchase of Oregon lands for himself. The charge was not proved, but it was so obviously true it damaged Tillman nationally.

But not at home. He largely controlled South Carolina's politics until he died, leaving many of the state's best traditions overturned and passions loosed which are endemic in the political life of the South. His state has never ceased to produce semi-reincarnations of him.

In all the Southern states there were those who early made him their hero. Many of these converts were young, and most of them were in families which had known and been frustrated by adversity.

James Kimble Vardaman was one of these. Texas-born, son of a Confederate veteran, he was a shirttail boy when his family moved to a farm in Yalobusha County, Mississippi. But at twenty-one, James Vardaman was admitted to the bar and began to practice law at Winona, and write for, and edit, the *Winona Advertiser*, a weekly. From 1890 to 1896 he edited the *Greenwood Enterprise* and served in the legislature. Later he founded his own newspaper, *The Commonwealth*.

The young editor began to hear, above the rumbles of bitter class factionalism in the Democratic Party of his own state, the thunder of Tillman in South Carolina. Vardaman early had the gift of invective speech. He was shrewd, coarse, vulgar, eloquent, ruthless, persuasive. Being a part of the unrest of his time, he decided to try the long leap from the legislature to the governorship.

When he began his campaign for the governorship he rode on a large eight-wheeled lumber wagon. Eight yokes of carefully selected white oxen pulled him to the hustings. It was drama and color in a land which knew little entertainment. His audiences were the discontented, the landless and the small farmer, the poor white man. The planters were the enemy — the planters on the Delta and the Negro, wherever they were. He had read Tillman.

"My friends," he would say to those first delighted audiences, "I know you will listen to me. My first audiences were barnyard animals and jackasses." He had the demagogue's necessary gift of communication. He easily established the tie of brotherhood with the discontented.

"The political dominions of the white race," he told them, week in and week out, "are threatened by the education of the Negro."

His attack on education for the Negro was then a shrewd political device, but there was no hypocrisy in his use of it. He believed it. He saw thus a force which might make him a personal power, above party.

Many of his audiences had bolted the Democratic ticket to vote Populist. Vardaman did not want to become identified with Populism. He believed its followers would in time return to the Democrats. He saw his real opposition as the planter class and he wanted to unite all other factions against it.

The Negro — and the danger of an educated Negro — were his unifying war cries.

His interest in the poor man seemed hotly sincere — so long as the poor man was white.

He, himself, noting how his yokes of white oxen caught on,

began to dress in symbolic white and to let his black hair grow long, brushed down to his shoulders for contrast.

He encouraged the descriptive phrase, "The Great White Chief." He became the hero of discontent, its spokesman, its leader.

In 1904 he was governor. Education for the Negro promptly was reduced to a vocational status, and there was not much of that. State schools for Negroes were closed.

He was defeated in a bid for the Senate in 1907. In 1908 he began to publish a weekly paper at Jackson, *The Issue*. It continued to stir racial passions, to protest education for the Negro.

In 1910 he was defeated by LeRoy Percy, gentleman and true aristocrat of the Delta, whose son, Will Percy, all his life was to fight the prejudices bequeathed Mississippi by Vardaman. It was a legislative choice, an earlier primary result having been declared invalid. Vardaman charged a steal by planters.

In 1911 Vardaman was elected in a primary and became a United States senator in 1912. "The bottom rail is on top," he shouted. And it was.

But power had corrupted. He began to lose his touch. He fought Woodrow Wilson and the war. In 1918 Pat Harrison defeated him. His health began to break. In 1922 he was unable to speak. He moved to Alabama and waited out death. Of him, too, it truly could be written that the evil that men do lives after them.

Tom Watson, another rallier and organizer of discontented men and prejudice in the South, was born in a small log house three miles north of Thomson, Georgia, on September 5, 1856.

Congressman, nominee for the vice presidency on the Populist's fusion ticket with William Jennings Bryan in 1896, and United States senator, Watson dwarfed the Tillmans and Vardamans in sheer genius of intellect and ability. He had, like them, all the black arts of the politics of violence.

But there was a time when the small farmers, owners, tenants, croppers, Negro and white, worshiped him next to God Himself, and, as one said, felt more sure of Watson. Negroes would crowd about him and touch his garments and go home and tell their families, "I seen him today. I seen him and heard him talk and touched his clothes."

He was the sworn foe of monopoly, not in the narrow sense of the word, but monopoly of power, of place, of privilege, of wealth, of progress.

He had, in his beginnings, to attack not merely the old social and political structures but the problem of race. His Populist struggle in the South was made more complex and bitter by it and the intellectual infamy of Tillman and Vardaman. But Watson attacked prejudice against the Negro fearlessly, and with an honesty never before seen in the political life of the cotton South . . . and not heard since from any man of his political stature.

His Populist program called for unity between the white and Negro farmers. Watson put his appeal in his usual simple but image-drawing words.

"Now, the People's Party says to these two men, 'You are kept apart that you may be separately fleeced of your earnings. You are made to hate each other because upon that hatred is rested the keystone of the arch of financial despotism which enslaves you both. You are deceived and blinded that you may not see how this race antagonism perpetuates a monetary system which beggars both.'"

Watson did not merely speak and write. He made public appearances before farmers deeply rooted in the old pattern of race hatreds and prejudices. They somehow were not made hostile to hear his voice crying out:

"It should be the object of the Populist party to make lynch law odious to the people. . . .

"I nominate this man [Negro] to the executive committee of

the Populist party as a man worthy to be on the executive committee of this party or any other party. . . .

"Tell me the use of educating these people as citizens if they are never to exercise the rights of citizens. . . ."

Watson spoke from platforms where sat white and colored men. He spoke to mixed audiences. He never advocated any easing of segregation in the schools. But he did insist, emphatically, upon political equality. He held the incident of color made no difference in the political interests of farmers, croppers and laborers. He was the first native Southerner, of political standing, to give intelligent and sympathetic ear to the legitimate aspirations of the Negro to full citizenship in post-reconstruction years. He urged that the Negro, with a third party open, become an independent voter and cease being a pawn in the hands of the city and county machines.

Trembling editors all over the state wrote of anarchy and communism. The entrenched Democratic party set out to defeat him for re-election in 1892 in the congressional primary. Another Watson victory and he would rule the whole state. Bloodshed and fighting grew apace as the primary day drew near. Killings became common. Watson was defeated by the results in Richmond County where the Democratic vote was almost double the number of legal voters.

Sandy Beaver, a distinguished educator in Georgia, head of a boys' school of note and a former member of the State Board of Regents, as a young boy watched that brazen steal. Negroes were hauled in wagons from farms and plantations into town and allowed to vote repeatedly by the Democratic county machine. Many more were brought across the Savannah River from South Carolina and voted.

"I remember," Colonel Beaver told me, "seeing the wagon-loads of Negroes brought into the wagon yards, the equivalent of our parking lots, the night before the election. There was whiskey there for them, and all night many drank, sang and fought. But the next morning they were herded to the polls and openly paid in cash, a dollar bill for each man as he handed in his ballot."

Watson ended his House career with the Fifty-second Congress and returned to Georgia to take up the Populist fight once more. In 1894 he angrily opposed Grover Cleveland's policies. The fiery Populist advocated nationalizing the railroads and any other corporation which was of a public nature. So, with bitterness and violence flaring once more, Watson declared again for Congress. Once more, he came to Richmond County with a comfortable lead. Once more it was wiped out. It was so callous a steal that even the winner agreed to a new election. It was delayed until a new registration law was passed and thousands disfranchised. Again Watson was counted out.

Many men who knew him say it was this which broke him and, almost overnight, turned him from a people's man into a reckless destroyer whose name became a byword for hate and fear and falsehood. Negroes who not long before had sought merely to touch his garments and had looked up to him with a reverence as to deities, became his targets. He became obsessed with hatred and flogged them with words and phrases which sent men to hunting them like animals. He who had sought to end lynchings defended them. He turned his hate equally on Jew, Catholic, Negro.

The splendid mind, once dedicated to people, by his own words, had always had a dark shadow over it. He began to be unstable. What the corrupt use of Negro votes in Richmond County had not done to his mind, the Populist convention of 1896 completed. He feared a sellout in all the talk of fusion. He would not attend the convention. Big money, he charged, was trying to persuade the Populists to join with the Democrats to ruin both. Bryan, the Democratic nominee, was nominated by the Populists. But they named Watson for vice president. The Populist convention impatiently waited while the slow telegraph relay brought word to Thomson, Georgia. Watson deliberated. At last, against his better judgment, he accepted, predicting political disaster to friends about him. He was right.

Watson retired to his home on Hickory Hill. He was in debt. He felt that his mind was going. For the first time in his life, he accepted defeat, and crept, brooding, into his tent. He began to write, with a brilliant, erratic style, books which sold well. His weekly paper, *The Jeffersonian*, was eloquently, if erratically and irresponsibly, filled with his writings.

Slowly, but surely, the last embers of the once-bright blue flames of the man's passion for truth and people burned out. Now and then he flared in the old manner. But it had less and less heat. By 1904 he was engaged in disfranchising the Negro. Georgia's notorious county unit system was a part of his plan. So violent were his tirades, in which others followed, that the Georgia election of 1906 led to the Atlanta race riot which lasted for four days, causing looting, brutality and murder.

Contradictions made the onetime flaming mind, bent on social and political justice, paradoxical in the extreme. In one issue of his magazine he defended the Russian revolution, attacked monopolists, the railroads, and Wall Street, and bitterly assailed Booker T. Washington, the Negro race, Jews, and Roman Catholics. National progressivism and Southern agrarianism no longer were going along together. To the dismay of men and women all over America who had followed him as the first compelling crusader for human rights to come in their generation, Watson sought to lead them into strange paths.

His tangents became pathological. The Populist Party disintegrated nationally. In Georgia, most of the originals, the "old Pops," were faithful to, though often confused by, the man they no longer knew. His flights of abuse and calumny were often incredible in ugly eloquence. God alone knows how many Negroes were lynched and murdered by his words. The Roman Catholic Church fought back. Men who sought to hold the sea wall against the tide of hate and helped defend Leo Frank in the circuslike trial and the lynching that followed were maligned and abused in Watson's paper, *The Jeffersonian.*

And so ran out the sands of decency, honor and greatness. The Tom Watson who walked into the house on Hickory Hill in 1896 after defeat never again emerged. The Watson who emerged had enough drama of vocabulary and prejudice to win election to the United States Senate in 1920 when reaction against the war years and the League of Nations was at its peak. By then, he was a drunken old man, racked with asthma, subject to colds, but still a dangerous opponent who knew no rules. He spoke out, now and then, for the underdog. Occasionally, his family saw flashes of the old sweetness they had known when he was the people's man. But mostly it was whiskey and bitterness and brooding melancholy which darkened and dominated his mind.

On the night of September 25, 1922, he died. His last words were, "I am not afraid of death." He wasn't.

The largest floral offering at the grave was from the Ku Klux Klan.

His legends still haunt the state. Twenty years ago I went to Thomson, seeking men who knew him, old Populists or their sons. At dusk we walked out of the town to his white pillared house, Hickory Hill, then shuttered and lonely.

"I remember him as a boy," said one of the younger men. "We used to run up this concrete pathway and yell, 'Hello, old crazy man!' We were shaking and scared, because he was a mean-looking old man and we were afraid of him."

"Tom wasn't mean," said an older man in the group. "Tom loved children, but Tom was fey . . . he could go off in his mind and leave his body walking around, and it was bad to cross him when his mind was off somewhere."

"I remember," said another of the older men, "one day I had gone to see him to get him to write a letter to Washington for me. We were sitting there talking when all at once he threw up his head like a setter dog smelling birds, and I could see

him listening. I listened, too, and I could hear a farm bell ringing the hands into dinner. His face got red and he said, 'God-
damn that man! He rings that bell just to worry me.'

"The damnedest sight I ever saw, and one to chill your blood,
and one that smelled of death though there was no death in it,
though it was close enough to smell it, was that day when the
word got out his opposition was going to kill Tom. All over this
part of the country men began to hitch up. They'd throw a
sack of corn and a tie or so of fodder in the wagon, and the
old lady would come out with some cooked-up cornbread, a
sack of meal, some ham meat and eggs, a skillet and some
quilts. For two days the roads coming to Hickory Hill emptied
themselves of grim-faced men, usually two of them to a wagon,
with two shotguns between 'em on the seat. They drove to
Hickory Hill, took out the mules and built little fires around
and cooked something to eat, and coffee. They didn't go up to
the house and they didn't talk with Tom. They just slept in
their wagons on some old quilts or sat hunkered around,
talkin'.

"They didn't nobody kill Tom, and the hotheads that usually
was willin' to shoot off their lip about him was quiet as sayin'
the blessin' at dinner. After two days, them fellers hitched up
and went home. They were the real Populists, the old Pops.
And you know, they never was one of them stories swept the
country again. Lots of people wanted to kill him, but they
talked it mighty low."

"What was he like?" I asked of one.

"Well, son," he said, looking at me with appraising eyes,
"when you heard Tom speak, you knew you were a man and
that God had made you for a man's work."

"But what was he *like?*" I persisted.

"Like that," he said. "Like I said. When you heard Tom bring
the opposition to the lick-log, your mind was on fire and you
were ready to do what he asked, because it was right."

"What do you think happened to him in his later years?"

"He died," he said, and those listening laughed hugely. But he did not mean it unkindly. He was sparring for time.

"Son," he said, "all his life Tom was fightin' the sons of bitches of this world, and there is a passel of sons of bitches, as maybe you know. They just ganged up on him. That's what happened in his later years."

These were old Pops talking. None would even say a critical word about their hero.

The Watson ghost will not let one rest. What might the South have become politically had Watson and his Populist coalition of Negroes and farmers, with their racially mixed executive committee, won control, as they almost did? What might the race problem have become if the Negro had won the ballot? What might the inheritance of that have meant, instead of the harvest of hate and disfranchisement?

His legend will not let that question die. . . .

These are the four.

It is not at all a coincidence that all the South's racist demagogues whose names became nationally known, were from four states — South Carolina, Mississippi, Alabama and Georgia. Alabama's contribution of a nationally recognized name was Thomas (Tom-Tom) Heflin. In all of them, and their lesser, local imitators, and in those who keep coming on, are reincarnated some of the phrases, thoughts, prejudices, invective, irrelevances and distortions of Dew, Tillman, Vardaman and Watson.

X

Ku Klux Klan

IN 1913 the Lyric Theater at Fifth and Market Streets in Chattanooga plastered its display areas with large lithographs depicting a rearing, pawing, hooded, sheet-covered horse, bearing on its back a man similarly garbed. The film *Birth of a Nation* was coming to town.

It played night after night to a packed house. All I can remember about the reaction to it is that some of the boys with whom I played told of hearing their fathers say there had been some trouble in the Negro section.

We did not know it then, but any Southerner born near, or after, the turn of the century was to know the revived Ku Klux Klan of the 1920's as a part of his educational processes.

As a young part-time reporter in Nashville, I saw my first big Klan parade and the numerous publicity stunts. A small group of rabid Klansmen would appear on a Saturday night at a Salvation Army street meeting, drop a roll of bills, usually twenty-five dollars or fifty dollars, on the drum, and silently walk away. On Sundays they would visit a church, walking in as the collection was being taken and depositing a roll made large by the presence of many one-dollar bills on the plate. So great was my innocence of the Klan that it did not occur to me in those first days of its public appearance that the ministers of the churches so visited were members of the Klan.

I was early inspired to wisdom by my managing editor,

Marmaduke B. Morton. He growled that the Klan was a lot of damned nonsense and that someone eventually would have to do what Nathan Bedford Forrest had done. General Forrest had disbanded the old reconstruction Klan because it had become a cover for rascals. But, beyond this, I knew little. A query brought from Mr. Morton a profane denunciation of the content and teaching of Southern history. Not to know of the crimes committed by the robed Klan, he said, was evidence of a native lack of curiosity, unpardonable in a newspaper reporter. A man might have had poor teaching, but he could not be excused for not teaching himself, he said. So, I went to the library and educated myself on the old Klan. It was more crime and brutality than it was romance. It got out of hand almost as soon as it was expanded beyond the social club created at Pulaski, Tennessee, by seven bored young men. It did not, as Southern legend has it, do more good than harm.

The 1920's saw the revived Klan become one of the major news sources — in politics, brutalities, murders and the activities of rascals. Atlanta was mecca for the faithful.

When I went to *The Atlanta Constitution* in the spring of 1929, with Mr. Morton's words still in my ears, I began to gather information about the Klan and the men who had reestablished it. I met, in the next several years, a half dozen or so men who had been a part of it and who were not merely willing to reminisce about it, but who enjoyed doing so. They gave me a picture of the rise and fall of the second "Invisible Empire."

They had a fine fund of stories, and they especially enjoyed talking about William Joseph (Doc) Simmons, who "revived" the original Ku Klux Klan. The story began about 1912. In that time Doc was, they said, a pious, prissy-walking, big man. Lodge badges and charms were heavy upon him, and he carried this burden joyously. Their weight was well distributed on lapel, vest, fingers, and hung pendant-fashion from the heavy gold watch chain, which was the hallmark of the salesman, or confidence man, of the times. His britches were rump-sprung, his old cronies recalled with laughter, from much sitting in the wooden chairs of lodge rooms, rural church pews, offices of county and municipal politicians, and the severe, high-backed chairs found behind pulpits. Mints and cloves wrestled with the bourbon on his breath, deceiving the good ladies of the W.C.T.U., but causing the knowing to speak of him with the half-condemning, half-affectionate, sometimes profane, phrases reserved for the amiably fraudulent who manage to be equally at home leading prayer, preaching, taking a dram, or making a fourth at poker. Doc Simmons was always proper. His gates-ajar collar was ever clean. The diamond pin, stuck just below the large, generous knot in his conservative tie, was small as befits gentility.

"Old Doc," they would say, "was a card — a real card. Too bad you didn't know him."

Behind him was failure as a medical student and as a minister of the Methodist faith and its rural circuits. He still is remembered as an arm-waver and an exhorter, who somehow never made the first division in what was, and is, in the South, at least, a very fast, highly competitive evangelical league.

By 1915, he was Colonel Simmons. The title had been conferred upon him as a leader of the uniformed drill team of the Woodmen of the World, for whom Colonel Simmons sold memberships with insurance burial benefits. He was a good salesman. Many an old rural graveyard in Alabama, Georgia and Florida yet includes, amid the conventional markers, the chiseled marble-tree-trunk section, which grave marker was thrown in with the coffin and the burial insurance payment.

Colonel Simmons was routinely in some sort of lodge meeting three or four nights a week. It was not surprising he began to think of an insurance-benefit secret order of his own from which he would receive the large profits, not merely the salesman's commission. At that time, the history-making movie

Birth of a Nation was playing at local theaters, and salesmen went to movies on lonely nights. Colonel Simmons was not considered an intellectual, but he saw and evaluated the enthusiasm aroused by the movie. This gave him an original idea. It was, so far as the record reveals, his first and last. But it was a big one.

In speeches that followed, he used to let his voice take on a deep solemnity, as befits discussion of visions, and say that one night, while sitting quietly before a window in spiritual meditation, he saw a vision of white horses riding across the sky with white-robed figures mounted on them, and from that derived the holy command to reorganize the Ku Klux Klan. But an old friend, of mine and Doc's, the late Bill Sharpe, an ancient showman who helped birth and rear the movie industry in the South, told often of how his fellow lodge member, Doc Simmons, would come and breathe upon him the aroma of bourbon and cloves and extract from him free admission to see, over and over again, the old Klan thriller.

"Doc told me many times he got the inspiration for the Klan revival from my free passes, a fact I lament no little," said Bill, "especially since I was always so mesmerized by Doc's yarns that I never cut myself in on it."

In the autumn of 1915, Colonel Simmons launched his plan. He approached a number of Atlantans, most of them prominent in politics. One of these, Bill Sharpe said, was city clerk Walter Taylor, a rotund, short-of-breath man later to go to jail for fraud.

"Walter," said Doc, in his best prayer-meeting voice, "I am asking a few carefully chosen friends to meet me atop Stone Mountain, Thanksgiving night, at midnight to be exact, to revive the ancient glories of the Ku Klux Klan."

"Jesus, Doc," Bill Sharpe heard Taylor say, "I can't climb Stone Mountain in the daytime. Can't you revive the ancient glories in the flatlands?"

Despite such facetiousness, the glories were revived atop the mountain. Fifteen men were present. But all, including Doc Simmons, were lacking in imagination. They didn't know what came next. Simmons was thinking of insurance policies and cash. But war was flaming in Europe. The Klan stagnated.

In 1920, Doc was still around with his somewhat anemic Klan. An uncertain destiny brought him to E. Y. Clarke, who, with a blowzy lady associate, was running a shoe-string advertising office. Clarke had a razor-sharp mind where the possibilities of a fast dollar were concerned, especially a shady dollar. A smartie in the con-man manner, Clarke was the perfect character to launch the Klan. Doc's speeches, like his sermons, had heretofore lacked substance, but as they poured from the pen and mind of Clarke, they became wondrous things, filled with God and Christ, the Ten Commandments, brotherly love, purity of womanhood, morality, patriotism, the flag and one hundred per cent Americanism. Speakers and organizers were trained to go about spreading the word. The Roman Catholic Church was the chief target. In rural churches and lodge rooms, organizers shouted Clarke's words of warning. The Pope was coming to America. The Catholic conspiracy was to destroy us all. Only the K.K.K. and one hundred per cent Americanism would save us. The Negro and any foreign-born man were also outside the pale. But it was the Pope and his church who served as the main target.

It was Clarke who saw also the political possibilities in the courthouse and state machines — the chance to sell and give jobs to Klan members. It was a pushover. The "climate" was right. America was disillusioned by the war. Isolationism, America-for-Americans, was in the air. Attorney General Palmer's hysteria about Reds; the depression of 1920-1921; the rural discontent; unemployment; the strikes; the explosion on Wall Street; the race riots in Eastern cities — all these created a perfect climate and soil for Klan development. The money poured in. "I remember seeing drawers full of greenbacks out there at headquarters," said Bill Sharpe. "God alone knows how much they took in in those years. They thought it would go on forever."

Within a short time, Clarke was the Klan. Doc Simmons was less and less careful about using cloves. He liked the ladies, and Clarke knew plenty.

"Hell," said Bill Sharpe. "In no time at all, Clarke had Doc hog-tied with indiscreet letters to certain ladies. He claimed to have what is called incriminating pictures of Doc, although this I never believed. But Clarke was running things and Doc was on a salary. Doc was sitting around daily in a perpetual state of bourbon-beatitude, no longer consulted by Clarke. He didn't seem to care. He had money; people called him Colonel. He belonged. People sort of loved old Doc and him there mellow-drunk, with his habitual courtesy and brotherhood. A lot of them hated Clarke.

"Some used to wonder, though," he continued, "why Doc didn't seem worried. Clarke knew. He knew, too, 'the boys' were after him. They wanted to be cut in deeper. That's why, when he figured the decline was at hand, he took all the cash he could and got out to begin his big real estate promotion that blew up with the depression. Clarke went on to go to jail in a Chicago song-book fraud. God knows how much money he got from the Klan, but it was plenty!

"When Hiram Evans and his rebels finally got enough power and prepared to oust Doc on a charge of having looted the Klan along with Clarke, they found out why he never worried. The name, property and everything it owned, except the members themselves, were copyrighted and registered in the name of William Joseph Simmons. That was the first time some of them knew Doc had a first and middle name."

The big-money glow was still on the Klan, so Hiram Wesley Evans, who left his dentist office to run the Texas Klan, formed a syndicate and bought out Simmons for $140,000. He was installed as Imperial Wizard on November 24, 1932. Evans had been a Klan figure in Georgia for years and was also a political maneuverer in Georgia, Alabama and Florida.

The depression of the thirties came on. Big money was ended. The invisible empire of the Klan, which had brought many states closer than they knew to control by a fascist organization, was dropping from an estimated 4,000,000 members to a few thousand. (Clarke had claimed state offices in forty-one states and members in forty-seven.) At its peak, it had elected many governors, senators, congressmen, judges, and countless local politicians. It had ruled with intimidation, terror and murder in such widely separated states as Indiana and Louisiana. It had controlled police and sheriffs where it did not have the governor or mayor. That was a critical period for the nation and a story never really told. The depression deepened. The climate of the amazing twenties, so favorable to the Klan, withered away.

Doc Evans — it is strange how that word "Doc" clung to the Klan — was in the asphalt and road material business. Old Klansmen still in control of county and state governments liked "the Wiz," as he came to be called, and bought hugely from him in several states. He saw that the big money from memberships was gone with the wind. But asphalt sales were good.

The Wiz began to liquidate. Some of the Klan property was sold to make payment on back taxes. The Roman Catholic Church bought the white-pillared, two-story house which had housed the Imperial offices of the Klan and remodeled it for use as a rectory. A cathedral even then was going up on adjoining land. This galled the old Klansmen, and they began to discuss ways and means to oust Evans, who had sold the property. What they did not know was that Doc Evans, himself, wanted out. An unexpected way out developed.

Bishop Gerald P. O'Hara had arrived in Atlanta a year or so after the publication of Margaret Mitchell's *Gone With the*

Wind. He was an immediate sentimental success, even with those who had their doubts about the bishop's church. After all, wasn't Scarlett O'Hara's very own father named Gerald O'Hara? A man of great charm, energy and intelligence, the bishop stirred the diocese to greater effort and enthusiasm than it had ever known. The cathedral was beautiful evidence of this energy.

One day the bishop telephoned and said he had a matter he wanted to discuss. The cathedral was to be consecrated within a few months. He was, he told me, with a great look of innocence on his face, considering inviting the Wizard of the Klan to be present. The magnificence of the idea overwhelmed me but did not cause me to overlook the transitory thought that the bishop, had he put his mind to it, could have become a master poker player. His idea was, I said, a stroke of genius, and he must certainly proceed. It was something which would become a national story for the newspapers, wire services, picture magazines and newsreels. Either way, I said, he had the Wizard. If he refused, the nation would learn what many persons in Georgia did not know; namely, that his church now owned the one-time Imperial Palace of the Klan. If he accepted, so much the better.

"You think so?" asked the bishop, but this time he did show a twinkle in his eye.

I said it couldn't fail.

"I would hope," he said, "that it would also be good for his soul to be with us when the cathedral is dedicated to the glory of God."

The invitation was sent and the Wizard, who was no fool, accepted. He came with his family. To have remained away would have been a complete humiliation. To be there was, of course, merely a lesser one. But as he later said to a friend, "I was there."

The service was, of course, one of consecration. There was

no reference to the K.K.K. But there was an electric quality in the air.

In addition, an almost unbelievable thing happened. In a movie script it would be rejected. But it is a literal truth that as the service began, the sun broke through a cloudy sky. The stained glass windows broke up the sun into shafts of light. All through that ritual of consecration a shaft of wheat-golden light was on the Wizard. This is one of my favorite memories of the Wiz — his benign, round, Halloween pumpkin face lighted by one of God's rays. I was awed by it, and that evening I said to Bishop O'Hara, "It was really unfair of you to arrange for that shaft of light to rest on the Wizard's head. You shouldn't have gone that far."

"Who are you and I," he said, "to question where the sun shall shine? God knows best."

So, we left it at that. (All through the years the bishop has been a person for whom I have had great affection.)

Days later, the Wiz sent word.

"You were hard on me," he said, "but not for publication, I will tell you, I was not a fool. I wanted out. This was a good exit."

The Wiz didn't just walk out. The K.K.K. has always been a commercial skin game, like the anti-Semitic rackets. The Wiz sold to Dr. James H. Colescott and Dr. Samuel Green. (The Docs were back again.) Colescott was a veterinarian. The wits said this was the first time the members had had one professionally trained to minister to them.

But the Klan slid downhill. Colescott ran into a demand for the balance due on back taxes from the federal government on monies collected across a long span of years. The Klan had believed itself above paying income taxes. In something of a panic, Colescott announced the Klan dissolved and surrendered its charter.

Grand Dragon Doc Green took out another charter and began trying to stop desertions, the formation of new and rival Klans, and to rally the faithful under his banner. Ironically, he often referred to one of the competing Klans, "The Original Southern Klans, Inc.," as a fascist group.

Green was not a bad man. He was a simple sort of person, with a burning desire for status. Early in his Klan career I editorially commended him for refusing to reveal to a political judge information given him by a patient. Both he and his family seemed to appreciate it. Two years later I had a call from a member of his family.

"Will you please talk to Dr. Green?" this person said. "You know he is not a bad man. But now he has people coming to the house to see him whom he would not have admitted a few months ago. They are bad people. They are deceiving him. They flatter him and call him the Wizard, and make him feel important. Please talk to him and make him understand."

I told her I couldn't.

"He wouldn't listen to me," I said.

"But he likes you," she said.

"I like him," I told her, "but Dr. Green is a captive of himself and those who know this use him."

And so he was. He died a sad and disillusioned man.

In Doc Green's time, and after, the Klans had become a haven for men as wicked and depraved as those who toiled for Adolf Hitler. The rascals, the ruffians, the sadists and the psychopaths found refuge in it. Among city memberships were found the worst elements of police, deputies, taxi drivers, bus drivers, city councilmen, minor police court judges, and so on. Law enforcement officers who enjoy beating prisoners inevitably were found to be enthusiastic members. Klan organizations still corrupt a few sheriffs' offices, and some rural juries in those communities where they are allowed to get a real foothold.

In the larger cities, it was relatively easy to get informers into Klans as members. They would, for a small sum, give reports on meetings. Such reports invariably indicate the low level of Klan intelligence. A sample report of a Klan meeting, by a member to whom we paid a weekly wage for acting as an informer, follows, taken from my files, and reproduced here as written:

Doc Green gave a long talk on the progress of the drive and said the Klansmen of Georgia were enthused about having another mass meeting and said he was yet undecided whether to begin the drive by using the applicants we were taking in now in this mass meeting. The boys in Atlanta are anxious for these new applicants to go into the drive. The Dr. promised them he would announce sometime soon if he thought this best to do at this time. ———— ———— [name of a minor city official supplied on separate sheet of paper] started off a series of talks on the decision a judge handed down in the Supreme Court in South Carolina in regards to letting the Negroes vote in that state. Several talks were made and all were suggesting how to beat this and how the people should keep the Negroes from voting. Some said the people of South Carolina should remember these people who were for the Negroes and on election day be prepared to vote them out of office. Some thought the people should take the law in hand and keep the Negroes away from the polls. ———— ———— said this [letting Negroes vote] was the same thing the Communist Party was trying to do in Georgia. He claimed the C. P. had men all over the state teaching the Negro that he was as good as anyone else and was entitled to vote and that they were being mistreated. He said rabble-rousers from the North had invaded the South and were here for no other purpose than to stir up the Negro and to cause trouble, and eventually it would cause a lot of Negroes to get killed. He also said rich Yankees were spending a large amount of money in the South supposedly to educate the Negro and all they were doing was trying to teach social equality, and in the end they were making trouble for the Southerner and were planting seeds of communism in the Negroes and that over half of the Negroes today are Communists. This he said the KKK was going to fight as long as there was a white man living. The Dr. reported robes would soon be available to all Klansmen.

Dr. also highly praised the Ladies Auxiliary of the East Atlanta Klavern and was telling the KKK men to take their wives out and enroll them in as they were needed in this fight.

Several newspaper clippings were read to the boys of what was happening over the country, rapes and attacks and everything against the Negro. Nothing was read that would mention any attacks by the whites against the Negro.

Nothing was mentioned about the cross-burning and I suppose the burning will be yet held. It might be pulled as a surprise. Yet, if it is announced, I will inform you at once.

After much talk we were dismissed and went our ways.

This banality was typical. But it must be remembered that except for the shrewd, cynical men who made money or political capital out of it, the Klan membership was made up of men whose lives were sterile and whose backgrounds were barren. This was true in city and county. One of the strengths of the Klan, and of other extremists groups, was, and is, the fact that the persons who made up its rank and file, often feel resentments and frustrations because of grievances, real or fancied. Often they are mere complaints. But they do not know how to go to their city councilman, or to the mayor. And so, some promoter tells them, it is the fault of Negroes, or Jews, and that if they will pay ten dollars to join the Klan they will have protection and power.

Some enjoyed the childish mumbo-jumbo of the robes and ritual. But there was nothing in the Klan for them. They were suckers. It used to grieve me, thinking of how badly their families could have used what went to the Klan promoters.

The state headquarters of the Klans did not have much control over the local klaverns. In the small rural towns and in the drab, decaying areas of urban industrial neighborhoods, the local klaverns were autonomous. They decided to flog or intimidate with a cross-burning. Sometimes they arranged to drive their cars through "Niggertown," with members robed — and armed.

Here and there industrial leaders used the Klan against labor organizers.

There were a number of human interest experiences in those years. One morning the brutally beaten body of a man was found in a field near an Atlanta suburb. He was identified as Ike Gaston, a barber given to drink and, of course, neglect of family. The Klan terrorist group had taken him out the night before. They, too, had, as usual, raised their courage with liquor and their sadistic enjoyment was thereby heightened. They overdid it and the unconscious victim, left in a field, died sometime thereafter. His body was found covered with the heavy white frost of the morning as if a merciful God was symbolizing a sort of forgiveness for the poor failure who lay there.

The work of an investigating reporter, a confession, and a vigorous young assistant solicitor general, Dan Duke, combined to send two men to jail for this crime.

Other of the more depressing features of the Klan was the appearance of a woman's auxiliary, and, later, most tragic of all, a children's division. Now and then there would be a demonstration. Cities grew used to seeing members appear in numbers of fifty or so, in which robed family groups would be prominent. There was an almost overwhelming pathos in seeing boys and girls of ages from about six to ten, walking along with their parents.

Looking at them, in the years after the Second World War, I remembered being in Germany and watching the Hitler Youth groups parade. They had strut and polish, whereas the Klan members plodded or strolled. But — and this was the point — the same sort of teaching was being put into their young heads.

One day after a reported beating, I wrote an imaginary conversation between a Klansman who had come home from such a foray and was boasting to his children about how he and a dozen or so other brave men had taken a lone man from his home and savagely beaten him. I had him gloating as he told of the screams and of the way the straps and sticks had thudded on the victim's body.

The next morning a call was put through to me. A woman began to talk but quickly broke into sobs. "My husband did what you wrote," she said. "God help us, but he did."

Another time a Klansman was convicted of involuntary manslaughter in an act of Klan violence. On paper he did not add up as an evil man. He was in his forties. He had worked steadily. He had three children. I did a piece in which it was suggested the convicted man was probably a simple sort of person, who had been led by shrewder men than he to do the dirty work. A tearful wife called to say, weeping, "Oh, he was, he was. He was a good husband and father until those awful men took him over."

As the Second World War rolled over Europe I became convinced that at least some Klan leaders were trying to effect some sort of association with Fritz Kuhn's German Bund groups in the East. Both raged against Franklin D. Roosevelt and were irrationally anti-Semitic. It was not possible to dig this out. But, in 1947, on a second visit to the Nuremberg trials, I learned that Kuhn was a prisoner there and obtained permission to talk with him.

It was a rewarding hour. Kuhn was brought in. He was a gross, coarse-looking man at best and the prison garb of khaki trousers and shirt emphasized these qualities of appearance. He had been brought from his job of peeling potatoes. It was difficult to believe that this bulking clod of a man had once swayed a crowd which filled Madison Square Garden. The first questions were about his visit to Hitler, taking a donation of American money. It was a fascinating thing to see excitement change his face and light his eyes as he retold the supreme moment of his life when Adolf Hitler had shaken his hand and congratulated him on his work in organizing a Nazi Bund in the United States.

It was after this that I asked him if the Ku Klux Klans
had ever approached him.

"Oh yes," he said. "We had two meetings about it. The
Southern Klans did not want to be known in it. So the nego-
tiations were between representatives of Klans in New Jersey
and Michigan, but it was understood the Southerners were
in. We all approved of what Hitler was doing. Had Roosevelt
not brought us into the war we would have got together
against the Jews and the Negroes."

Kuhn went back to his potatoes.

In the Nuremberg courtrooms one could hear the evidence
of Hitler's crimes and see some of the victims testifying as witnesses.

In the postwar years, in which Adolf Hitler's super-race
philosophy and the brutal excesses of it were so thoroughly
exposed, the Klan became more and more preposterous. There
was no longer any real money to be made from it, and this,
more than morality, accelerated the decline. Also, the Klan
had ceased to be a mystery. Somehow, everyone knew what
was behind those masks. In cities Negroes began to look on
casually and to jest about the parades. It was different, of
course, in the rural areas where the sheriff and the deputies,
and perhaps the judge, were members. There the terror still
lived.

But the Klan was dying.

The White Citizens Councils, which sprang up like weeds
in the wake of the 1954 school decision, finished the K.K.K. as
a major force. What was left of it became a refuge for the
small group of violent anti-Semitic and anti-Negro crackpots.
Among these were the terrorists who did the dynamiting of
schools, homes and churches. It was dangerous because of
this. But as an organization with political influence, it was
done.

So discredited was it that the secret Citizens Councils suffered from the fact the public equated them with the various

K.K.K.'s. In Alabama, Mississippi, and South Carolina, the Councils and Klans in some areas had near-duplicate membership. There were exceptions, but in general, the White Citizens Councils were so tarred with K.K.K-ism that they did not flourish save in a handful of states. Try as they would, the Councils could not escape the appropriateness of their description as "the White-Collar K.K.K."

It seems to me, looking back on it, that over-all, the K.K.K. had one asset. It forced Southerners to a decision, pro or con. By its excesses it proved what General Forrest had found in the reconstruction years; namely, that it, or any other such organization, provided a refuge for scoundrels.

The fact that the anti-Negro rights forces have always included a heavy strain of anti-Semitism, made it easier for those of a mind and will so to do, to expose the old Typhoid Marys of the hate business who were operating in the climate created by the Klan and their white-collar contemporaries. No matter what new, high-sounding patriotic names they gave to their new traps for suckers, it was possible for the diligent to expose them. Life had an added zest for those who could laugh at the absurdity of its rituals and titles, who could feel compassion for the men whose lives were so sterile they felt themselves men only when they were robed and masked and in the presence of the phony mysteries of the order, and who could see and expose the contradiction in the Klan's claims to Americanism and its subversion of American principles, and who knew the cover it gave to scoundrels.

In their own peculiar way, the Klans were educational.

XI

Butler Island Plantation

O NE DAY in the early 1930's I went down to the Butler
Island plantation of Colonel Tillinghast L'Hommedieu
Huston to attend a college graduation party for a Guernsey
bull. Before I came home I had met and talked with an old
man who had been a slave errand boy for Fanny Kemble,
Britain's magnificent actress whose antislavery writings from
the Georgia coast had stirred abolitionist sentiments in England and America.

Colonel Huston was a Falstaffian man of great good humor,
with a vast appetite for baseball, food, drink, fellowship and
fun. He was one of the most warmhearted, entertaining characters possible to meet in life's journeyings. He had been an
engineer at the time of the Spanish-American War and had
done an immense deal of work in Cuba, at home and around
the world. He also had served in the engineers in the First
World War and was very proud of his army career. Along the
way he had accumulated wealth. He had become a partner
with Colonel Jake Ruppert at the time the New York Yankees were being built up to begin the climb to baseball's
Olympus. From that time on, he spent much of his time with
baseball people and those who wrote of it.

His particular devotion was to Wilbert (Your Uncle Wilbert) Robinson, legendary manager of Brooklyn's Daffiness

Boys, and to William O. McGeehan, the *New York Herald Tribune's* brilliant sports columnist.

Leaders of the baseball clans gathered for some weeks of each winter at a hunting lodge near Darien, Georgia, called Dover Hall, an old English holding which the Colonel had acquired. It was my happy lot to visit there often and hear the tall tales. They ran, naturally, to baseball and hunting. The mornings were usually sharp in winter, though by noon each day it was pleasant. Colonel Huston had a ritual for waking his guests. A fat venerable colored man would arrive in the sleeping quarters and turn on the light. On a tray would be a strong hot toddy. "The Colonel say this is to start the blood," he'd announce, grinning broadly, putting the steaming glass on a table within reach and going on to the next visitor.

Breakfast, for those whose blood had been thus started, was gargantuan. There would be massive cake pork sausage, seasoned with sage and red pepper. Usually, if a meat-hunter or so had been a recent visitor, there was venison sausage as well. Platters of fried and scrambled eggs, rashers of bacon, and hot cakes with heavy sorghum syrup were on Dover Hall's unvarying morning menu.

After such a breakfast, which was to sustain hunters trudging all day after quail, or waiting in blinds for ducks, some residents and guests chose to sit all day in the rocking chairs on the veranda. An artesian well flowed up through a pipe and splashed down to form a small pool of fresh clean water. A gaggle of domestic geese and a flock of ducks frequented the pool. The three largest geese were named "The Brooklyn Directors," this being a period when the owners of the Dodgers were feuding and giving Uncle Robbie trouble.

Only the foolhardy and valiant went hunting at Dover Hall when guests in great plenty were present. Many visitors coming to Dover Hall had never handled a shotgun, much less fired one. Such men on deer stands, with their blood well started, were likely to fire at anything which moved. On one deer drive a New York photographer, Izzy Kaplan, killed the lead hound in the pack as it broke cover near him, swearing later it looked like a deer he had photographed in a zoo.

Babe Ruth once gunned down a scrawny range cow, and explained he took it for an elk.

Some of the baseball players who came were excellent hunters, and it was they who kept the larder well stocked.

Bill McGeehan was a fine teller of stories and had an abiding affection for the place. In the last year of his illness, with his legs swollen and his damaged heart slowing down, he talked and wrote happily of a dog trainer who had a new brand of conditioning pills which the keeper of the kennel believed would bring him around. McGeehan wanted to die at the old hall, but the end came in a Brunswick hospital.

To the consternation and near heartbreak of the Colonel and Uncle Robbie, the widow determined to have a private cremation. The nearest crematorium was at Jacksonville, Florida. A local hearse was hired and the journey begun. It halted at the ball park. The Brunswick team was in a championship series and the driver was determined to see at least part of the game. He did, with the hearse parked outside the ball park. When the Colonel and Robbie heard of this, they were somewhat mollified.

"What a perfect happening," said the Colonel. "I'll bet old Bill's ghost was in the park laughing to beat hell. What a story he could do about it."

"Yes," said Robbie, "and it wasn't a bad game, even for a ghost."

When the driver belatedly arrived at Jacksonville, a disagreement had developed and he was directed to return all that was mortal of the great McGeehan to Brunswick.

He was buried hard by the majestic old oaks beneath which John Wesley had preached. Mrs. McGeehan had only the briefest of private ceremonies, a fact the Colonel deplored. After her departure the Huston dudgeon rose. He summoned a squad of the National Guard, dignitaries and friends. He had the Episcopal service read and three volleys fired. In the following silence, the Colonel, resplendent in striped pants and afternoon coat, clapped a derby on his head and said, in a voice heavy with satisfaction and contentment, "Now, by God, Bill's buried."

Not many miles from Dover Hall was historic Butler Island, one of three large ones formed in the delta of the Altamaha River at the Georgia coast. The Colonel had seen it, deserted and neglected, on visits to the Hall. Its dikes had long been broken and marshes had intruded. His engineer's eyes saw the possibilities and he purchased and restored it. With a fine, typical defiance of tradition, he built on that semitropical island a comfortable, two-story New England colonial house, with dormer windows and a gabled roof, steep enough for snow, which would never fall there, to slip down easily. In the years before the Civil War, Pierce Butler had inherited the plantation from his father, who had assumed control of the island and other land in the early days of the Republic. He maintained a home in Philadelphia, but visited his large holdings each winter. It had gone to ruin in the postwar years.

The place delighted the Colonel. He managed to grow flowers in profusion, limes, lemons, satsuma oranges, and fruits. He also awed all the local wiseacres by producing commercial crops of iceberg lettuce. His herd of registered Guernseys was the talk of South Georgia, as was his glass-walled milking parlor and his special maternity house.

The Colonel cooperated with the University of Georgia School of Agriculture. A parsimonious legislature did not provide breeding animals to match his, and so he lent them. It was the return of a bull, valued at some thirty thousand dollars or more, after nine months at the University, which created the opportunity for a graduation party.

I arrived early one morning, having taken an overnight

sleeper car to nearby Brunswick where the Colonel's foreman had met me. At the house I found the bull being moored inside a straw-bedded, fenced area on the lawn. A mortarboard had been firmly attached to the huge head of the animal and a black gown spread across his ample back. This was in the corn whiskey days and there was a plentiful supply of it and cold milk. The Colonel urged any who felt driven to milk to lace it well.

The invitation to the graduation party had included Dover Hall and a few days of hunting. The next morning, before moving to the lodge, we took a look at the Colonel's island plantation.

"Over there," he said, as we drove along a back road, "was Pierce Butler's house. You should have seen it. The fact he brought an elegant lady like Fanny Kemble to such a house proved he was no gentleman."

"It was the overseer's house," I said. "I read about it in a book. He didn't even build her a house — just moved the overseer out."

The Colonel's reaction was profane.

"It didn't even have a clothes closet in it," he said, "just pegs behind the door."

"Maybe they had wardrobes," I suggested.

"No," snorted the Colonel. "He was a bum. He didn't know how to treat a lady."

One of Mr. McGeehan's stories came to mind. The Colonel had, around ladies, a natural courtesy of the Chesterfieldian sort. It could, however, be aroused to emotional peaks. McGeehan had told of a visit to the Tower of London with Colonel Huston. They had fortified themselves for the encounter with history and culture at several of the more historic pubs. At the Tower the guide seemed, to the Colonel at least, unusually abusive of Mary Queen of Scots, whom he repeatedly referred to as Bloody Mary. At length the Colonel could endure it no more. "My good man," he said. "I will not hear you insult a lady any longer. She could not have been as bad as you say. How much do we owe you?"

They departed in a taxi to meet a British sportswriter at a hotel on the Strand. As they reached the door, a tall and imposingly uniformed doorman made ready to open it.

The Colonel halted. He removed his hat.

"Hurrah for Bloody Mary," he shouted, bringing several startled passersby to a halt.

The doorman did not bat an eye.

"Quite so, sir. Quite so," said he, and swung open the door.

"What," I asked McGeehan, "did the Colonel say next?"

"Well," said McGeehan, "in the lobby he glowered at me and said, 'I guess that squared it a little.'"

The Colonel and I talked in the parked car for a while about how it must have seemed to be cultured, intellectual young woman to live there amid slavery in one of its more callous aspects. Suddenly the Colonel brightened.

"There is an old man over near Darien who was an errand boy for Fanny Kemble," he said. "He makes out by what people give him to talk of the old days. You ought to go see him. He is well over a hundred years old and can't last much longer."

And that is why, an hour later, I was sitting in a straight kitchen chair before a small cabin talking to an old Negro man named Liverpool Hazard, who was then, he said, one hundred nine years old. It seemed incredible to me then, and is the more so now as I look back on it, that the withered old figure before me had been a young slave assigned to Fanny Kemble, the magnificent and magnetic British actress who, after one of those whirlwind courtships in the East, had married Pierce Butler and shortly thereafter had come with him to Butler Island.

How much imagination and how much fact were in the mind of the gaunt, ancient man before me, I could not divine. He was obviously very old. He could neither read nor write. If, through the long, empty years some fantasy had crept in with the facts inside that aged skull with its frizzle of white hair and the weary veins bulging large beneath the skin, who could complain? He tried, he said, to please tourists who hunted him out, wishing to see a man who had been a slave. If they asked him foolish questions as they focused their cameras, he gave them foolish answers, he said, chuckling.

Local records established him as one of the slaves from Butler Island. After Fanny Kemble had come and gone from that island, a kinsman of Pierce, named Hazard, had taken the boy to Liverpool, England. He was a servant, but also, the old man thought, it pleased Hazard's vanity to attract attention to himself by having a black boy follow him about the streets. Hazard had dressed the boy in a specially made uniform. After he returned to the island from that journey he soon came to be called Liverpool Hazard.

"I talked about it so much they teased me with the name," the old man said, chuckling again, as the weary old mind reproduced some pleasant image in his memory.

In 1935, Lady Alice Butler, a granddaughter of Fanny Kemble, visited Butler Island and gave a dinner for the few old slaves who had been on Butler Island and for their descendants.

"She give me back Miss Fanny's flower," Liverpool told me, fingering a white paper flower pinned to his cotton jacket. "She give me a real one," he said. "When it died I got the folks to git me this 'un. When I was a errand boy for Miss Fanny I wore one. When I told her granddaughter she give me a new one."

I was impatient to hear about Fanny Kemble, whose *Journal of a Residence on a Georgian Plantation,* to my mind, is still the most condemning indictment of slavery written by a white observer. Fanny Kemble brought to Butler Island no preconceived prejudices or opinions about slavery save the instinctive dislike of it as an institution. A daughter of Mr. and Mrs. Charles Kemble, themselves distinguished actors, she was a star at Covent Garden at nineteen. Queen Victoria was one of her admirers and had received her to express her appreciation and respect.

At twenty-three, she came to New York on tour. Walt Whitman, a boy of thirteen, slipped into the balcony every night she played. In Boston, the Harvard student body attended her performances as did many notables of the city. In the still new, raw Washington she was the guest of President Andrew Jackson at the White House. She played before John Quincy Adams, John Marshall, Henry Clay, Daniel Webster, and Dolly Madison. She had made John Marshall weep. Henry Clay was especially charmed.

It astonishes the reader of history that Old Hickory found time to receive her. He had even then prepared his proclamation calling for thirty thousand troops to put down John Calhoun's nullification move in South Carolina, and was hourly expecting to release it. Some of this tension must have been in his face as the young actress saw him.

"Very tall and thin," Miss Kemble wrote, "but erect and dignified in his carriage. A good specimen of a fine old well-battered soldier — his manners are perfectly simple and quiet, therefore good. . . . Of his measures I know nothing, but firmness, determination, decision, I respect above all things; and if the old general is, as they say, very obstinate, why obstinacy is so far more estimable than weakness, especially in a ruler, that I think he sins on the right side of the question."

She had a good, comprehending eye. There were many of Old Hickory's qualities in her. They were among the reasons she could not remain as Pierce Butler's wife. He was a vain, cruel man, lacking in any firmness or decision save that of the martinet.

Pierce Butler's attitude and the austere plight of his slaves were too much for her. She saw slavery in the raw. The myth persists. Much fiction and some history well mixed with the former, have sought to make the exceptions the rule. A meager few of the truly told stories of plantation life fit, and sustain, the myth. Those which are not replete with harshness and misery, bleakness and cruelty, are callous in the full meaning of the word. Some of the worst of these stories are from the rice plantations. Even at this late date fishing guides on the St. Marys River know the way through the slave-cut tidal canals of old rice fields and can take one on rides through them. There are miles and miles of such passages, the marsh grasses growing high about them.

The stories of the digging of them by slaves standing knee- and waist-deep in tidal slime and muck, and the knowledge that the task required years of such toil, have no beauty in them. The death rate from fevers, malaria and yellow jack, was high. The working and living conditions of such slaves were invariably bad. Fanny Kemble's description of their living quarters, their food, clothing and the primitive medical care available, does not make one think of magnolias and juleps in silver goblets. No banjo tunes of happy, movielike scenes in "de quarters," rise from her accurate pages.

The canals were cut so that when the brackish tides came up the St. Marys, the rice fields would be flooded twice daily. In those days sailing vessels from England came up the river to the plantation docks. South Carolina produced about two-thirds of the South's crop. Georgia was next.

Rice planters looked down their noses at the cotton grow- ers — anyone could grow cotton. This was not far off the mark. A beginning in cotton required little capital and no slaves, if one had a large, working family. But as one ambitious grower wrote in a diary, "each bale, to the energetic, is a step in a stairway to a white-pillared mansion, to slaves and grand tours to Europe." Those with drive and capital soon pushed the less vigorous whites back into the piney woods or the uplands. If one looks at the statistics one finds that from 1820 to 1861 the cotton crop doubled with each decade. It was the cotton planter who put his stamp on the land, its customs, its culture, thought and politics.

The counties sent their legislators to the state capital and there they elected their United States senators. The planters were powerful enough in Washington to make it legal to add three-fifths of the slave population to the free population for the purpose of determining the number of congressional representatives to which each state was entitled. The slaves had no vote or civil rights, but they were a very real political asset in Congress. Not even the rise of cities, with their considerable commerce and trade, could dull the image of "the plantation South." It held to the end and in our time the myths of it die hard.

These things ran through my mind as I sat there with the old man — a relic, a symbol, a voice, an accusation out of that "old South." It had not provided a good life for many planter families. Fanny Kemble wrote of Darien, the city near Butler Island, that it was "a place of desolation." The intelligent, cultured London girl was bored by the "vapid conversation," its "slave slobber," with the "sameness and stupidity of it," which would "deaden any amount of intelligence."

She poured out her experiences in letters to Elizabeth Dwight Sedgwick in Boston, to whom she dedicated her book. Household slaves, who loved her, as, indeed, did all the miserable ones of the wretched quarters, would slip quietly into the room and squat in a corner in silence, watching their mistress write letters whose content they did not know. They were satisfied to watch a human being who was like no other person they had known. The old man before me had been one of those worshiping ones before the fire — a small boy watching a woman write pages in what would become a moving, eloquent book, condemning man's inhumanity.

I reached over and patted his bony knee and said, gently, as to a child, "Don't try to tell me anything important. Just talk to me about Miss Fanny."

"I remember Miss Fanny well," he said, sitting forward and leaning on his walking stick. "I was just a boy. I was told to wait on her, to carry messages, and do what she asked me to do. She was a good lady, but sad a lot of the time. She hadn't been there long before all of us on the place knew she wasn't happy. I heard talk. Mr. Butler he wanted her to stay away from the quarters. But she went there, and me with her. I guess I was a problem, too. I wore a white flower, like I said. That was my badge. I could go places others couldn't, because I belonged to Miss Fanny. The women, when they was sick or in need, they'd get me to tell Miss Fanny. She'd go to them. The overseer he complained. And Mr. Butler he would get mad with her. But she went."

I told him I had read her writings of her months on the island and that she had written of how she had been troubled by the hard life of the slaves.

He nodded. "I heard about the book," he said, "a long time ago." He was silent. "I wish I could have read it," he said. "But I never learned."

"Was Pierce Butler a hard man?" The old head affirmed it.

"Mr. Butler," he said, "was a hard man. The others [neighboring slave owners] wasn't all as hard. There used to be boat races on the river. But Mr. Butler, he never let his boatmen race."

The old man was growing tired. I changed the subject. "You had some fun as a boy?"

"Oh, yes, sir. I was the proudest of all. I could go to town on one of the boats if Miss Fanny sent me. And when someone in town asked who I was they'd say, 'Don't you see that flower? He belongs to Miss Fanny!' "

"What is the most pleasant memory you have, Liverpool?"

He thought a moment or so, his aged mind on the border of, but not yet in, the morass of senility.

"Well, sir," he said, grinning, "I remember the rice birds and how we trapped them and how good they smelled cooking on sticks over the coals. They came by the thousands, sir, millions. It seemed so to a boy, and I don't know how many is a million. But we trapped them through the months when the rice heads were forming and the harvest time. That's when they really come. And every night in the quarters there'd be little fires before the cabins and women holding the sticks full of birds, turning them over the coals. The smell of them would fill the air. My mouth still waters, thinking of them."

I asked him if he remembered Miss Fanny's leaving.

"No, sir," he said, "I didn't know. She left now and then and this last time she didn't come back. I can remember crying when I knew she wouldn't ever come back."

I never saw Liverpool Hazard again. He died soon after. Coming, as I did, from a background of farm people who had a profound religious dislike of slavery and almost a contempt for those who lived off the sweat and labor of slaves, I never had any patience with those who accepted the myth that the peculiar institution of the South was a soft thing. I dissented from this view from the time I was old enough to reason about it. Along the way someone placed in my hands Frederick Olmstead's *Cotton Kingdom*, Fanny Kemble's book, and other books of fact, not "spoony, fancy pictures," as Olmstead called them.

When I read Stephen Vincent Benét's *John Brown's Body*, in 1928, I liked the concluding verses, especially the lines:

> Bury the South together with this man,
> Bury the bygone South.

Bury the minstrel with the honey-mouth,
Bury the broadsword virtues of the clan,
Bury the unmachined, the planters' pride,
The courtesy and the bitter arrogance.
The pistol-hearted horsemen who could ride
Like jolly centaurs under the hot stars.
Bury the whip, bury the branding-bars,
Bury the unjust thing
That some tamed into mercy, being wise,
But could not starve the tiger from its eyes,
Bury the fiddle-music and the dance,
The sick magnolias of the false romance
And all the chivalry that went to seed
Before its ripening.

Talking that day with Liverpool Hazard I remembered those lines. Hazard's weary old eyes, deep in their sockets, had seen the tiger. Fanny Kemble had seen it, seeing the helpless old die alone with flies settling on their mouths and eyes; hearing the weeping, watching a slave, sold to another owner, leave his wife and children behind.

The chloroforming myths lie yet on the land, and in the pages of novels and histories. Worse still, they have held in attitudes toward the Negro. He was never again, after 1930, when change began to gather speed, to fit the image the white man had of him. And this was bad because this meant the image the white man had of himself wasn't true either. And this was disturbing.

I had never really seen plantation country, save in passing, until after I came to Georgia in the spring of 1929. It was a bad time to see it. It was still struggling with the boll weevil plague which had come with the twenties. And it was soon to fall into the demoralization of land and people which the depression of the thirties brought. A second cotton kingdom died then. The cabins began to empty, their doors and shutters sagging. Looking back at it now, I know that segregation began to die then, too, though it was twenty-odd long years until May 17, 1954.

I left Liverpool Hazard, shamefacedly putting what money I could spare in his hand, feeling the weight of guilt and knowing there could be no repayment, and went on to Dover Hall. There I could step from the accusing "old South" into a small, comforting world where baseball and laughter ruled. Colonel Huston greeted me loudly, stopping a story to ask, "You saw the old man?"

I nodded. He waved toward a table where the drinks were, and resumed his tale.

"Bill and I decided," he said, "to go to St. Andrews to see Bobby Jones play. We registered at this little hotel, and then Bill went down to the clerk.

" 'Young lady,' he said, to the fine, handsome young Scottish girl who was there, 'I belong to the old sheep-stealing clan of McGregor. If any sheep are stolen in the neighborhood, charge them to room 127. If any whiskey is ordered, charge it to Mr. Huston in 129.' "

I laughed louder than anyone else, wanting to exorcise from my memory old Liverpool Hazard and all the thinking he had put in my mind.

XII

What the Depression Taught Us

THERE WAS in the South an excitement about the early depression years of the 1930's which ameliorated the harshness of them. There was a mighty surge of discussion, debate, self-examination, confession and release.

Few towns were too small to have their study groups.
The demand for panel members and speakers was steady.
Aligned with faculty members from Emory University and
Georgia Tech, I traveled much of the state to spend a day
investigating and half a night in argument and in question-
and-answer hours. There were sharecroppers and tenants to
visit. Their wretched cabins and the pitiful meagerness of
their possessions and existence were eloquent evidence of the
inequities of an agricultural social and economic system
which had ground to a halt. I recall thinking, with a surge of
pity, on seeing them on the roads, sometimes whole families
of them ragged, now and then barefooted, I had never before
seen despair. There was the rough, scaly skin of pellagra victims, the thin bodies and hot eyes of the chronic malaria
sufferers. We got to know U.S. Public Health doctors and
technicians who encouraged us to peer through microscopes
and learn to identify hookworms. We saw and we talked.
There was a stimulation in those days. Gone, finally, were
the myths of white-pillared mansions, and a magnolia-
scented civilization. There were days, as we drove along the

rural roads, when it seemed as if distorting veils had been removed and we could, for the first time, see the cotton South plain.

There was another side of the coin. Traveling through Georgia and adjoining states, one could see, too, the general store or commissary which dominated the economy of the smaller towns which lived off the farm people around them. Many of these towns even then were drying up, as the colloquialism had it. One learned about the brutal mark-ups on every item that had been sold in these stores. Now and then men who had clerked, or "kept books," in those stores would come to a discussion meeting and, in a sort of confessional mood of repentance, tell the story of how credit was extended to illiterate tenants and croppers so that it was, in effect, a sort of peonage. There were cruel mark-ups on each sack of flour or meal, on every slab of bacon, or pair of work shoes or pants.

The old arrogance was gone, or going, from the commissaries. The 1930 census had shown a substantial ten-year decline in Negro population during those years of the boll weevil, and a lesser one for whites. There already had been tens of thousands of foreclosures, thousands of bankruptcies, hundreds of bank failures.

So, we talked of new directions, of cattle and dairying, of improved corn and cover crops. And we argued the history which had brought us to that time.

It had been the harsh pressure of credit rates which had brought on the Populist rebellion. It was put down. The "New Departure Democrats," or "The Redeemers," joined in with the speculative capital which came South and began to preach a "New South."

Booker T. Washington, for reasons even now not fully comprehended (but likely pragmatic), participated in what was the establishment of a new caste system. Within the newly developing economy the Negro was fixed as a sharecropper, tenant, small landowner, or in the more menial jobs in the cities and towns. With few exceptions, he was excluded from skilled employment.

This South of the 1880's-1890's was bankrupt of capital. Public services, including education, were starved, or simply not provided. The professional schools and universities were few. They, too, were neglected. Low wages, low taxes and a "contented Anglo-Saxon" labor force were promised those who wanted to invest in the industrialization of the New South. One sees something of the same sort of thing happening in the newly emerging countries of Africa and Asia, and in some of the Latin American countries where there is a new demand to industrialize.

The social costs to the South and nation were — and are — great. The lag then created in education, in public health, and public services persists into the last half of the twentieth century.

I remember one day, in the small South Georgia town of Waverly Hall, a man said, "The real enemy we have had in the rural, cotton South has been a certain type, small-town rich man." He oversimplified, but he was speaking out of a lifetime of experience with such men. Until the depression of the thirties was piled atop that of the boll-weevil twenties, every town in the South had at least one of this certain type. He was a fascinating study, now and then charming of manner, but more often repellent and hard.

Usually he lived in the best house, on the best hill in the town, or at the shadiest corner, a block or so off the main street — and always his home sought to sustain the legend of the South as a place of many mansions.

He owned, according to his geographic location, the gin, the turpentine works, the cotton warehouses, the tobacco warehouses. He was a director in the bank.

He was the owner of all, or part of, the biggest store. From it he sold fertilizer, plows, machinery, food, fencing, seeds, patent medicines, poultry and livestock remedies. He sold on credit, taking liens on crops and mortgages on livestock.

At least one of the popular automobile agencies was in his name, or owned by a brother, uncle, or son.

He controlled credit. He knew the financial predicament of every man in his section of the county. He knew the United States senators and the congressman from his district was always a "friend." He could write to Washington about a job for someone in his community. He could do the same with the governor. He called at the governor's office when he journeyed to the state capital. He made a contribution at campaign time, always to the right man, and if in doubt, to both candidates. He had a hand in the political patronage in his county. He "advised," or selected, the men who ran for the legislature.

He was, more often than not, a deacon in his church. If not a deacon, he was a "pillar," in that he gave liberally. He was wont to speak humorously, and with a certain condescension, of "my preacher." (In more ways than one, it usually was *his* preacher.)

He hadn't much time for books himself, but took a tolerant pride in the fact his wife belonged to the new Book-of-the-Month Club and collected antiques. He liked to tell the boys at the drugstore or at the office about the time his wife stopped him walking along a street in New York and made him go in with her and buy "some damned antique thing she saw in a window."

He usually owned and operated a few farms, taken in on foreclosures. If he "farmed" one or more of these farms he drove a hard bargain with his tenants, kept them in debt as much as possible, and let the tenant shacks go until the wind blew them over. He enjoyed saying he wished he were half as well off and as happy as "his niggers" who didn't know any better than to be happy. These men had a saying common to them all — "Nigger is Nigger and cotton is cotton, and that's the way it will always be."

If this certain type of rich man lived in one of the small, tightly held, back counties, he not infrequently indulged in the illegal luxury of using paroled Negro prisoners as farm laborers. In a county where perhaps one hundred fifty persons vote in a race for governor, this type of man owned the sheriff. He and a friend or so would pay the fines of Negroes and let them work out "the costs on the farms." Now and then they would see to it that on a Saturday night before the fine was worked out, a little "trouble" in town would give cause to have the Negroes arrested again and burdened with new fines and costs to work out.

As late as 1935 there were federal peonage cases made and convictions attained in some of the cotton states.

This certain type, small-town rich man hated Roosevelt, the New Deal, the triple A (Agricultural Adjustment Act), and the Federal Land Bank, which took mortgages and farm loans out of his hands.

He damned the WPA because it took away farm labor. In the towns he cursed it because his handy man, who had been taking what compensation he could get, now accepted the WPA's six dollars and eight dollars per week instead of his fifty cents or seventy-five cents per day. When war came and labor went into the war plants, he became nearly apoplectic about "labor" and the government paying high wages which, of course, was causing the happy, contented farm tenants and croppers to be discontented, or worse, to move away.

He saw the small farmers about him, defeated because they didn't know about markets and couldn't find out. Before the depression he usually spent a day or so each week in the nearest city doing a little gambling on cotton.

He hated all union labor. If the organizers came to his cotton mill, as they did in the late thirties, he encouraged the Ku Klux Klan to run them out of town. He did not want new industries in "his" town. They competed for "his" labor.

He fondly regarded himself as the bulwark of all that was "best" and of the Southern "traditions." If one asked him to delineate the traditions, he would flounder and stammer and find no words, save to say, "You know damn well what the Southern traditions are." He would turn away, mentally marking the questioner down as a person possessing "leftish" tendencies. If he were of the more arrogant type, he would condemn you as one of those "god-damned Reds."

He was willing to corrupt, to debase politics, to fight with all his weapons anything which seemed likely to diminish his power in his domain.

In those years I came to know many of these men. Some had admirable traits. Some had so much personality and charm it was impossible not to have an undeceived liking for their company. Yet, I do not recall one who could be called wholly admirable.

Their counterparts existed, of course, in other regions. They were, in a sort of malignant rural miniature, like the giant figures of the robber barons, who operated on a national and international scale. They never questioned their belief that the country belongs to him who can exploit it.

But since the South had for so long lived with the poverty of a one-crop system, one-party politics, and a small percentage of voters, these men of the type described were incredibly ruthless and lacking in conscience when it came to exploiting those dependent on them, colored or white. They saw the taking of a tenant's mule or wagon to satisfy some unmet crop or credit lien as merely part of an agreement. That they had made, and set its terms, and perhaps made impossible its fulfillment by exorbitant rates of interest and price mark-ups, was a satisfying piece of business.

I not recall one of these who could be described as a Southern aristocrat to fit the legend. Sometimes they had married the daughter of an old family which was of the planter aristocracy. But, almost without exception, these men were of the yeoman, small farmer, class who had clawed their way up through cotton with shrewd, unconscionable practices.

They could be, and were, generous to friends. They were not miserly. But they, like all exploiters, were corrupted by power and they had a sort of contempt for those whom they had used.

But, as the thirties began, they and their feudal holdings and practices were in trouble.

No matter what the 1930 census showed about the decline in Negro farm population, the Negro was still there in great numbers, the most helpless, the most exploited. The cotton, the timber, and the naval stores were based on his labor. He did not vote. He had no voice in decisions about government, schools, or policies which controlled his life. He could not serve on juries, and for justice, in the more rural areas, he depended on the whim or friendship of some white man.

To the average man in the South, this was merely the way life always had been. This was a part of the "tradition." It was a way ordered by history and custom. God and law so ordained it. Nor was there any intellectual exercise involved in this conclusion. That's the way it was.

There were genuine aristocrats in some few of the pillared plantation homes or old town houses. Some of them knew better. One of these was Will Percy, the planter, scholar and poet of one of the Mississippi Delta's historic plantations. This gentle, much-loved man, whose beautifully done book, *Lanterns on the Levee*, was the last, warming, contribution of a life spent in alternative, courageous struggle with the reality of his time, and who escaped into poetry and travel, said it better than anyone else:

To live habitually as a superior among inferiors, [he said,] be the the superiority intellectual or economic, is a temptation and hubris, inevitably deteriorating. To live among a people, whom because of their needs, one must in common decency protect and defend, is a sore burden in a world where one's own troubles are about all that one can shoulder. To live in the pretense that whites and blacks share a single, identical culture and way of life is not only hypocritical but illusory and obfuscating. And, last, to live among a people deceptively but deeply alien and unknowable guarantees heartaches, unjust expectations, undeserved condemnations. Yet, such living is the fate of the white man in the South.

It is true in the South that whites and blacks live side by side, exchange affection liberally, and believe they have an innate and miraculous understanding of one another. But the sober fact is we understand one another not at all. Just about the time our proximity appears most harmonious something happens . . . and to our astonishment we sense a barrier between. To make it more bewildering, the barrier is of glass; you can't see it, you only strike it.

Will Percy's magnificent father, as has previously been noted, had been defeated for Congress by James K. Vardaman, the one who, in the moment of victory, had cried out, "The bottom rail's on top. And it's going to stay there." He was, alas, a very accurate prophet, insofar as political rails are concerned. After Vardaman in Mississippi came Theodore Bilbo, James O. Eastland and Ross Barnett, to name three whose names became nationally known.

Will Percy could sense, even on his plantation where always a kindly, just paternalism and an old-fashioned concept of *noblesse oblige* prevailed, that clamorous change was coming. He talked of it, dreading, he said, to live through it. A heart attack, not long after his book had won national acclaim, spared him what he dreaded.

Almost everything and everyone seemed to join to accelerate change in the 1930's. Southern politicians embraced the New Deal and its props for agriculture, its WPA, PWA, and its patronage with all the ardor of a bridegroom.

One of the favorite subjects of the professors of political

science, sociology and economics with whom I went to college and study group discussions in 1932-1937 was the Hawley-Smoot Tariff Act. As a Woodrow Wilson Democrat, I had read all his writings on the folly of excessively restrictive tariffs.

My attempts to discuss tariffs at the community meetings were not always well received. I was then writing a daily sports column, and in the fall covered football games. One evening at La Grange, Georgia, an irritated cotton mill man arose at the question and answer hour, and said, "I enjoyed your story on the game last Saturday, but what in the hell do you think you know about tariffs on cotton?"

It was a blow to my pride, but I persisted. For one thing, I learned more about it. The Hawley-Smoot Act, most severe of a series of tariff acts begun in 1921, was ratified in 1930. Sir Arthur Salter, British business leader and economist, later said, "The ratification of that tariff was a turning point in world history." I think it was. Certainly it was for American agriculture, and, more especially, cotton. Before the First World War, we exported about sixty-five per cent of our cotton crop. In the period 1926-1930, we exported fifty-nine per cent of it. Other of the nation's crops were also heavily involved in foreign trade, including tobacco and wheat.

In a talk with President Roosevelt at Warm Springs, he said that the response he had from farmers after an autumn speech at Des Moines, Iowa, by President Herbert Hoover, convinced him the Republicans had lost the farm vote. In the fall of 1932 farmers everywhere were losing their farms through foreclosures and evictions. The foreign market was being lost and the home one paralyzed.

President Hoover told them he would save American agriculture by raising farm tariffs. "Ninety per cent of your market is at home," he said, "and I propose to reserve this market to the American farmer."

Cotton farmers knew this was not true. Their market had always been largely a foreign one. At the time Mr. Hoover spoke, wheat was thirty-five cents a bushel at Chicago and twenty cents on many local farm markets. The tariff was forty-two cents a bushel. In that year our millers and manufacturers of special products imported only 241,000 bushels of wheat and about 230,000 barrels of flour. United States production was 24 million barrels of flour.

Cotton then began to lose its export market. Not long thereafter United States capital moved abroad to grow cotton. Foreign production was encouraged. Nationalism, as we have seen all too plainly, breeds nationalism. The cruel depression set many forces in action. There were revolutions in agriculture as well as in technology and the structure of world power. The cotton South would never again be the same. We knew that by 1933. The Second World War reaffirmed that conclusion. It was on a scale terrifyingly vast and expensive in dollars and lives. Much of the war capital flowed South to create new pressures. As usual, the members of the old oligarchy rallied wherever they could to keep wages in the new war plants held to the local scale. But there were others who could be heard in Washington, and they said, "For God's sake, be sure the national wage rates are paid. Low wages have been the South's curse. Help us break out of the past."

Suddenly, it seemed, by 1942, everyone had money. The situation was not without humor and exposure of selfish folly at its preposterous worst for a while became front-page news in all the nation's newspapers. By the summer of 1942, the South surprisingly found itself almost out of cooks. Since there had always been a surplus of cooks, who as a consequence were poorly paid, the shortage became an outlet for all the frustrations produced by the changing South. It was, many angry wives said, caused by all the New Deal coddling of Negroes. That was the season the stories about Mrs. Eleanor Roosevelt began to be heard in drugstores, Pullman smoking rooms, in the lulls between the songs at the civic clubs, and in all the homes where cookless ladies met at tea or lunch.

Nor was it merely that Southern kitchens were out of cooks. Maids were also scarce. And this was, of course, too much to endure. Not to have a cook, or at least a girl who came to "clean" two or three days a week, was a sign of social inferiority. It became very easy to decide that Mrs. Roosevelt, who had interested herself in the issue of civil and economic rights, was an awful person when the cook telephoned to quit, or, as was more often the case, simply didn't show up at all, because she had a job in a war plant — or her husband did.

The summer of 1942 also saw first Southern hearings of the Fair Employment Practices Committee. These deliberations, which some editors and community leaders said threatened the traditions, were the subject of many outraged editorials, speeches and resolutions.

The outbursts with preposterous irrelevancy centered on Mrs. Roosevelt. She became the issue. It was ridiculous and, occasionally, frightening. All the resentment at the very idea of an FEPC, at the lack of a cook, a yard man, or a butler, was concentrated in spiteful talk about Mrs. Roosevelt. It found outlet in epithets and stories of all degrees of silliness and bad taste in which she was the central theme. The newspaper editorials were even worse. They ran all the way from that of the *Jackson* (Mississippi) *News*, which began, "It is blood on your hands, Mrs. Roosevelt," to "Back to Harlem for Eleanor." The nation has known no more disgraceful, hysterical display of immaturity.

The rumors were endless. Chief among them was the "Eleanor Club" myth. No one ever discovered an Eleanor club of Negro cooks and housemaids. Here and there an amateur effort to form a labor union was discovered but Mrs. Roosevelt had no part in it. Vereen Bell, well-known Georgia novelist, who was killed late in the war in the Pacific theater invasion, discovered one such "club" in Thomasville, Georgia. It was directed at one wealthy matron in the town who had a habit of being drunk on too many cocktails by late afternoon and berating her cook. The town's cooks held no meeting, but one day they had decided not to work for the lady. This decision received the hearty applause and support of all white persons who learned about it.

Later on, the Eleanor club rumors were to give way to the "Disappoint You" clubs. This was supposed to consist of at least ten colored cooks who would telephone at least ten want ad addresses and promise to come to work. They would then disappoint the cookless ladies by failing to show up. This, too, was a myth, although some good matrons likely will go to their deathbeds believing it.

"I can't wait for this war to end and to have them [the cooks] come crawling back," wrote one small-town matron to her local paper.

Resentment took even more curious forms. One woman was outraged because her cook, who had worked for twenty years at wages from three dollars to five dollars a week, quit and "just sat on her porch and rocked" when her two sons went into the army and began sending home allotment checks.

Few there were who understood they were seeing the visible beginnings of the Negro's effort to have some voice in decisions involving his welfare. They were small beginnings, but they were plain to all who were willing to see.

The kitchens were never to fill up again, at least not in the old way, any more than would the empty tenant cabins. The forces loosed by the depression, the war, and Franklin Roosevelt's political coalition had already rubbed out "Nigger is Nigger and cotton is cotton" and all that this crude inanity implied, though some time would be needed to make that clear.

The war engulfed us, and only a handful of persons noted that some preparations had been made to file suits testing the segregation laws which kept Negro students out of schools of law, medicine and dentistry in those states which did not provide such institutions for colored students. Another old South was passing before our eyes, but we had to get the war behind us before that became apparent. And then, as in other times of change, there were many who did not want to see it, and who insisted things could be kept the way they had been.

XIII

Southerners Overseas

THERE WAS a South Georgia afternoon I can't, and don't
want to, forget. It was late in August, 1939. Heat lay
heavily on the land. There was dust on the goldenrod bloom-
ing on the edges of the roadside ditches. The leaves on the
lower branches of trees along the way were dusty. The weeds
were heavy with it.

The Negro county agent, who was driving, talked of the
farm and the farmer we had just left. A young Negro agricul-
tural-school graduate had bought land on the tenant purchase
plan.

"He'll make it," said the agent. "His wife has sense. He has
those nice pigs. He has corn and a field of peanuts into which
he can turn the pigs. He'll make a bale and a half of cotton.
He has a tractor. He'll do all right."

I nodded, remembering the young man and his wife who
had been surprised and a little self-conscious to have a newspaperman walk over their land, look at the pigs, and ask questions about the hybrid corn. (I spent most of that summer
going around, writing about farmers selected by the county
agents as having done good boot-strap jobs.)

"I live just down the road a piece," said the agent, as the car
bumped along. "Would you like to stop for a glass of iced tea
and some cake before I take you into town?"

I said I would. He was silent for a minute. We had never met until that morning.

"There is something I need to tell you," he said, "that I hope you will understand."

"About what?"

"My house. I don't want you to be surprised or not understand."

"I'm not sure what you mean, but don't worry about it."

He nodded.

He was silent as we crested a rise, drove on down the slope and halfway up another, pulled off to a small, weather-stained house, unprepossessing in its fading brown paint. The yard was clean-swept dirt. We got out of the dusty Chevrolet. His wife had opened the door and stood on the top of the steps.

"It's Mr. McGill," he said.

"Come in," she said, "it's been real hot, hasn't it?"

We went in. And then I understood what he had been driving at, and couldn't bring himself to say. I stood there, shame crowding through me, and a heavy sadness on me.

"We'd like some tea," he said, and his wife turned and went to fetch it.

The room was paneled with a stained, native pine. There were some bright rag rugs on the floor. There was an upright piano at one corner. Three or four conventional prints, of the cheerful rural-scene type, were on the wall.

"You did all this yourself?"

"The wife and I — and our son, before he went to the army."

"It's awfully nice."

"We like it," he said.

"I understand what you were trying to say, and I'm ashamed you felt you had to say it."

"Well," he said, "you know how it is."

"Yes, I know, but I never felt it this way before."

"Well, I didn't want you to be surprised by the inside. But it's best this way. A lot of people wouldn't understand. A lot of people are funny about things. They think you are getting too big for your place, or putting on airs. Some didn't like it. So, we just don't attract attention. We leave the outside like it is. But we live on the inside. They don't come in, you know. They holler and I go out."

The tall glass of tea sweated in my hand; and my shirt, wet across the back and about the neck with the sweat of the day, seemed tight and uncomfortable.

Here was a man and his wife, with a son in the army of their country, and mine. The husband and father was a Negro county agent — not simply a county agent. He could work only with Negroes. He was so earnest a worker, and so well grounded in agriculture, and with a sort of passion to teach it, that Negro farmers in his county had attained a reputation for modest successes. They won prizes in the Negro section at the county fair. Their wives canned vegetables and put up pickles and preserves. The farms all had a look of neatness about them. There was use of REA electricity, and pumps in many of the wells.

But it would not do for the man who was responsible for all of this to appear "uppity," by making his place attractive to the passerby. It had to be almost a secret, "inside" thing. The white people in the county seat liked him. They spoke well of him. But he never wore a good suit to town, except on Sundays, and he did not let it be known that the rooms of his house were paneled, nor that there was a piano in the living room and framed prints on the wall. There would have been some, as he said, who wouldn't have liked it. It was one of those things which he and I understood — a dark, mysterious, hateful thing, never written out, or said, but a part of what was meant, in rural sections, by that well-rounded phrase, "Southern customs," or "ways."

All this was known to me. It was present in the homes of Negro faculty members at universities, or of professional or business men in the cities. In cities it could be discussed with a certain abstraction. They could have what they pleased in their houses or apartments. But not there — not in that neat, attractive room, hot with the deep, sweltering heat of August in South Georgia. The house was alone there near the road. And those in it were alone.

We talked, sitting there, drinking the iced tea, and eating oatmeal cookies, of how cotton was not what it used to be, of what a blessing a tractor was, but of how something vital was lost when the mules went. He was a man with a cause, and he talked powerfully of the need to keep the family-type farms. I listened, nodding affirmatively. But I could not shake off the feeling of shame and responsibility for a situation in which a man and his family — in the United States — could not fix the outside of his home as he wanted it — could not live simply and freely as any other person. It was wrong, terribly wrong. The injustice of it was unspoken, but it was heavy in the room and though neither of us spoke of it, there was communication between us. They knew that I knew.

He took me into town to the hot sultry little hotel where the small coffee shop was air-conditioned, but the rooms were not. A fan buzzed from a table in my room. Sleep was slow in coming. Memory went over and over again the agent's halting sentences in the car, and the wave of comprehension that came over me as we stepped in the room. I long had known that we did not have a free and ordered society in America. It was obvious in the cities where we discussed the Southerner's substitution of humanitarian philanthropy and paternalism for the deeper values of human life and an ordered society.

In the Southern cities there was no first-class restaurant to which the Negro doctor of philosophy could take his wife and family if they wanted to eat out. If he wanted to take his family to a movie it was necessary to go to a side entrance and climb up a flight or so of stairs to a gallery. If he rode the city buses he and his children went to the rear. In most towns, if he took a taxi it had to be one for Negroes only. The schools were not equal. All this, too, was wrong. But we discussed it intellectually, with sociological terms and with understanding of why this was so, and why it would have to end. But somehow, it had never hit me like a blow until that hot afternoon in a rural county when the county agent had brought me to his home.

I think it was because when we talked in study groups or at teas or dinners at the universities or at some homes, we never felt alone. In the hot hotel room that night I could picture the agent and his wife sitting at home talking about the day, their son in the army of his country, and the visits we had made to the farms. They were alone. There were no neighbors. They were vulnerable — there in the secret tastefulness of their own house. For them, more than anyone in the town, the routine of their lives depended on maintaining a careful balance of things never said, but known.

Hitler's voice could be heard in those days on American short-wave radios. In New York Fritz Kuhn and the German Bund secretly were plotting with the Klan groups in anti-Semitic tirades and demands that America stay out of war. The South was interventionist-minded. There was talk everywhere of freedom and the dignity of man. At breakfast the next morning with the white county agent with whom I was to be that day, he talked mostly of letters from the Department of Agriculture asking that farmers be encouraged to produce more food. He was planning a big meeting at the schoolhouse.

"Will the Negro farmers be there?"

"Oh, no," he said, "they'll get the word from their agent — the one you were with yesterday."

There was no guile in him. The talk of American democracy and the dignity of man did not have a crack in it insofar as he was concerned. And he was not a bad man.

The war came on with a rush and many times in those years I thought back to that late afternoon when we returned, sweaty and tired, to the Negro agent's house on a farm-to-market road out from the county seat of a town which had known the glories of the days when cotton was king, and the South had a monopoly — "Ours and our sons' forever."

In England in the summer of 1943 I saw young Southerners in the compelling classrooms of the war. Those I saw were, for the most part, aviators, fighter pilots and bomber crews at the bases scattered over the British Isles. I spent my first week in England at General Curtis E. LeMay's headquarters near Cambridge, and developed in those days a lasting admiration and respect for him. No matter how late or early one was up, he seemed always about, a slightly stooped man, with a gray sweater over his army shirt, plodding about setting up the next B-17 raid.

Among the Southerners I noted a grudging respect for a severe disciplinarian who was allergic to mistakes and who accepted perfection as the norm. They knew he had faced all the dangers which were theirs. He had created the tight-formation flights for the big unescorted B-17's. They flew, relatively as close as fighter planes, to mass firepower and to make more difficult the breaking up of the flight into separated craft which could be the more easily picked off. General LeMay ruthlessly removed commanders and pilots who flew sloppy, loose missions.

Seeing them go, and sweating out the long wait, was a thrill and agony which grew more intense as one watched the skies for their return.

Public information officers always brought forth, as a sort of captive audience, the men from a visiting correspondent's home state. I met many Georgians, and through them other Southerners. We talked, as men in foreign countries will, of home and hometowns, and of people we knew in common.

The war had not then turned toward victory. The hard pounding of the Nazi-held cities, and of Germany itself, daily was being stepped up. The men who flew the B-17's and the B-45's were magnificent. Life at the attack air bases was at a high, shared level, such as the foot soldiers and tank battalions later were to know. There were death and suffering and incredible danger in it, but there was something else, too; something not seen, but felt, experienced. Life on the days of the great raids was something like a Book of Common Prayer, with readings of the exalted Psalms of battle, of praise and thanksgivings; and prayers for deliverance from evil and danger, and for those who died in duty.

We Southerners talked of the South, of course, of how we loved it, and of how it must learn to be a part of the nation, and not withdrawn. We laughed at the folkway posturing of our politicians and wondered why we all had a not-quite-understood affection for the most gifted and worst of them. Service in the Second World War opened the eyes and minds of thousands of Southerners. But truth to tell, we were all so lifted up by the daily challenge of war that we talked mostly of it. It was to be somewhat different two years later.

On January 10, 1945, Wilbur Forrest, the associate editor of the *New York Herald Tribune;* Carl Ackerman, then dean of Columbia University's School of Journalism, and I were sent out from New York on a journey which was to take us around the world. We represented the American Society of Newspaper Editors in a sort of Johnny Appleseed mission of trying to organize and interest journalists in being prepared to demand and participate in a freer flow of news and an exchange of news ideas and problems once the war ended and the world was put together again. We traveled in planes of the Air Transport Command, without priority. (It was offered, but we refused.) The way led us to London, where the V-2 bombs were coming; to Paris, newly liberated; Rome, with fighting in the north; Athens, with the Communist-directed ELAS troops a few miles away, to Cairo, to Ankara and Istanbul, to Moscow where there were rockets and gun salutes each night to the victorious push against the Germans; to Karachi and New Delhi; to Chiang's wartime capital of Chunking, and to Aus tralia, via Ceylon; and then on to San Francisco, where, in the hopeful sun of a beautiful April, the delegates were gathering to write a charter for the United Nations.

The journey was a magnificent panorama. We talked with generals, and heads of governments, with soldiers of all nations, with newspapermen and government press officers; with princes and queens in exile. We saw American soldiers under many conditions. It was a thought-provoking trip. There were prophetic stirrings. None who saw the world in the last months of that earth-girdling war could fail to sense that the forces unloosed by it would not die out with the fighting. There would be a new environment requiring new responses. Yet, it was not a journey without humor. Forrest and Ackerman, not quite comprehending that in the more provincial journalism of the South a byline that had been appearing in *The Atlanta Constitution* for sixteen years would have become known to a great many Georgians and Southerners, early began to note how many of them sought me out for news of home. The *Stars and Stripes,* in whatever theater we were, gave notice of our presence. And, truthfully, there was a run of Georgians. On the way over we were delayed at Stephenville, Newfoundland, before testing the Atlantic. The duty officer, a Georgian, seeing our names on the manifest, became our guide. He took us to one of the Air Force's ubiquitous DeGink hotels and warmed us with hospitality and Scotch until departure time. We landed at Prestwick, Scotland. As we changed money at the army finance office, the corporal said he had met me at Rigg Ware's home in Hogansville, Georgia, and we chatted about him, a mighty fox hunter. In London and Paris other homesick Georgians came around to ask about home. Crawford Ware, a nephew of Rigg Ware, was one. At Paris, where I had a good visit with Mary Welch and Ernest Hemingway, there were more Georgians.

Forrest began to complain that the flood of visitors was, of course, rigged. On the way out to Versailles to see General

Eisenhower, he said to Ackerman, "Well, Carl, at least Ike is a Middle West Dutchman with no Georgia connections." When we had completed a very helpful briefing with the General, I told him I had seen his son John about ten days before. He was coming up to Atlanta from Fort Benning for weekend liberty and was having dates with the attractive daughter of one of my neighbors. The General was delighted to have news of him, and showed us a cutting from a Columbus, Georgia, newspaper in which there was a picture of the young ladies who had attended a dance there and asked me to identify his son's date. This I did, not failing to pass it on to my associates for a look.

Rome was next; and there an ATC colonel, a Medical Corps major, both Georgians; a WAC, a member of *The Atlanta Constitution* staff, then on the *Stars and Stripes*, came to call. On our drive to the Vatican, accompanied by the late Myron Taylor, then U.S. representative to the Holy See, Forrest told the story of the Georgia callers and said, "Ike let us down. But one thing is sure. The Holy Father hasn't got a son who has dates with the daughter of one of McGill's neighbors."

Pope Pius XII received us at the appointed time, and as I was presented, he said, "Mr. McGill, we have had a nice letter about you from Bishop O'Hara in Atlanta."

This was so unexpected that it was with the greatest of difficulty that Forrest and I kept straight faces. The audience was a most pleasant one. For a half hour the Holy Father asked questions and answered ours. Before we left, he blessed us each, and prayed for a safe journey. (No three Protestants ever felt more reassured by a prayer than by this one, and the rest of our journey, especially one night out of Abadan when the controls on our DC-4 stuck, we leaned on it mightily.)

Georgia's triumph was complete when, on quitting Pope Pius's chambers, we were met by two young priests from Atlanta, then studying in the North American College, who asked us out to dinner.

In talks with Georgians and Southerners from neighboring states, one of the most common statements was, "The world won't ever be the same again, will it?" Those whom I met in Teheran, in China and India were, like all other men who served there, shocked by the poverty and misery of the people. Scraps of conversations and conclusions have stayed in my mind. The meetings were brief — an hour or so — and most of the talk was of home and the progress of war. The American soldier, like his generals, is not very politically minded.

I remember talking with a Negro truck driver at Dum Dum airport, Calcutta.

"I write my daddy and mother about this place [India]," he said, "and they won't believe it. We are farm folks, never had nothing. But this sort of thing is really wrong. I'm going back to school when I get home and I'm going to try to do something about helping my own folks. I hear we are going to start a United Nations. I'm for it. I hope it can help these people."

Teheran, where the Persian Gulf Command had headquarters, was the inland terminal for an American-operated rail line which brought supplies and equipment along a tortuous route from Khorramshahr. The railroad shops were in Teheran and a number of railroad men from railway shops at Waycross, Georgia, were there. One day one of those took me to see the machine shop. A number of dark-skinned Iranian helpers were busy about the place. The railroader pointed them out. "You know," he said, "I've learned something here. You see these 'wogs'? When we first came here I thought they were all trifling and no-account. But you know," he said, honest astonishment in his voice, "you train them and give them a chance and they do damned good work."

They were still "wogs" to him, but he was learning.

"You know," I said, "we may have to learn that same thing

about the Negro back home." He looked at me, startled. "By God," he said, "we might at that."

The better-educated Southerners, white and colored, knew that never again would there be a slipping back into the old restraints, and an acceptance of the cynical fiction of the separate but equal status.

One night in Rome a young officer from Georgia said, as a group of us sat around a table in the ATC-requisitioned Hassler Hotel, "We have been living a lie back home for a long, long time. I guess it's caught up with us. And I guess I'm glad of it."

There was one thread which ran through talks with Southern men in service all around the world. They had been shaken out of any isolationist ideas they may have had. And if some of them would return to, and re-embrace, parochialism and the old "ways" they would never again feel comfortable in them.

From Teheran, after long delays, we at last obtained seats on one of the two C-47's which the Soviets shuttled back and forth on the busy run to Moscow. By then we were familiar with this wonderful little workhorse aircraft, but it looked different because of the red star painted on it.

We took off after taxiing to the head of the runway, with no preliminary warm-up tests of the motors, and began a steep climb to the thirteen-thousand-foot pass through the hurdle of the Elburz Mountains. On the take-off all the passengers leaned forward from their no-safety-belt bucket seats and steadied the freight and baggage piled in the aisle. The American and British military services carefully lashed theirs lest it slide back into the tail on take-off, or forward on landing and upset the craft's balance, causing a crash. Apparently, the Russians, knowing that air travelers really have nothing to do, allowed them to perform this simple service, which they, knowing what an abrupt shift in load means on take-off, required no urging to provide.

Memories of that flight have remained with me.

We were a mixed crowd of Russians and Americans, all very amiable. We kept climbing. There were still gas fumes in the cabin from the take-off. A tall, friendly Russian, who had helped us with translations, moved forward to sit on one of the extra gas tanks, installed forward, and lit a cigarette as he began a conversation with a friend.

I tugged nervously at the sleeve of a small sergeant in a fur cap, who seemed to be a sort of flight officer. He followed my eyes. His face wreathed itself in smiles. He threw up one thumb: "Boom!" he said, happily. And still smiling, he reversed his hand and swept it downward in a swift gesture. "Boom! Boom!" he said, and, still smiling happily, he leaned back and resumed his nap.

The tall Russian left his seat on the gas tank and came back to say we soon would see the Caspian Sea. We flew across one long corner of the sea, out of sight of land. Not until then did I notice that the usual load of rafts and radio equipment found in American planes crossing large stretches of water was missing. I understood it was superfluous. Nevertheless, I mentioned it casually to the tall Russian. He translated, smiling, to the blond, cheerful pilot, who was back in the cabin speaking briefly with friends, the co-pilot having taken over.

The pilot spoke rapidly, smiling, and the tall Russian grinned and relayed it on: "He says tell you he never lost a foreigner yet."

So, with stops for refueling, and a thirty-six-hour weather delay in a small, new, plaster-smelling airport building at Stalingrad, we came to Moscow; then to the National Hotel and old newspaper friends — Eddie Gilmore and Daniel De Luce, of the Associated Press — vodka and cheese and warmth.

Moscow provided an experience that has been a puzzle all the years since. The second night after our arrival, Ambassador Averell Harriman gave a dinner. (My notes record it as March 11, and say that late that evening there were salutes fired from guns about the Kremlin, and a display of rockets followed to announce a further Soviet advance against the Germans.) The Ambassador's invitations were to the press officers and to the Russian writers and editors. All invited came, somewhat to the surprise of the Embassy staff. This was the first attempt at a get-together with Americans. It was a pleasant evening of toasts and responses. (The notes say that twenty-seven toasts were given and responses made.)

On the evening of March 14, the Russians gave a return dinner. It was a large affair, preceded by trays of vodka and the most plentiful and excellent hors d'oeuvres. Among those present was Michael Borodin. He looked old. There was about him an almost tangible air of indifference, but also of enough patience to endure it. It was like meeting a legend. Somehow I had supposed him dead. Memory of books read raced through my head. He had been a central figure in the Russian effort to convert and subvert Dr. Sun Yat-sen's Kuomintang program into Communism. It began in 1923 after Dr. Sun previously had failed to get help from Europe and America. Russia signed an agreement of friendship and aid. In September, 1923, Borodin arrived in Canton. To this day, not a great deal is known about him. Yet, in his time he unquestionably must have been regarded as one of the party's most able men. They otherwise would not have sent him on so important a mission. He began with success. By January, 1924, both Russian and Chinese Communists were admitted to the Kuomintang. Organization of the Nationalist Party followed. The skilled hand of Borodin was evident. He created a Central Committee. It replaced Dr. Sun. Chiang Kai-shek, Russian-trained, became the military leader.

By 1926 the Communist wing was in control of the party, with civil headquarters in Hankow. Borodin was the civil leader.

Later that year, after the capture of Nanking and the murder and mistreatment of foreigners, Chiang broke with the

Communists and seized power. By July, Borodin and Madame Sun Yat-sen escaped to Russia.

Borodin disappeared into the vast unknown of Russia, presumably in disgrace, though historians believe the errors which led to Chiang's move and enabled it to succeed were more Stalin's than Borodin's. To find this legend alive and present was an unexpected fillip to the evening. He spoke English. I told him I had read much of him. He said he was editing a small weekly, printed in English. We managed a few remarks of no consequence before I was surrounded by questioners. Ilya Ehrenburg was among them. They sought to give me a bad time of it. Ehrenburg, after a tirade against the American press in general, which he said had a Fascist heart, asked me to explain the psychology of Southerners who opposed intermarriage. He wandered away after I had said that the business of intermarriage was not, after all, a philosophy, but a very personal matter and further had said that demagogic use of it by Southern racist extremists had exacerbated it out of all proportions. Two or three others hung on for a while. Some of their information was distorted. But there were enough true stories of racial violence to make it an uncomfortable time. I rolled with the punches and never showed any loss of patience or failed to make a full comment. After a while, they wandered over to another of the several eddies one finds at all cocktail parties.

It was then that Borodin leaned over and said, *sotto voce,* "These damned fools don't know what they are talking about." I was startled. He had, in a very real sense, made himself vulnerable. Had I written about it he would have suffered. It was an impulsive, bold thing for him to do. I was grateful for his understanding, and said so. He shrugged. Thinking about it in the days that followed I could only conclude that he, with his years of perspective, was bored with the whole thing and with what it had become. He was then a very minor figure, who had once been so prominent a one. None of the other editors or writers did more than speak with him. He was supremely indifferent. When the dinner was ended I looked around to say goodbye to Borodin. But he had slipped away.

His name never thereafter appeared in print until after Stalin's death. Then, one day, I saw it. Khrushchev's new regime had "rehabilitated" a great many Russians who unjustly had been convicted and imprisoned or killed by Stalin and Beria. Borodin's name was in the list. He had died, the report said, in Siberia.

In the summer of 1959 I was one of the newspaper men accompanying Vice President Nixon to Russia. I made inquiries among the Soviet journalists who covered the vice president's tour and was told only that Borodin had been arrested after the war ended and sent to prison. They did not know why, but pointed out that he had been rehabilitated. I can imagine his ghost smiling wryly at the use of that word.

Once the war was ended, it seemed to me the South began to stir. It was only nine years before the U. S. Supreme Court decision was to be handed down.

Nor were those years empty of action. The late forties produced President Truman's civil rights committee. In 1947 it flatly recommended "the elimination of segregation, based on race, color, creed, or national origin, from American life."

The Congress evaded action on recommended legislation. But in the humid summer of 1948, in the oppressive non-air-conditioned climate of Philadelphia's convention hall, Minnesota's young Senator Hubert Humphrey smashed through the hypocrisy of double talk with a demand for an honest civil rights plank in the Democratic party platform. It was like flashes of lightning in one of those sudden heat storms. The committee compromise plank was cast aside. The substitute called for an end to discriminatory segregation practices. I will always remember Senator Humphrey, how he looked and sounded, and the roar of the crowd. Most of Alabama's delegation quit the floor, followed by the more angry delegates of other Deep South states. They soon formed the Dixiecrat Party. It was, at heart, the most infamously hypocritical and intellectually dishonest political organization ever created. While it sought to conceal its real motives with the cynical old shibboleth of states' rights, its real principles were those later espoused and practiced by the worst of the White Citizens Councils. Indeed, many of the Dixiecrat leaders became the chief organizers and supporters of these councils.

In 1953 school segregation was ended in all schools operated by the Defense Department, many of them in the several Southern states.

The courts also were interpreting the separate-but-equal phrase in the 1896 "Plessy v. Ferguson" case. The rights created by the Fourteenth Amendment required equalization, and there had been none. In 1952 five cases were brought before the U. S. Supreme Court challenging the Plessy doctrine.

There was something shameful in the hurry of the Southern states to equalize their schools. They knew, but would not admit, the truth. I sought to put it into words in a column:

What the various state legislatures are doing, as they busy themselves with plans to carry on school segregation without legal compulsion, is admitting segregation by law is finished . . . either this year, next or within the next few to come. . . .

As a matter of fact, segregation has been on its way out for a good long time and has been breaking down at the edges for more than a generation. . . . Two great forces have been at work on segregation and the problem of race. One is secular, the other religious. The Christian of today cannot help but wince at the full implications, and the jarring clash of his creed, with discrimination against any person because of color. . . . Christianity cannot well afford to be on the wrong side of a moral force, as it was in some areas when it defended slavery.

The other influence is secular. Segregation implies inferiority. There are those who argue that it does not. But those segregated believe it does. . . . Across two great wars now we, along with other free peoples, have preached the rights of men everywhere to be free and equal — we have encouraged long-oppressed peoples to rise . . .

An end to segregation — when it comes — will not, of course, force people to associate socially. That will remain, as now, personal choice. But it will bring on change — and this is what state legislatures in South Carolina, Georgia, Mississippi, Virginia and Alabama are, or will be, considering. They consider not how to retain legal segregation — which they see soon ending — but how to effect it without legal compulsion. . . . Segregation is on the way out and he who tries to tell the people otherwise does them great disservice. The problem of the future is how to live with the change.

It was obvious, too, that the old tradition of *noblesse oblige* was fading fast. There had never been much of nobility in it. It was paternalistic and, with some few exceptions, the Negro was quite right to reject it because of its connotations of inferiority. (During the sit-in demonstrations one merchant who had provided a basement lunch counter for Negroes, said, with honest indignation, "I don't see how they could do this to us after all we've done for them.")

That the school decision of May, 1954, came as a surprise to many Southerners, evoking furious protests, and shameful slanders on a unanimous court, indicated how deeply convinced many persons were that the Negro was not a citizen and even if he were, he shouldn't be. Since 1945 there had been yearly reminders that the United States could no longer ignore its own principles, its Fourteenth constitutional amendment, and the demands of civilization and morality.

The decision was, all in one, fulcrum and lever. Customs, traditions, and political structures began to find themselves moved out of the way.

In all America no one was so lucky as the Southerner who was a part of this social revolution — of this determination to reaffirm the principles of what we have called the American dream. My county agent was a symbol of this dream.

XIV

Industry and Labor's Search
for a New South

S OMEHOW, when I think of the South's long struggle for industry, memory turns first, not to the incredibly ruthless sweatshop exploitation which followed the Supreme Court's nullification of the National Recovery Act in 1935, the cotton bale barricades and the machine guns of the bitter textile strikes, nor today's gleaming new plants on terraced lawns, but to Miss Lucy Randolph Mason, daughter of one of Richmond's beloved Episcopal ministers, and a true FFV from Virginia, who, in 1937, at age fifty-five, came to the regional headquarters in Atlanta as an organizer for the newly created CIO.

It was impossible that this sweet, gentle lady, who blushed when you paid her a compliment, should have been a part of the Congress of Industrial Organizations at a time when hired evangelists were going about the South, in the small towns and on the fringes of the larger ones, thundering that the people must choose between God and the CIO. Even in the cities pastors of major churches found it convenient to condemn the new union as inspired by evil and wicked forces. Organizers frequently were driven from town and city. Some were brutally beaten.

In many ways it was hilarious that Miss Lucy was with the CIO. Many a tough sheriff in a small town that had a CIO organizer in jail looked up to see a small lady in a dark suit, wearing a little white-trimmed black hat on gray hair, come smiling into his office. Being, of course, sure of his image of himself as a Southern gentleman, and a protector of Southern womanhood, he would offer a chair before he heard even her name. Some, legend has it, swallowed their cuds of chewing tobacco on hearing that she was with the CIO and had come to talk about civil rights. One or two cursed her from their offices, but most of them heard her out with a certain awe at their own control.

Here and there unctuous bankers, bosses of their towns, went forward to greet her when she came in, wondering what sort of account this widow wished to open. Their consternation was complete on hearing a stern lecture, in a girl-like voice, on the wickedness and illegality of beating up organizers and of permitting workers in their towns to toil a week for five dollars or less.

Many a Southern newspaper editor, author of fiery anti-CIO editorials, found himself tongue-tied and humble as Miss Lucy corrected his published errors and exposed with carefully researched facts his ignorance of his own town's economics.

But it remained for a political boss in her native state of Virginia to receive, the one and only time Miss Lucy ever gave it, what might be called the full treatment. There was a new textile mill in a city far up the James River where workers twice had managed to obtain a Labor Board election. Each time a local civic club had campaigned against the union and brought about its defeat. Miss Lucy was dispatched to the city. A doctor was regarded as the town's unofficial political boss and Miss Lucy was in his office lecturing him on the civil rights of workers, when a friend of the doctor's walked in. He wasn't introduced, but listened. At last he said, with brusque rudeness, "Lady, let me ask you this. What's back of you? Who sent you here anyhow? And by what right do you come into the state of Virginia to make trouble about civil rights?"

This was too much to take. And, so Miss Lucy told him. She ticked off her ancestors. George Mason, who wrote the Virginia Declaration of human rights, was her great-great-great-grandfather. Three of her ancestors signed the Declaration of Independence. Chief Justice John Marshall was her mother's great-great uncle. The Randolphs, the Carters, the Beverleys, the Bollings, and the Chichesters of the colonial days were of her family. And if he wanted to come down to the Confederacy, her great-grandfather, James Murray Mason, had gone with John Slidell as Confederate envoy to Britain; General Robert E. Lee was her father's cousin and her father himself had served in the Confederate army. And, she concluded, her brothers had served in the First World War and one had been killed in action in France. Drawing a deep breath, Miss Lucy said, "Young man, I believe I have a right to come into Virginia to talk civil rights to her people."

"Madam," said the visitor as he walked to the door, "whatever the CIO pays you, you are worth it."

And she was — many times over. The American labor movement never saw anything quite like Miss Lucy. To see her with a group of up-from-the-ranks steel or textile organizers, some of them scarred from beatings, and to hear her cultured Virginia accent and impeccable enunciation amid their grits-and-gravy Dixie drawls, were unforgettable experiences.

Miss Lucy was one of those symbols of conscience which the South continually has produced in time of need. Her presence in the CIO's turbulent efforts to gain a foothold in the South's old industries and her new beginnings, also symbolized something else — an awakening of Southern women to the basic problems of their communities. The old Southern traditions could not ignore Miss Lucy as she attended and worked in the League of Women Voters, as she participated (as a CIO member, mind you) in the DAR. Her blood was bluer than any present, and when it came to ancestors she made all the others seem parvenus.

"Dammit," wailed a textile owner, shaken by a lecture by Miss Lucy, "she *is* a lady, so you have to listen to her. This makes you boil. Also, she always has her facts right, and that is infuriating. All you can do is walk out on her." (Some did.)

Miss Lucy came at a time when the Old South of cotton was sick near to death of the boll weevil and depression, and when the New South was struggling toward the promised land of industrialization. It had a long way to go. Just how long it was had been revealed by a University of Georgia economics department study. It revealed that in 1930 the South's percentage share of the nation's industry had been just about what it was in 1860. This meant, of course, that for three decades the South had suffered economically from this tremendous industrial lag.

Both the industry-seeking committees and the unions had a difficult time in the 1930's. In retrospect, the CIO, still not greatly beloved, probably made the most important contribution. It went to the grass roots — and the grass roots were where the South's economic and spiritual sickness was. After Roosevelt's National Recovery Act was declared unconstitutional, its twelve-dollar minimum wage requirements also were ended. There were almost literally no labor laws. Unions were few. There grew out of the collapse of cotton and the depressed economy one of the most shameful stories of the South's economic history. Governors, chambers of commerce, committees of boosters, began to exploit "a surplus of white, Anglo-Saxon labor." Mississippi, which was most vigorous in this form of industrializing, offers the best illustration, although all Southern states were as avidly eager and guilty. Her governor, Hugh White, in the mid-1930's, eagerly supported by political leaders, chiefly those of the smaller cities, produced a plan which he said would "balance industry with agriculture." His legislature enacted a law that permitted cities, subject to a referendum, to bond themselves to finance new buildings as a lure to industries, and to grant five-year tax exemptions.

Only slightly varying forms of this plan were adopted in Tennessee, Alabama, and Georgia.

In his message to the legislature, which was panting to pass the bill, Governor White said: "Our high percentage of native Anglo-Saxon citizenship, with an absence of the disturbing elements so common to larger industrial centers, offers a great attraction for those looking for new fields in which to establish their factories."

This was an invitation to employers — the good and the bad — in all regions. Both knew what he meant. There would be no unions. And if a surplus of "native, Anglo-Saxon citizenship" was to be docile, accepting gratefully what was offered, then just how cheap could one hire a huge Negro labor force to do the common labor? The answer to that also was quite clear.

There was an almost immediate deluge of shysters, most of them with a truckload or so of old machines which could be set up in small buildings and put to making shirts and cheap cotton work pants. Small shoe plants, producing women's shoes of low quality and price, also sprang up. These fly-by-night operators were from the areas in the East where their exploitive practices had been exposed.

"Learners" were in demand. They were exploited in a most inhuman manner. There are records of payments of as little as ninety-seven cents for two weeks' work. The operators gave credit for so many shirts to be produced per "standard hour." A person might — and many did — work six twelve-hour days per week and receive pay for only a few "standard hours." The explanation of the employer was that the employee's work was not up to standard.

Sometimes the learner's period was dragged on and on — only to have the factory close. Often, when their standard hours began to mount as their skill increased, they would be fired and replaced by another "learner."

The political and business leadership in the many Southern

towns with such "industries" made much of their work and civic virtue in constructing a plant to provide jobs. But they rarely let it cost them anything. The money subscribed for construction was deducted from the pay checks of the employees, usually at five per cent, but sometimes at six or seven per cent. Consent to this deduction was required of each person hired. I remember yet the signs posted in the stores of the communities that had put up a factory building, warning merchants to deduct the specified percentage on each check handled; if they did not, the bank would do so and the merchant would lose.

The files reveal a typical worker's agreement of that period:

I the undersigned hereby make application for employment at the garment factory erected by the town of Manchester, Tenn., and agree with the said town of Manchester, Tenn., that in the event of employment at the said town of Manchester, Tenn., securing employment for me with operator of said factory, I will pay to the said town of Manchester, Tenn., 6 per cent of my weekly salary or wage to be paid as directed by the aforesaid town.

Always a local committee passed on each applicant to be sure "the right sort" of contented, compliant Anglo-Saxons were hired. The human aspect of this may not really be put into words or photographed. One had to see them, the listless men and women, dozens of them for every job open, shabby and gaunt, their feet sometimes wrapped in guano sacks. Illiterate, ill-fed, and sick of hookworm or worse, they waited patiently, hopefully. It made a person's mouth taste salty to see them, already degraded, being pushed down a bit deeper. No Southerner of any sensitivity who saw them could ever again believe in the myth of Southern paternalism. One day an observer said, "The masters are selling their slaves." It was not too far wrong — especially in those towns where the screening committees and the leadership dismissed them casually in conversations as "poor white trash."

I knew then — and at other times — that the South would always be in my blood and mind. Its rivers and pines, its red rural roads, its hills and fields, its people — they would always be part of me. I wanted it so. But I already had learned, and was often thereafter to have confirmed, that I never wanted to be "Southern" as the word applied to those on the hiring committees, as it was interpreted by those at the top of the caste system who could exploit their own people so callously, who could speak of them publicly as "trash" and in the labor ads as "Anglo-Saxon citizenship, with an absence of the disturbing elements so common to larger industrial centers. . . ."

The focus was on white labor. Even it could hardly be called "a citizenship." Few were registered to vote. (A poll tax had been designed to make it too costly for them and the Negro.) Nor could it be said they were good advertisements for the Southern system of agriculture, of state government, of education, which had produced them as they were. And assuredly, those ignorant, sick, ragged and helpless people were not good illustrations of American democracy.

They had come originally from a self-reliant, independent, free-holding, yeoman stock. They were, for the most part, afraid, or suspicious of unions. When the crash of the 1930's forced them off the land, or left them there in a sort of peonage, they came to the towns with what was a genuine innocence.

There was an ill-advised textile strike in September, 1935. The AFL's United Textile Workers Union had called it and was unprepared to sustain it. I remember yet the barbed wire about the entrances to mills where armed guards were on duty. At some plants management placed barricades of cotton bales about their mills and had men who had learned to use machine guns in the First World War armed with them doing guard duty. A few had machine guns on the roofs of their plants. The guns were zeroed in on the main gates to stop any rush on them. After a while wholesale arrests by the police, and in some states the National Guard, broke a resistance already weakened by hunger.

Because of this union debacle textile workers and those on the new jobs were even more suspicious of unions. It was the bad luck of the unions that all the early organizational campaigns and many of those later projected an image of weakness and failure, rather than strength and success. This image has been one of the several psychological roadblocks to the inability of labor to make an organizational breakthrough in the region.

In that time the Negro was taking what he could find. What he was finding in industry were jobs which paid as little as ten cents per hour. In one of the NRA wage hearings Southern representatives of the quarry and gravel industry and of the timber and turpentine industries testified that a wage of twenty-five cents an hour for Negro labor would bankrupt industry in the South.

This was the grass roots background of the rural states of the old cotton South in 1937 when Miss Lucy and the CIO arrived on the scene. Both the unions and industry were to experience severe difficulties because of the interests which had fattened on a low-income economy, in part made possible by the suspicions of a long depressed, landless people and the liabilities of one-party politics. The impoverished school systems and the violent prejudices were bound up in a race problem about which almost no alleviating move had been made.

Communism found the going even harder during these years. Its organizers originally came with a certain jauntiness. They felt that the harsh injustices and indignities imposed on the poor whites and Negroes would cause them to follow the Marxist Pied Piper. They were especially confident of the Negro. Communist organizers were in Alabama, Georgia, North Carolina, Tennessee, Arkansas, Louisiana and Florida. From there they worked the entire Southeast. Their failure was conspicuous. To this day the American Communist Party (and perhaps even Russia's) cannot understand why the Negro was not attracted to Communism. This example of the Negro's faith in what is his country, too, is one of the more inspiring stories of our time. As late as 1951 party members in an annual meeting in New York were harangued by then Secretary Gus Hill for failure to bring in more solid members. A new committee was created and directed to give first consideration to "the working class and Negro comrades."

The Communists have endorsed every issue which seemed to have possibilities. It was their support of the Supreme Court's school desegregation decision which caused the White Citizens Councils and voices for other court-defying organizations to charge that Communists were behind it and that it was, and is, a Russian plot.

Communists also have intervened in court cases involving Negroes. Without exception, they sought propaganda rather than justice. Morris Ernst, a well-known attorney in defense of civil rights, charged, for example, that most of the money raised by Communists for defense purposes in the Scottsboro Case (a famous one of the 1930's), and later cases as well, went largely to finance the deficit of the *Daily Worker* and to pay organizers. The American Negro has been intelligent enough to see that only when some legitimate grievance of the Negro was in accord with the party's propaganda possibilities was there any activity in his behalf. Peak Negro membership in the party was reached in the late 1930's and was estimated at about eight thousand. Few were in the South where the deepest wrongs were.

Despite the Negro's exceptional record of remaining American, individuals and organizations opposed to allowing him equal opportunity have spread the word among the more uninformed workers that the Communists seek to put Negroes in control of Southern unions. Indeed, some labor organizers believe that Communism, in an effort to damage unions, is responsible for the several variations of such propaganda as "Do you want your wife (or daughter) to have a Negro foreman?"

Labor's concern about organizing the South grows with its industrialization, and the Negro is an increasing part of the skilled work force. A good many million of dollars have been spent, a shocking amount of blood shed, and perhaps a hundred men killed, and yet only about seventeen per cent of the region's goods-producing and service workers are in unions as compared with about thirty-three per cent for the United States.

There has been no lack of trying. In 1946 CIO strategists decided that what was needed was a massive coordinated drive. Van A. Bettner, an able, intelligent man and a skilled organizer, was placed in charge of "Operation Dixie." The AFL, more firmly entrenched, placed a competitive drive in the field. From the viewpoint of organized labor this competition, revealing as it did labor's bitter division, was an error. The AFL announced a gain of 200,000 members in one year. The CIO drive was more widespread, but less successful.

Once the two huge unions were merged (1955) as the AFL–CIO, another Southern drive was planned. Its edge was blunted by the many, varied, sometimes preposterous and irrational reactions to the 1954 Supreme Court school decision. Most Southern union members were segregationists. Great was the CIO's embarrassment, for example, when the race-baiting wizard in one of the Klan revivals which came in the wake of the school case, turned out to be a United Automobile Workers member. Some unions lost locals whose majority membership was rabid segregationist and opposed integrated membership by withdrawal. The American Federation of Teachers expelled locals in Atlanta, Chattanooga and New Orleans for refusing to accept the merger of Negro locals. The large craft and industrial unions, after expelling one local, found expulsion no answer. Negro and white members had thereby lost a union. Anti-union forces quickly and gleefully moved into the vacuum. In a few unions defiant segregationists persuaded members to halt contributions to the political action committee. Organization has been a frustrating business all around for the unions. Efforts have met with other obstacles. The larger textile mills learned to keep wages up to, or above, union demands. State governments, by enacting right-to-work laws, reflected the union hostility of rural legislators and the farmers and small towns they represent.

A major handicap to the union organizational drives and industrial progress has been the lack of balance in the South's new industrial picture. In 1961 about sixty-five per cent of all the region's industrial workers were in textiles, including apparel plants, lumber and wood products (excluding furniture), food and allied products, and chemicals. The larger textile complexes, long established and with fringe benefit plans which match the unions', have been a constant thorn in labor's flesh. Employers in many of the other industries usually have come South to localities where wages are below the national average and all-out resistance to unions could be expected from the political powers of the town and county.

From the time of the first attempts by the unions, it has been the large, constant surplus of unskilled labor, eager to take any sort of job at almost any wage, which, in the final analysis, has frustrated organization of the South's labor force. Agricultural income in the South is still only about one-third the national average. A young man coming off an eroded, worn-out farm, or out of a sharecropper or renter's house, can triple or quadruple his annual cash income by taking a relatively poor-paying job. What is more, he will have little interest in joining a union which he hears (or sees) has not been able to do much about working conditions or wages in a contract plant.

By 1961 the unions everywhere were up against the increase in service and white-collar jobs, and a decline in blue-collar jobs. This was not so profound in the South, but it was an influence.

All indications are that until the surplus of agricultural workers, who have never known a regular cash income, has been absorbed, and until labor presents a new and more attractive image, free of its internal problems, the South will continue to lag well behind the national average in union members.

While labor had its problems, the industrial planners were not without theirs. It was ironic that some of the conditions which frustrated union organizers also were detrimental to the development of a sounder industrial base. Among these were the South's politics and its race problem.

Without question, the revolution in technology is presenting the South with opportunity to attain that New South which the orators and prophets of early generations hailed and proclaimed.

The same thread runs through the stories of the many "New Souths." There was the New South of 1840. It emerged out of the sectionalism which had begun to grow heated by 1830. Railroads had been built, steamboats were on the rivers. As anger grew against the abolitionists in the North, the South silenced her antislavery voices. There began what historians have called "an affirmation of Southern perfection." Editors and politicians began to see an independent New South. They saw it more plainly in 1850. By then they openly were preparing a "New South" for secession. In 1861 they did it. The 1880's, however, were the prolific "New South" years. Military rule was ended and the carpetbaggers driven out. The Democratic party, by joining hands with Northern industrialists and promoters, had "redeemed" their region. Its members had, indeed, described themselves as redeemers.

In redeeming the South from military rule and carpetbag government, they set up what, in honesty, must be called a caste system. The Negro was relegated to a subordinate rank. He was, as fast as legislatures in the South could act, deprived of civil rights and equal protection of the law. The system also excluded him from most of the skilled crafts. By the end of the nineteenth century the caste status was written into segregation laws. Disfranchisement, while not literally total, was virtually so. Nor was it thought necessary to offer the Negro much education. The white man was to provide the labor for the jobs in the new factories.

This exclusion of the Negro was not to go entirely unnoted. Southern editors and leaders saw the Negro as a farmer or farm worker "contentedly" jogging his mule down the cotton rows. A number of writers in New England and the East condemned what they called the abandonment of the principles established by the defeat of the slave states. Few paid any attention to them. The South was the big opportunity for quick returns.

The guarantee of low wages to any who would set up an industry was to become an enduring regional curse. The redeemers, however, could be honest about it, and were. Publications of the time contained ads and articles not unlike Governor Hugh White's (and those in other Southern states in the mid-1930's): "Long hours of labor and moderate wages will continue to be the rule. . . . Supplementing this compliant white labor is a large body of strong, hardy, active, docile and easily contented Negro laborers who have no disposition to strike. . . ."

A credo began to be formed and proclaimed. One industrial promoter wrote, "The white laboring classes here are separated from the Negroes . . . by an innate consciousness of race superiority. This excites a sentiment of sympathy and equality on their part with the classes above them and in this way becomes a wholesome social leavener."

In the 1890's, continuing well into the next century, the average wage of adult male workers was about fifty cents per day. Thousands of women — and children between the ages of ten and fifteen — worked seventy hours a week in the textile mills. I have talked with old men who remembered how there were those whose job it was to go about the mill with a long stick or cane, rapping or punching the weary, sleepy children.

The one-party political system which had emerged from the "redemption," further entrenched itself with unit systems, poll taxes and white primaries. The credo began to be more and more refined. It was that only the Southerner understood the Negro; that political equality meant social equality, and could not be permitted; and further, that the South must be "let alone" to handle its problem.

The historic effects of this redemption were plainly visible in 1937 and thereafter when Miss Lucy Mason was startling and discomfiting sheriffs, mayors, mill owners and bankers with lectures on the Fourteenth Amendment and civil rights in general.

In 1895 Clark Howell, Sr., publisher of *The Atlanta Constitution*, outlasted opposition and had Booker T. Washington, of the new Tuskegee Institute, at Tuskegee, Alabama, invited to speak at the Atlanta Cotton States and International Exposition. (The Exposition was designed to attract industry and did.)

The speech became — as publisher Howell believed it would — a Southern sensation and a national story.

Washington was an eloquent man of splendid appearance. He declared his love for the South and his faith in improved conditions. He reminded the South of the fidelity of most of the slaves during the Civil War. He identified his people with the industrial hopes of the region. But what excited his audience to wild cheering was his acceptance of the status quo. He declared himself and the Negro to be more interested in learning trades and jobs than in political rights. He strongly intimated that the Negro did not want to join unions. He spoke of the Negro worker who (without strikes or labor wars) had helped build the South's new industries and who would continue as a strong labor force.

In a later interview he told Alabama industrialists that in the South alone, by reason of the presence of the Negro, capital was freed from the tyranny and despotism that "prevents you from employing whom you please."

The speech became known as the "Atlanta Compromise." The speech, which identified Washington as the national voice of the Negro, and as endorsing the segregation policies and attitudes of the South, had profound effects. It pleased Eastern promoters and industrialists as well. It should not be overlooked, for example, that just a year later the U. S. Supreme Court handed down its separate-but-equal decision in the case of Plessy v. Ferguson. It involved not schools, but railroad travel. But the die of caste was cast.

Booker T. Washington continues into our time as something of a mystery. In the East he identified himself socially and in a consultant capacity with Northern capitalists who were, or were about to become, interested in Southern properties and enterprises which were, or would be, large employers of Negro labor. He submitted some of his speeches in advance to William H. Baldwin, Jr., vice president of the Southern Railroad, which employed thousands of Negroes. He was a welcome guest of Collis P. Huntington, railroad official and builder of Newport News. Andrew Carnegie invited him to Skibo Castle. More than once he was a guest aboard the yacht of H. H. Rogers of Standard Oil. These were his circles in the East, open to few, if any Southern white men of the time. To his own people he preached, "patience, forbearance and self control in the midst of trying conditions." From 1895 to his death in 1915 his influence was thrown behind that of the dominant political and economic forces of his time. That this power had very considerable influence in determining federal policies in matters of race relations in labor, education and in encouraging Southern states to proceed with disfranchisement is unquestioned.

What he really thought and sought none may say with assurance. His policies did enable Tuskegee to have support. It did open to Negroes some vocational fields such as those of carpenters, harness-makers, tinsmiths, blacksmiths, brickmakers and bricklayers — though not without objection from the white workers in these fields.

Some years before publisher Clark Howell's death in 1937, I asked him his opinion of Washington's position. He believed it to have been one of realism. Washington, he said, did what he knew was possible — to improve the economic position of as many Negroes as was achievable through Tuskegee and his influence with industrialists.

Some of the Cotton States Exposition buildings became a cotton mill. There is no doubt that the South attracted industry. But its chief attraction — low wages — also was most alluring to those industries that produced goods or materials to which little value had been added. A majority of the textile mills of the 1880's and 1890's manufactured the cheaper quality fabrics such as osnaburg and canvas.

Freight rates were rigged as another aid to perpetuation of colonial conditions in the region. The raw products were shipped to the East at low cost. The higher-paid skilled labor in the East and New England turned out the higher-valued finished goods. The rates on these to Southern businessmen were higher than those in the East. The freight rate inequities persisted into the late 1940's. Ellis Arnall, as governor of Georgia from 1943 through 1947, took a case to the U. S. Supreme Court which breached the rate barrier. This also led to the end of what the steel industry called "Pittsburgh plus." An example of the plus system were charge practices at the large steel plant near Birmingham, Alabama. A purchaser of steel in nearby Atlanta had to pay the rate for that distance plus what it would have cost to have the steel shipped from Pittsburgh.

The social price paid for the low-wage type of industrialization which was attracted to the South, and of the political and caste systems which were established to protect it, are spelled out in our time in the crippling lag in expenditures for public education, public health, public services, in per capita income, wage differentials, lack of research facilities, and in political attitudes which deter industry. (Even tax manipulations and anti-union activities are not reassuring to all. If a state will change its tax laws to induce an industry to come, a succeeding administration may have other ideas.)

It was not until the Second World War that the South made a substantial advance in absolute and relative income gains. During the five years from 1940 through 1944, Southern income payments rose from 12.5 billion dollars to 29.7 billion, an increase of one hundred fifteen per cent. But in those years of advancement, Southern agriculture did not, by any means, keep pace.

It is against this often harsh travail of human beings in transition that the exciting and swift-moving story of the industrial gains since 1945 must be viewed and told. To tell it in any other fashion would be to distort and prevent understanding of what is becoming a progressive, exciting New South.

With such a background it was impossible that the history of Southern industrial development should have continuity. But the Second World War supplied a new start. Somehow, when the fighting was ended and the huge camps emptied and most of the air bases stilled, there was a substantial residue of capital, management, and skills that the South never before had possessed. The old Confederate South then began to enter the first stages of modern industrialization. There already were, to be sure, pockets of advanced industry here and there (The more enthusiastic proclaimers of this newest New South for example, always included the oil, the petro-chemicals and chemical fertilizers of Oklahoma and Texas, to make their statistical studies the more attractive.) But the cold, explanatory statistical truth is that it was not until after 1945 that regional progress in the old South began to move in a pattern of continuity.

By 1954 the South began annually to earn a larger share of the national industrial income. In 1939 the South's goods-producing industry had an output valued at $11,000,000,000. By 1954 this had increased to $60,000,000,000.

Between 1956 and 1959, almost five thousand new industrial plants were located in the South. It was an exciting, stimulating experience. Expansion continued to be largely concentrated in textiles, timbering and its related products, petroleum and chemical manufacturing. The rivers were polluted with chemical wastes, and some Florida beaches began to have sudsy, foamy days when nearby pulp mills released their chemical residues into the sea. But the fishermen who protested about the disappearance or death of fish were frowned upon. The few beaches affected suffered only temporary inconvenience, and no real objections were made. Conservation would have to come later — if at all.

The textile industry, by 1960, had begun to go through a wringing-out process. Perhaps forty per cent of its machinery was either not competitively modern, or was obsolete. Many of the smaller mills, enticed from New England in the 1930's and early 1940's, brought their old machines along. With low wages they still could do well. But as the 1960's began, they, and some of the larger mills which had failed to modernize, were "liquidating." The human story of what happens in a small, one-industry town when the mill closes is not an easy one to see, or tell. Chemicals and lumber (including pulp and paper) were the two happiest stories. Newsprint mills in Alabama and Tennessee were enlarging and becoming important suppliers to Southern newspapers.

In other industries large and magnificent assembly complexes had added Midaslike touches to payrolls. Distribution plants contributed their millions to the regional income as the Southern market responded. Banks flourished. The more imaginative bankers began to do intelligent, competent jobs in bringing in new industries and the accounts that came with them.

The national image of the South inevitably began to change. Even more important, the region's image of itself was changing. Progress by bulldozer came South of the Mason–Dixon line. Expressways, skyscrapers, generating and atomic plants, factories, ever-extending suburbs, began to obliterate the old South, or to bypass it in back eddies of rural, small-town life. Surviving Fugitive contributors to *I'll Take My Stand* were largely silent. Only Donald Davidson put on armor and rode out to challenge the snorting bulldozer dragon. He is a kindly and scholarly man, is Professor Davidson, and no part of a Saint George. Also, the bulldozer is a tougher dragon than those which dwelt in caves.

There was, as 1962 ended, a picture and pattern of material progress that would have had Henry Grady dancing editorial jigs. There was continuity of growth and there was momentum. In mid-year the U. S. Supreme Court ordered reapportionment of legislatures in those states which had ignored population changes. In Georgia the iniquitous county unit system, which made it possible for the candidate with a large majority to be defeated by rural unit votes, was ruled out.

But the Southern leadership that looked beneath the surface could see that the New South had by no means arrived The more proper description is that of an emerging South — a South at last breaking out of the cocoon of its past. The progress of the sixteen years since the end of World War II had been a glittering triumph. But there still was much to be done. Of the thousands of new plants that had come, most were organized and managed by outside corporations. No slight ob jection is implied. Indeed, one reason for the astonishing sixteen years of progress was the enrichment of the Southern communities by the executives, young and old, who poured into the South to direct the new assembly and production plants and the burgeoning retail businesses. The harsh truth was that too many of the second- and third-generation Southerners, heirs of the tough and resourceful men who had made comfortable or vast fortunes in the days of the "Redeemers," had gone to seed, insofar as risk or venture capital was concerned. They had put their inherited wealth in real estate or tax-free municipal bonds and they preferred to play it safe. There are, of course, the exceptions. There were Southern merchants and managers who became national figures in their respective fields. There were still too many others who had no managerial skills, and none of grandpa's toughness and financial boldness. They were willing, often eager, to have the makers of the New South buy out the old family mill or plant, or the long-held, long-unimproved real estate.

There could have been no postwar surge toward a new South without the new managerial breed, the executives who came with the new industries, and the young, equally competent Southerners who had long wanted to cut the umbilical cord to all that was lazy and indefensible in the old South — and the old Southerners, too, for that matter.

One of the strengths of the several booming cities of the South is a revolution in their populations. As the physical face of the region has changed, so has the makeup of its people. We have heard much of the out-migration from the South. The over-all in-migration has been considerable and important. It has beefed up the South's industrial business and cultural energies. It has enabled the extremely able Southern managers and administrators to assemble efficient staffs. As a matter of cold reality, while the in-migration is smaller, it almost certainly is of a higher quality, insofar as the ability to make a contribution is concerned, than is the native population out-migration loss. Those coming in are, on the average better educated and trained.

For generations the South has watched many of her best young men and women leave — along with the poorly pre pared — for cities in the East and West where there was more opportunity. Georgia's excellent Georgia Institute of Technol ogy annually is made proud of the fact that the nation's large corporations snap up its graduates. But there is a frus tration in the fact that a heavy majority of the positions are outside the South. The tide has not yet turned — but the flow of it has slowed.

Some of these young Southerners, after experience in other areas, are coming back as part of the new breed.

The 1960 census statistics, which began to be available in detail in late 1961, had some surprises for the South. Those for Georgia, which were superior to most of her neighbors, revealed that the "typical Georgian" has completed only nine years of school, and lives not on a farm, as have "typi cal Georgians" of the past, but in an urban area. If he lives in one of the larger cities this typical citizen will have slightly more schooling. (In Atlanta, the average was 11.1 years. While over one million Georgians were in school in 1960 (47,450 in college), a melancholy 66,668 over twenty-five years of age had not completed even one year in school. Some 288,585 had not gone beyond the fourth grade. With the state's typical citizen possessed of but nine years' schooling, there was no joy in considering the educational average in the many poorer, rural counties. (It is in these that one finds the serious weak spots in the South's progress.)

Another shock of the 1960 census breakdowns to some Southerners was the discovery that the old Confederacy is becoming more cosmopolitan. Georgia, for example, was star tled to discover that two per cent of her population is foreign born or of foreign parentage. The total was 60,771.

Germany had the largest representation in the state, with 14,814. The United Kingdom came next, with 11,851 and Canada had 7462, with the USSR, of all places, having 3783, and Poland 4669.

Other countries represented by more than 1000 persons each were Italy, Ireland, Greece, Austria, France, Sweden, Czechoslovakia, and Hungary. Norway, Mexico, Denmark, Lithuania, the Netherlands, and Rumania provided more than 500 each. Switzerland, Yugoslavia, Finland, and other European countries were counted in lesser numbers, as were Latin Americans and Asians. More than half of the almost 61,000 residents from thirty foreign countries are in the state's five largest cities. They already are providing a new leaven in the life of those cities.

They are a small part of the many new features of the emerging South which the region's aggressive managers, merchants, and financiers see and understand.

The banks have flourished mightily in the years since 1945. The Sixth Federal Reserve Bank System, which serves the heart of the South, reported that in December, 1961, the District's banks had total assets of roughly $16,478,800,000. Demand deposits were a whopping $10,121,000,000. This is wealth beyond the dreams of prophets of two decades before.

Yet, the realistic, sophisticated men who now are creating an emerging South know that these figures represented, respectively, six and a half per cent and seven per cent of the national total.

"We still are borrowing," said a leading banker, "but we are closing the gap and when we do we will have that New South."

The realists know, too, that to close it the South will need to reform its one-party politics, bring common sense and morality to bear on its race problem, and break away from the still-clinging dead hand of the status quo Southerners.

This can be done — and will be — without losing anything of the old South which had integrity and merit — as much of it did.

Looking at the continuity and progress of the years since 1945, I like to imagine a scene in Heaven: Miss Lucy Mason, modest and neat, is giving Henry Grady a lecture, and Grady, always the courtly gentleman, with a weakness for Virginians, is listening patiently, albeit with a certain restless wish to reply. He liked to say that he came by talking naturally because his father was Irish and his mother a woman.

I hope they can both peer over the balustrade when the New South at last arrives.

XV

The Conscience of the South

QUIETLY and with no advance discussion, the Georgia Institute of Technology announced in the spring of 1961
that three young Negro men had been accepted for entry in
the fall term. Each was a graduate of local high schools and
his qualifications were well above average. They had been
routinely selected and were the first of their race to become
engineering students not merely in Georgia, but in the South.

An evening or so after this announcement, my wife and I
attended a buffet dinner in honor of some visiting artists at the
home of Arthur Harris, an executive of one of the nation's
largest paper manufacturing corporations. At least one in
three of the arriving guests, after a welcome by the host and
hostess, made unerringly for the kitchen where James H. Williams, chauffeur and houseman for the family, was assisting
the staff with the hors d'oeuvres to be served with cocktails in
the garden. There were so many visitors seeking him out that
he had to stop work and become a one-man receiving line.

James Williams's son, Lawrence (Mike) Williams, was one
of the three young men admitted to Georgia Tech. Their story
was an especially happy one because they were approved
normally, without delays or resort to courts. Friends of the
Harrises' knew Lawrence's father to be a well-educated, kindly,
gentlemanly person, and his mother to be an unusually com-

petent and fine woman. Their obvious pride and joy in the success of their son, though entirely controlled, were so deeply felt that their eyes and faces literally seemed to glow.

After a buffet dinner was served some of us took our plates to the library. There one of the men raised the remnants of a Scotch and soda and said, "To James and Mike, who have eased the Southern conscience."

We agreed that this was what had happened. Admission of the three young men had made us each feel that Lawrence was somehow an advocate for the sins of the region.

James Williams and his nice wife are very tangible symbols of Southern guilt. They illustrate the enormous injustice segregation has imposed. There is, of course, discrimination in other areas, but the South is the only region to have written it into state laws and constitutions. It would not be possible to find a couple whose life stories better exemplify the inequities of such a system. James was born in Atlanta, one of two children. Despite family need, which made it necessary for him to begin seeking and taking part-time work at thirteen (delivery boy, odd-jobs boy at a tourist camp and nightclub, cook's helper, and waiter), he was an honor student in his high-school years. He completed his sophomore courses at Morris Brown College before going into the army in March, 1941. A year later, to the month, he married Narvel Odom. Mrs. Williams was one of fourteen children of a tenant cotton farmer in Eatonton, Georgia.

When cotton was king, Eatonton was an almost storybook Old South center. The town was settled by owners of large plantations. It became one of the small, self-contained seats of ante-bellum culture. Joel Chandler Harris, author of the Uncle Remus stories, was born there and lived in the county until a young man. His character Uncle Remus was a composite of several of the ex-slaves whom he knew in Eatonton.

Narvel Odom's father left the weevil-devastated plantations

and came to Atlanta seeking work opportunity for his children when she was five years old. Narvel was an honor high-school student. She attended Morris Brown College three and one half years. After marrying James, she taught business English, spelling, and secretarial procedure at West Side Business College, one of the few such vocational schools available to Negroes.

Married, and with added ambitions, James Williams worked hard. He served four years and eight months in the army. He was for three years enlisted chief of his section, performing all duties involved in the testing classification and assignment of over 500,000 men. The army gave him technical training and rated him as a skilled personnel consultant, placement specialist, vocational counselor, job analyst and office manager.

After discharge from the army he returned to Atlanta and was the first Negro employed by the War Department at nearby Fort McPherson as an occupation counselor. He had civil service scores from 82 to 93. He and his wife became leaders in their community. Mrs. Williams was for seven years president of a chapter working with retarded children. She was a Girl Scout leader, and a summer senior counselor at the city parks recreation day camps. She has been a PTA president, and a volunteer worker with the American Cancer Society.

In July, 1946, the department that had engaged Williams was deactivated. His home city had no job for him. Segregation barred him from all but the most meager employment search. The discouragement of this period was like a sickness; at times it almost overwhelmed him. A cousin one day told him that Mr. Harris wanted a chauffeur. He applied and was hired.

Williams recalls that his first two years with Harris were filled with bitterness, resentment and "utter frustration" because of the existing mores, which would not allow him to obtain a job in which he could use his skills. A warm and friendly relationship, typical of many such, developed, however, between him and his employer. With it came a philosophy of doing what had to be done without losing one's perspective or hopes.

"Undoubtedly," Harris says of the years of the relationship, "James has had to sublimate certain of his abilities and ambitions over the years through no fault of his own. My family and I have been the beneficiaries of this sublimation in the same manner, I presume, that a career woman suddenly turned housewife might pay more attention to her family than a non-career woman, if she feels that she has given up something or failed to attain something on her own and therefore sublimates to the family."

The night we rejoiced with James Williams and felt a lessening of the weight of conscience, not too much change could be seen in the South. Three young men had made history by being admitted to Georgia Tech. In January a year earlier, a young Negro woman and man had entered the University of Georgia after a long court fight. At one large aircraft company near Atlanta, Negro engineers, designers, and technicians were at work in an entirely desegregated industrial operation. There would be a job for Lawrence Williams as there had not been for his father. The immense inertia of custom, tradition and prejudice had moved ever so slightly. But more significant to the observant Southerner was that the people of his region were showing signs of making moral judgments — as opposed to purely legalistic ones. "Segregation is the law," many had said. "The Supreme Court decision may have been tested elsewhere, but not in my town. I'll wait." But the Regents of Georgia Tech had permitted the young Negroes to enter without a test, and against the demands of extremists that they "fight." There were other signs, too, that decisions involving race could be made on the issue of right and wrong. The conscience of the South here and there had begun to thaw. The South's guilt-feeling is a complex thing, not easily delineated, as Southerners know only too well. But even in those areas where conscience was not thawing, it was showing signs of uneasiness.

Not long after the appearance of the novel *The Heart Is a Lonely Hunter*, a slender young Carson McCullers and her mother came up from their home in Columbus, Georgia, to Atlanta, en route to New York. We had lunch and a long talk about our state and the South. (Southerners enjoy talking shop.)

"There was something of the conscience of the South in the theme and characters of the book," she said. "All of us seek a time and a way to communicate something of the sense of loneliness and solitude that is in us — the human heart is a lonely hunter — but the search of us Southerners is more anguished. There is a special guilt in us, a seeking for something had — and lost. It is a consciousness of guilt not fully knowable, or communicable. Southerners are the more lonely and spiritually estranged, I think, because we have lived so long in an artificial social system that we insisted was natural and right and just — when all along we knew it wasn't.

"The fact we bolstered it with laws and developed a secular liturgy and sacraments for it is evidence of how little we believed our own deceits."

Carson was, of course, quite right.

In its literature, its national and local politics, its fierce insistence on regional identification, its self-conscious regionalism, and its fierce chip-on-the-shoulder defensiveness, the South has consistently and almost embarrassingly revealed its troubled conscience. Now and then, indeed, Southerners, weary of their own uses of the subject, have been known to ask with a profane or exasperated plaintiveness (and a sort of perverse pride in their unique state of affairs): "Why isn't it possible to discuss the conscience of the Rocky Mountain states, the West or East?"

It is the fate of the Southerner to be involved in his region, always to feel himself held by it. He may never have believed the myths. The often cruel injustices of the rigid formula of race may have offended him and aroused him to open opposition. The cost of parochialism and injustice, not merely to the Negro but to the material and spiritual welfare of his own people, may long have been on his conscience. But nonetheless, he is a part of what he has met, and been. And the past, in tales of his grandparents, his great-aunts and uncles, has been in his ears from birth.

Nor is this all. He has absorbed much by what might be called cultural osmosis. The more sensitive Southerner often is self-embarrassed by a realization that he has accepted unquestioningly some aspect of his community life which he rejects. The Southerner suffers, too, from having estranged himself from much of the life about him. Segregation is estrangement. It is a withdrawal from humanity that is close at hand, that passes in the streets, that lives just over the way. Life in separate, side-by-side compartments, as events of the last half of the twentieth century already have demonstrated with such devastating emphasis, is productive of results both explosive and tragic. This is a part of the guilt and accusation that make up the mosaic of Southern conscience.

Many observers and researchers have oversimplified the subject of psychological guilt and uneasy consciences as being merely a sociological malaise inherited by each generation following those who defended slavery as a moral institution. It is not quite that simple.

The Fourteenth Amendment was ratified in 1868. It was, admittedly, a coercion of the radical reconstruction. But it is necessary to say that the South had played into the hands of the much vilified "Black Republicanism," by a stubborn refusal even to consider suggestions that a start be made in preparing the Negro for the right of franchise. When the amendment became a part of the Constitution, the masses of just recently freed men and women were not ready for citizenship. Even then a start could have been made.

The South, however, set out to bypass the Fourteenth Amendment entirely. Various schemes were devised. Without exception, they were dishonorable in purpose. The various "Black Codes" and the "grandfather-father" amendment that were written into the constitutions of the Deep South states committed Southern politics to a succession of dishonest improvisations that soon had to be supported as props and pillars of all that was good and traditional in the region's life.

The grandfather clauses in the constitutions or statutes of the several states excused from literacy tests, a prerequisite to suffrage, all who were descendants of citizens who were qualified to vote before 1867. Its purpose, of course, was to disqualify illiterate Negroes, as most of them were, since schooling had been denied the overwhelming majority of slaves, but to grant the ballot to all illiterate whites. As the years went on, this clause, like the later white primary acts and the poll tax, came to be regarded as a sacred Southern principle. It meant that to permit the Negro to attain the rights of citizenship was against Southern principles and that to argue the contrary was to be disloyal to the South. White supremacy, said the political leaders, depended on white unity. The nation soon came to speak of "the Solid South."

This building of a political system based on fraud and deceit was hardly the stuff of Jefferson, the Virginia giants, or others from the Southern states who before the Civil War had given the region distinguished leadership and supplied the nation with Presidents. As is always the case, fraudulent methods begat others. In time, the originals and those spawned by them ceased to be admittedly sly and dishonorable devices and became shields of the Southern way of life — honored, hallowed customs "tried and tested by our forefathers." Segregation became, not a ruthlessly pragmatic mechanism to disfranchise and economically depress and exploit the Negro, but "two separate societies existing side by side for the protection of each." Segregation was "best" for both. The Negro was "happier" with it. The old customs, "proved by experience," were best. And, anyhow, they were a part of legend, custom, and tradition.

The "Redeemer Democrats," having begun, or encouraged, dishonest procedures, found they could not control them. Having enfranchised white illiteracy, the Redeemers were soon destroyed by it, or obliged to compromise and join with the worst products of it. The harsh but inescapable conclusion is that the Southern politics in those years lost the character it had before the Civil War. An example of what happened was the elimination from South Carolina politics of the Confederate hero and planter-aristocrat Wade Hampton in 1890. The barbarians came over the political walls. There were to be no more eloquent voices to match those of the past. Wade Hampton was replaced by Pitchfork Ben Tillman. After this crude and powerful man came Cole Blease, Cotton Ed Smith and J. Strom Thurmond. With all too few exceptions, this was the story in other Deep South states.

Out of this melancholy deterioration came a Greek tragedy that has never left the South's political stage. The effect of it further has sickened the region's politics. The South has continued to send a number of really able men to Congress. Once there they invariably have found themselves caught up in a dilemma which continually confronted them with the need to compromise along the lines laid down by their forebears. To survive politically they were required to conform to the mores of their states. They could never fully attain the national respect and stature for which they so admirably were equipped. The most excellent of these were fully competent to have become Presidents of their country. Yet, their states demanded of them that they — the senators and congressmen — publicly, and with vigor, go counter to the mainstream of national life and values; and proclaim, instead, the virtues of white supremacy, uphold segregation in its most rigid form, including the evils and injustices so plainly seen and condemned by national and world judgment. The most able and honorable of them were condemned to be bound to a Prometheus rock, or like Sisyphus, eternally to push an unrewarding stone up the hills of bitterness.

Some endured with all the courage and will of Prometheus or Sisyphus. Some broke under it, and became embittered, sterile men. A few cried aloud. One of these can speak for all. Tom Watson, the famous Populist leader of the tumultuous years of agrarian revolt, was a United States senator when he died in 1922.

Watson's life had been a violent one. The Populist struggle in the South was one of incredible bitterness and brutal campaigning, physical and verbal. Indeed, the uses to which demagogic politicians put race prejudice in those years, from the 1880's to the early 1900's, explain much of the Deep South's enduring agony. There are states which quite literally have never been free of deliberate agitation of race for political ends.

In his later years Watson wrote a candid comparison of his career with that of William Jennings Bryan, who, for a time, was not as well-known or popular as Watson.

"Consider the advantage of position that Bryan had over me," the Populist leader wrote. "His field of work was the plastic, restless and growing West: Mine was the hidebound, rock-ribbed bourbon South. Besides, Bryan had no everlasting and overshadowing Negro question to hamper and handicap his progress: I had."

For Watson the race problem was "the dark Nemesis of his career." It has remained so ever since for all those who enter Southern politics.

One encounters this goddess of retributive justice daily in small, yet revealing, ways, as it affects attitudes and conscience.

Outside a cathedral one Sunday morning in 1961, a man, whose name runs back to a distinguished officer on General Lee's staff, took me by the arm, his face agitated.

"Why can't they stop those damned Freedom Riders?" he said. "This thing has gone too far. Agitators are bound to be behind it."

"They are all agitators," I said, as gently as possible. "Maybe they will help us to stop being so stubbornly wrong."

"Wrong?"

"Yes, surely you will agree that an American citizen who is sold a ticket for travel on a bus has a right to equal use of public bus facilities."

"Well," he said, "why don't they wait? Things are changing. Why are they in such a hurry?"

"How much time would you want to wait?"

He paused, his face grave.

"Two or three hundred years," he said, flinging out the words with frustration and impatience in the sound of them. "I guess I'm getting old. They annoy me, the Freedom Riders, and I know they shouldn't. . . ."

Sometimes there is a malevolent innocence. A taxi driver talked as we rode: "I read you. Some of it makes me mad. I figure you've led a sheltered sort of life. I doubt if you know it's dangerous for a white man to go down into Niggertown after dark." (By this he meant a Negro slum area of Atlanta.)

"Perhaps it depends on where one goes," I suggested.

"No, they got it in for the white man," he said. "Like I said, you been sheltered, to write what you do."

"Why do you think they have it in for the white man?"

"It's all this Congo and civil rights business. It's getting just like the Congo. They want to get back at white people."

"Get back at them?"

"Sure, get back. Just like in the Congo." (He was utterly unaware of his admission of guilt — that he felt the Negro was "getting back" at white people for wrongs done his race.)

"The Congo is in a chaotic, demoralized state. Only a stable government can have law. We have law here."

"It won't be enough. You been too sheltered. I'm telling you, it's gonna be like the Congo. You think it over."

One brief letter sometimes can tell a long story. Two weeks after a church in Augusta, Georgia, had turned away two Negro college students who sought to attend a service, a woman wrote:

I somehow felt I had to write. I cannot talk here because there is so much feeling and one is misunderstood and misquoted. The strangest thing has happened. It is sad and grows the more so. Our church is not the same since we turned those people away. I am convinced it will never be the same. We go to church. We explain it away. We say they (the students) tried to get in just to show off or to get into the newspapers. We say all that and we nod and agree that this is how it was. And perhaps it was.

I must confess, I was one who originally approved denying admission. I knew it would disturb our church if they were admitted. But what I did not know was that it would disturb it more deeply and fundamentally to keep them out. But it is true. It has happened.

One or two of us have talked about this. We are sure many feel it. Even the more angry and determined members protest too much. They reveal by their very anger and protestation their own sense of guilt and the uncomfortable fact that a Christian church can do what we have done. . . . We will never again feel so warm and good about our church . . . or about one another. Worst of all, I am sure our pastor, poor man, knows this — and like us, is troubled.

Troubled minds are a sign of change.

Rare, for example, was the person who did not admire the courage and vitality of the ideals made visible by the sit-in students. Many angry, ugly things were said of them and their techniques. But that they symbolized a really inspiring surge of the human spirit could not be argued away. It was not at all unexpected that the sit-ins attracted admiration and respect around the world.

The moral strength of their action was great. Yet, in some cities, where hastily and ingeniously drawn municipal or state trespass ordinances and statutes had been enacted, the sit-ins became technically trespasses. Those who had been demanding that the processes of law be honored in the school cases were impaled on the hook of this dilemma. The comparison was not, of course, exact. Injustice and affronts to human dignity were given sudden legal status by the new laws. Mobs, which engaged in vicious violence in which men and women were brutally beaten, insisted their "demonstrations" were no more illegal than those of peaceful sit-ins or bus riders.

The moral question became: Was morality thereby estopped from further sit-in demonstrations?

The Southerner likes to think of himself as churchgoing. The church has often urged, and commended, civil disobedience. Martin Luther precipitated the Reformation by violating civil and church law. The famous Old Testament story of the fiery furnace is concerned with the refusal of Shadrach, Meshach and Abednego to obey Nebuchadnezzar's law. As a young student-reporter I was thrilled by John T. Scopes's civil disobedience in teaching evolution despite the statute against it. I recall how a packed chapel at Vanderbilt University had cheered when the chancellor announced the theory of evolution would continue to be taught.

Was the merchant who was licensed by a city and state to do a public business, and who placed ads in newspapers, on television, and radio appealing to the public to buy his goods, protected by law in his prejudice against barring persons of color from one counter in his store — while selling to them at all others? Could it really be said that a publicly licensed business could switch from private to public selling as the owner or management pleased? Could such an enterprise be private business at one counter while a colored person was in the store and public business when he departed? Is a colored customer really guilty of violating a trespass law if he seeks to buy a cup of coffee or a sandwich in a publicly licensed department or variety store — or in a restaurant?

As the Freedom Riders and the sit-ins made sociological and political history, one fact became clear to all but the most hopelessly obtuse. It was that the South could not win. It was again on the wrong side of another morally discredited "peculiar institution." When Negroes decided not to trade where they were unwelcome, the trespass laws, of course, ceased to have meaning. Merchants and operators of bus lines who were saying, "The trespass laws give me the right to insult you, but I expect you to trade with me anyhow," actually became enraged when Negroes did withhold patronage. (In Mississippi Negroes were arrested for encouraging refusal to trade under such segregated conditions.)

Communities that saw how immature their position was, and that the legal trespass status was untenable because of the moral issue involved, went ahead and ended discriminations.

There was no general answer. The adage that the letter of the law killeth was glorified in an increasing number of cities, large and small, where the business community insisted it could, as it wished, switch at will from a public business to a private one — and back again. It was, they insisted, "their right."

The idea that the South has rights or privileges not common to other Americans is held by a surprising number of persons. There still are governors and spellbinders who speak defiantly of the sovereign state, even though the Civil War was fought over that issue. The mythology that persists about the word "sovereignty" is irrational — but it is there.

The United States Constitution presumably is easily available to any interested person. It says what the states may and may not do. They may not, for example, secede; they cannot determine the composition of their citizens; they cannot forbid exit and entry; they cannot coin money, or make war; they cannot enact laws which conflict with federal laws. These are only some of the many illustrations of nonsovereignty. This does not deter the extremist leadership. It goes right ahead assuring its audiences that the states are sovereign. One of the hallmarks of Southern demagogues is their sometimes magnificent irrelevancy, often entertaining — but by no means always so.

Perhaps an even more serious example of mythology and deceit, which has prevented logical discussion, is the charge, repeated over and over by a shocking number of Deep South political leaders, as well as some of its press and pulpit and laymen, that a constitutional interpretation is not binding — that a constitutional decision does not have the effect of law, even when made part of a court order.

The nation could not, of course, have been formed without the indispensable ingredient of federal law. There would have been no need to go through the great travail of ratifying the federal Constitution if it were not to establish its primacy over state laws and constitutions.

Article VI, Clause 2, of the United States Constitution clearly says that, "This Constitution, and the laws of the United States which shall be made in pursuance thereof . . . shall be the supreme law of the land, and the judges in every state shall be bound thereby, anything in the Constitution or laws of any state to the contrary notwithstanding."

That alone is plain enough. Without it, there is no national sovereignty.

Yet, even now, many thousands of Southerners have been sold the idea that the Supreme Court acted illegally in segregation cases, that the Constitution is not a part of law, and that the sovereign states are not really bound by it.

Still another bit of deceit which has been hard-pushed to the detriment of rational discussion is the assertion that the United States Supreme Court can't make law. The facts are that the court interpreted the Fourteenth Amendment in the school decision exactly as it had handed down interpretations on many former occasions when corporate rights, not those of children, were in dispute. In reality, some of these decisions concerned with corporations begin in almost the same language as the school decree. Lawyers know, though this fact has not been widely advertised by those seeking orderly compliance, that one of the earliest acts of Congress itself was to give the Supreme Court sovereignty over state law. In the judiciary act of 1789 Congress enacted legislation giving the top federal judiciary jurisdiction when the courts of a state have upheld the action of that state in a case involving interpretation of the federal Constitution.

All the evasive legal delays and extremist defiance, much of it entirely cynical and self-serving, have combined to create public confusion and misunderstanding.

This is a great pity because, from the decision of 1954 on, the South (and the nation) was engaged in a struggle to do by law and the courts what men of free will had not been able, or willing, to do by themselves.

The greatest social reform of our time was, and is, being implemented by courts. They and the legal profession inescapably were, and are, a focus of attention. In the light of this emphasis, it is clear that in the past twenty years, but more particularly since the United States Supreme Court decision of May, 1954, the leadership of the Southern bar has not lived up to its responsibility. It was not until the spring of 1960 that the Georgia Bar Association heard one of its members publicly state the truth about necessary compliance with decisions of the court. Nor was the speaker encouraged by the considerable number of fellow lawyers who later came to him to express appreciation and to say they wished they could have said what he did. "My clients do not want either themselves or their attorneys to be in controversy," they told him.

As late as January, 1962, not a single Southern state bar association had gone on record with a resolution of court support and an analysis of the processes of law which would have provided the people with an alternative to the peddlers of defiance. Only one city bar association in the South (Atlanta's) made a public statement affirming the validity of court orders as they apply to schools.

While the bar associations in the South were silent, individual attorneys, described glowingly by the segregationist press as "constitutional authorities," were publicly and slanderously denouncing the federal judiciary and assuring a troubled and indecisive public that the U. S. Supreme Court's school decision was not legal, did not have the force of law, and was Communistically inspired. That this stoked the fires of violence is unquestioned.

One of the saddest aspects of the Southern race problem has been that governors have, by plan, had lawyers, paid out of public funds, join with them in public pronouncements which deceived the people. Some of these seemed eager to distort and falsify the facts and deny the primacy of the Constitution. All too often this alliance has been assisted by lawyer-members on the floor of Congress. One reluctantly concludes all concerned know better, because they, as lawyers, could hardly have been ignorant of the meaning of Supreme Court decisions. I recall one governor saying three months after the 1954 school decision, "The path we are going to have to take has been laid out. My policy will be to do everything I can to avoid putting our feet in it." The lawyers, however, like the governors, were and are prisoners of their own excesses, the best illustrations I know, in our time, of Frankenstein and his monster. And some, in private, are men deeply ashamed of themselves.

I do not, of course, mean to suggest that bar associations, or lawyers, should have agreed with the court on the school case, or with other decisions in this field, although, to be candid, I hoped for it. But what the South has needed, from the bar, and from public leadership generally, has been a continuing defense of the integrity of the federal judiciary. Had the people been told by bar associations that court orders require compliance, we would, I believe, have escaped much of the trouble caused by the deliberate deceit of the people by political leaders who invariably were loudly seconded by a "leading constitutional authority" that they could, and would, deny the courts.

Another aspect of this agonizing dilemma requires thoughtful consideration. It concerns corporations doing business nationally. One dislikes to believe lawyers advised companies doing business across the nation, during the moral dilemma of the student sit-ins, to follow local custom in the South, while in other areas the same companies were told to practice no discrimination.

A second conclusion is equally inescapable.

A national public philosophy, including the morality of our problem of race, held in common by American business, would have prevented economic losses, social disorders, and bitterness. In this day of specialization, every branch of learning, including the law, is indeed divided into compartments. This, I think, explains a part of the dilemma of lawyers. One of the legal compartments represents business clients. It is perhaps inevitable that lawyers should take on the neutral coloration of their clients and delay any advice about law until the public relations council has determined what the public policy shall be. The lawyer technically is not supposed to make moral decisions. We are told that this is the function of management. But, must the lawyer always be the neutralist in representing corporate clients whose scope is national? Is there not something lost here which is necessary to the law, management and society? It is likely that American business will regret that its role in the drama of social change was more influenced by the slowing down of cash register bells than by morality.

One day at the outset of the student picketing of variety and department store lunch counters and tea rooms, the public relations representative of one of the firms involved telephoned for an appointment for himself and the company's local attorney. They came, they said, for advice. But what they chiefly wanted was the comfort of talking to someone about their problem. Officially, they were divided as to procedure. Personally, they were not. The public relations man said that business was badly hurt. He had recommended that the eating places in their several stores be desegregated immediately, without any public notice. "I am a realist," he said. "Business will not improve until we desegregate." The attorney admitted as much. He, too, was all for reality. But his took another direction. "I have to think," he said, "of stores in neighboring states. I have advised the head office to resist here as long as they can. If we seem to give in in Atlanta, then our white customers in Alabama, Mississippi, and other states where we haven't yet had any picketing will be angry and the White Citizens Councils may declare a boycott. We don't want that. So," concluded the attorney, "I have urged that we hold out until the courts force us to act. Then we can say in the other states that we went down fighting."

I suggested that this wasn't quite fair to the government and was an encouragement to those committed to defiance and violence. He gestured with his hands. "What else can you do?" he asked.

Neither had ever considered the morality of the issue. The attorney certainly did not think of himself, or the bar association to which he belonged, as being arms of the courts. He was not at all adverse to stultifying the judges of the United States Supreme Court and those of lower courts who handed down decisions based on findings of the top court. When this was mentioned, he said, "Look, in the competitive system you can't take chances."

It was not at all unusual to have lawyers say privately that they knew desegregation to be morally long overdue, and inevitable, but that they could not do other than recommend to their clients that they force the courts to "make them give in."

"Look," said one. "I'm just an old prostitute. When I hired

out I took pay for it. My personal principles aren't important."

The government has a large responsibility but it is certainly true there are large areas left to private choice. In a totalitarian society the state is all-pervasive. In our society only a modicum of political, moral and economic order is imposed by government. Our kind of national community, therefore, depends partially on law but in a large measure on the private decisions of millions of people. Our government has a limited authority but within these limits it must be obeyed. Large areas, however, are left open for private action and choice. If a free society is to reach an established goal, across the board, it must do so to a great extent through individual decisions. This freedom implies a moral responsibility. This responsibility is that of free business, a free press, free labor, free civic groups, a free bar, and free men. If free Americans do not act responsibly, our nation suffers, particularly in comparison with monolithic states where an established policy is quickly translated into practice. The painful fact of this is a nagging feature of our daily life. It is the reason behind many of our national fears, suspicions and frustrations. We cannot equate the moral value of the just deed of a free man with the same deed of a state automaton. If a group in a totalitarian society acts responsibly — there being no moral choice — there can be no moral credit.

A people who value a free society must, therefore, act responsibly and strive to adjust their practices to their professions. When the decisions involved are legitimately private, not public, the only compulsion is conscience. Therefore, failure to act on the part of the bar associations, of corporations, newspapers, labor, the clergy and other elements of our national community has been a grievous disservice to our principles. This is true not only in a moral sense but in the more important one that makes for the viability of the whole society.

I must enter a *mea culpa* plea for my own profession of journalism and that of local television and radio. Some of the failures of our regional press and the other media to offer truthful, honest leadership have been tragic and contemptible in spirit and in the encouragement of extremists to violent defiance of law. The fact that the business communities, the chambers of commerce, and the professions also share in this guilt does not reduce journalism's accusing conscience.

Fixing or attributing blame, however, is an unprofitable exercise. It is too ancient and widespread to pin down and say, "Here are the culprits." Also, we Southerners are all involved in our region, in its guilt, its weaknesses, its strengths and hopes, our long failure to face the realities of our problems, and our fumbling of the early school issues.

The solution is really relatively simple if we would but admit it to ourselves. It is no longer as complex as it was. Much of the undergrowth of myth and self-deceit has been cleared away. The clamor of mongrelization of race, of supremacy, and of tradition has not ceased, but more and more it is known to be noise, not fact. The problems were aggravated because they were made into more than they were. The remedy is no longer as difficult. It is to grant to the Negro the rights and privileges of full citizenship. It is to look at the Negro and see another human being.

One night I was asked to talk to the men's Bible class of a small-town church. I tried to speak casually, yet seriously, noting that we Southerners have a reputation for being Bible-oriented, for quoting from it, and for using it in our politics. I said that somehow along the way we had managed to exclude the Negro from our concept of the Fatherhood of God and the brotherhood of man. We did not appraise the Negro, I said, as being the same sort of human beings as ourselves. I went on to talk of visits to the United Nations, of some of the American leadership in our delegation, of the rise of intelligent, competent men in the new nations of Africa — but also of the critical shortage of such men. Our basic national problem, but more especially ours in the South, was to accept the Negro as one with us in human brotherhood. We need him in the South, and in the nation, as an educated, trained, participating citizen. This did not mean, I insisted, that anyone's privacy would be disturbed. It was only necessary for us to grant the full rights of citizenship and to see the Negro as just another human being — as we already saw the brown and yellow peoples of earth.

There was polite applause. Later, when the meeting was concluded, an old man came up to me. "I just want you to know," he said, and there was no heat in his voice, "that I believe in white supremacy. Even the Bible says as much. I hold with our traditions."

I patted him on the shoulder and said, "Well, the Bible is interpreted many ways."

He was old and troubled and on the defensive. Also, there was genuine pathos in him. There are many like him, young and old. If they cannot hold on to the concept of their superiority their small universe will crumble.

That particular old man was a product of the Southern system as established in the post-reconstruction years. Looking at him I thought: Old man, Southern traditions for you have been those of the one-mule farmer, the tenant, the sharecropper, the renter of land, or the small acreage of depleted land — of cotton and boll weevils, of one-party politics, the poll tax, the white primary, of educational lacks, of harsh and unrewarding toil. They have left you poor indeed. These things are passed, or passing, and yet you stand here and are impelled to speak of white supremacy and of Southern traditions. You are lucky because you will die before all the old landmarks that made us feel "different" are gone. The young generation of Southerners will have other yardsticks of regional identification. They will not wear their skin as a badge.

There was an impulse to put my arms about his frail shoulders, showing so beneath his worn, clean, church-supper coat, and to say to him, Everything will be all right. Don't you try to change. You go right on clinging to what gives you strength.

I put out my hand and he took it. I went away thinking

about all the cynical and bitter men, in politics and out, of this generation and of those of the past who have had a part in making that old man (and the thousands like him) what he was.

This was a thing of conscience.

There was change on every hand — the revolution was all about us at the men's Bible class dinner. Twenty years before, the small town was a placid, pastoral village. Now, on its outskirts, the lights blazed in the windows of a metals plant working three shifts on a defense order. Housing was springing up along the highway.

All over the South the old Confederate monuments still are standing on the town squares (although a few cities, with great embarrassment, have moved them in order to make traffic easier for downtown shopping). But the old monuments of "Southernism" — of what made us "different" — are falling. This is not everywhere true in the same degree. But they are going.

In the summer of 1961, for example, suits were filed by the United States Department of Justice in Clarke and Forrest Counties, Mississippi. Clarke County, in the east-central area, had more than fifty per cent of her white citizens registered. Not a single one of the 2988 eligible Negroes was on the registration books. In Forrest County, in south-central Mississippi, about half the 22,431 eligible whites were registered. Only twenty-five of the 7495 Negroes had been able to become qualified. There was, in the Justice Department files, a long record of attempted registrations that failed.

At the time the suits were filed, U. S. Attorney General Robert Kennedy said, "Negroes in those two counties still are being deprived of the right to vote — the fundamental right of all American citizens. It is our responsibility under law to guarantee this right and we will meet the responsibility in these counties and elsewhere."

Vast was the anger in Mississippi. Governor Ross Barnett

issued a statement. "I don't understand why they [the federal government] want to interfere with local self-government," he said, "local government is the thing that has made this government great."

This was irrelevant in the grand, magnificent style, in which the traditional Southern politician is so skilled. Yet, it also was ruthlessly revealing. Governor Barnett did not refute the facts as alleged in the suit. It was evident that he was both angry and puzzled by the government's interest in the Negro's right to vote. It was a sincere puzzlement. His words plainly indicated he did not equate the Negro with citizenship. He and the others who were irritated by the suit apparently could, and did, exclude the Negro from the privileges of citizenship without question or any slight twinge of conscience. Why did the federal government want to bother with Mississippi's local laws and customs? What Mississippi did to Negroes was Mississippi's business. Nor did the Mississippi State Bar Association commend the U.S. attorney general and remind the people of the constitutional guarantees involved in the suits. There was only the old clamor of states' rights, the ugly abuse of the attorney general and the U. S. Supreme Court. The conscience of the Magnolia State was not touched.

In January of 1962 the State Democratic Committee of Alabama adopted a resolution condemning the attorney general of the United States for interfering with the "historic rights of white Southern Democrats," and for interfering with the voting laws of the state.

Here again was the angrily asserted belief that Southerners have special rights not shared by other Americans. The resolution did not spell out what rights white Alabama Democrats felt they possessed that were not also the rights of Eastern or Western Democrats — or Negro Democrats, for that matter.

Race discrimination — and the local "right" to practice it, was implicit in the anger in Mississippi, Alabama, and in other

areas where, for the first time, the Constitution of the United
States was beginning to be felt in protection of the most basic
right — that of participating in the choice of one's representatives in government.

The men whom the civil rights cases stirred to angry, vulgar
and childish slurs made themselves thereby more naked than
they knew. The events in Asia, Africa and Latin America were
without meaning to them. But the winds of history were blowing harder and colder, and it seemed that perhaps those whose
perspectives were so limited might, very soon, discover their
nakedness.

The conscience of even those Southerners whose identity has
been with the old landmarks is beginning to show signs of uneasiness. Southernism, or "The South," increasingly is being
equated with the mobs burning buses and rioting over the effort of Negro passengers to be accepted as other travelers.
Southernism suddenly has become the screaming, cursing
mothers in the New Orleans school troubles; or the dynamiters
of schools and churches, all of whom defiantly shout their loyalty to "The South" and their determination to protect "Southern traditions."

The Confederate flag, borne in honor by valiant troops on
many battlefields, has become degraded to the place where it
is sold in variety stores for sideburned, leather-jacketed teen-
agers to tie on the radio aerial or windshield of their hot rods.
The flags so reverently furled at Appomattox now are compan-
ions of the burning cross of Ku Kluxers. In one K.K.K. convention the tough boys on the discipline squad wore leather jack-
ets each with a Confederate flag sewed across the back. In the
murder-committing mob at the University of Mississippi in
the autumn of 1962, some of its members carried Confederate
banners.

The young Southerner, seeing what "Southernism" has become, or at least is about to become, will be extremely unlikely

to assume the weight of the old myths. Certainly he wants none of the heritage that made his region poor and so burdened that all its public institutions lagged behind those of other regions. Past generations have known scarcity and want — the young Southerner wants a new heritage. He wishes to eliminate the lags in his region's living and educational standards. He does not want the deprivations of other citizens on his conscience or that of his generation. He may have a new heritage — though attainment will not come without hardship and disappointments. But as he looks about him, he sees the old shibboleths, the old customs are disappearing. Negroes have breached the walls of segregation in universities, secondary and elementary schools, in restaurants, concert halls, in travel and in public facilities generally.

The walls are broken — not down. But each day there is a further crumbling of them. Segregation is a Humpty-Dumpty. It will not be put back together again. It lies there in the ruins. Guerrilla fighting will go on in some areas for an unpredictable time. Extreme racial attitudes will not easily be diffused. But, curiously, it is they that are becoming segregated in today's society.

History reminds us of the aftermath of the hanging of John Brown. When the trap was sprung on that violent man, the defenders of slavery were very sure their position was strengthened. They were confident that the attack on the United States arsenal, the killing of the citizens and federal soldiers, "would bring the North to its senses" and "cause the abolitionists to lose face." They did not, or would not, understand that the conscience of the world had condemned slavery. So it is with segregation. Civilization and morality are bored with it.

Happily, the chambers of commerce are increasingly aware that segregation no longer is economically practical. Nothing better illustrates changes in the South than that the voice of the chamber of commerce is becoming more influential than that of the demagogues of politics and extremist organizations. Conscience accusingly reminds business that it and the South have waited an unconscionably long time in moving to end a long discredited institution.

Without question, the South is on the move. It is experiencing an economic growth and a reorganization such as the East experienced at least two generations ago. Here and there, where communities and states have taken a good hard look at themselves, there are exciting advances and a release from much of the fear, guilt and frustration of the past. At a time in history when the American people desperately need to comprehend themselves as a people and the culture they have produced, the South's lack of self-understanding is the more acute. A shocking number of its newspapers had failed in the responsibility of leadership — to reveal a region to itself. Painfully few had ever dissected the so-called Southern way of life or stripped the myths from the Southerner's belief that he was somehow different from other Americans and entitled to special rights, including that of being "let alone" in the ugliest practices of discrimination. Here, too, conscience is nagging.

The economic advance and its reorganization and direction by the new breed of managers — Southerners and "outsiders," are undenied. Its fulfillment awaits that moment when conscience catches up with a regional commitment to place at the disposal of the nation the vast wealth of the South's human resources as well as her material. There is a Southern wisdom and a heritage, born of experiences which only the South has known. There is a contribution of mind and spirit that will be a transfusion of strength for our common country.

After all, as the region's historians have pointed out, the South was American long before it isolated itself as "Southern." Thomas Jefferson did not think of himself as Southern when he wrote out for the struggling, jealous colonies their Declaration of Independence that was to make them a nation. After Apponattox, General Robert E. Lee did not think of himself as Southern when he accepted the presidency of a small, desperately poor college in Virginia so that he might teach young men of the South to become builders of a stronger Union, which he bade them love and serve.

One thinks of the poet Robert Frost at the lectern before the national capitol on the day the slender young senator from Massachusetts became President of the United States. The poet's white hair was blown by a snow-cold wind. A brilliant January sun was in his eyes:

"The land was ours before we were the land's. . . ."

So it is with the Southerner. His was a national identity before we were a nation. (He never lost it, as the testing of war and faith so eloquently reveals.)

And now as the twentieth century moves toward its exit, there is coming to true national identity that other Southerner, the Negro, who for so long and painful a time has been identified by a stereotype or as a problem. It is relatively a slow movement, but it is a steady, increasing one. As he takes on a firm, positive national status, it is wise to understand how very Southern he is. His contribution is so closely interwoven with that of the region so long associated with him that it may not be dissected out. His labor has built much of the physical South, the old and the new. In the slave cotton South, it was his work in the fields and at the cotton gins that made possible the European-oriented centers of culture. Where kindly paternalism flourished he provided an example of loyalty and good manners that became a shining legend. Where cruelty and the lash were he became a moral indictment that yet plagues the conscience of mankind. There is a trace of his inflections in the Southern tongue. His laughter, the haunting music of his spirituals, his slave-period superstitions, are in the Southern personality. The Negro is an essential ingredient in the regional character of the South and the Southerner.

As the region loses its fateful uniqueness, based on a subordinate position for a third of its people, the best human qualities of both races can move into the mainstream of American life and the promise of equal opportunity — the American hope and dream in which both Southerners at last may share fully.

XVI

Sacrifice of the Children

ALL OF US have words that call up images, and for me, "education" brings to mind not my own schooling, but a visit made to a small backwoods community in the fall of 1938. I ad returned from Europe late that summer after having been one for almost a year. Seeing Hitler in Germany and in the ustrian Anschluss action had been a part of the experience of hose months, and this generated a great many invitations to peak to civic clubs and schools. A letter came one day from a eorgia town of which I had never heard. A map revealed it s a tiny south-central village of about one hundred population, located in one of the poorest counties in the state. The rincipal of the high school earnestly requested that I come own and tell his students, the parents and the community bout what I had seen. It was, he said, his first teaching job nd he was seeking to make the school mean more to the children and parents. His words had an unusual appeal, and I rote I would be there.

It was a drive of more than one hundred miles, and the way t last turned off from the main highway some twenty-six miles long a rutted, sandy dirt road. The county was one noted for he poor quality of its soil. There was a common saying among s discouraged small farmers that the only reason the Lord had ut any land there at all was to hide hell.

The unincorporated town was little more than a crossroads

collection of a few shabby stores. Two of them boasted gasoline
pumps. There was no pavement. It was dirty, slovenly, and
lacking in any single attractive physical feature. Each house
had its well, and there were, of course, no sewers. Drop cord
electric lights were in the houses and a few metal-shaded bulbs
on poles provided light in the crossroads area.

The young teacher-principal and two middle-aged "lady
teachers"— the total staff — were waiting for us. (My wife
accompanied me.) We had a pleasant country dinner at a table
in the "run" of a shotgun house. Notice had been sent far and
wide and an ambitious program had been prepared, including
an exhibition of tumbling, folk-dancing, and a guitar quartet.
After this I was to speak. The principal roomed and boarded at
the house where we had dinner, and after it was done we went
to his room and talked until it was time to go to the school. He
was in a discouraged, yet defensive, mood. The school board
was made up of three men. None had been past the fifth grade.
One, who kept one of the small stores, was also a moonshine
tycoon. The community was desperately poor. Its people and
their cultural level represented several generations of poverty
of spirit and body, of wants and needs not comprehended.
"And yet," said the young man, "the kids are wonderful. God,
how eager and grateful they are for attention and challenge.
They love coming to school. This is the first time a parents-and-
friends program has ever been held. They have swept the gym
and decorated it. They'll be a little bit self-conscious, as will
their parents. But you'll see. They are wonderful."

There were perhaps two hundred adults in the audience. (I
recall especially two old women in the front row who had snuff
sticks in their mouths.) The principal warmly welcomed the
audience, the homemade curtain was pulled back, and there
were the tumblers, all lined up, wearing basketball shorts and
new white T-shirts. (I later learned the principal had bought
the T-shirts with his own money.) Their mats tugged at the
heart. They were a series of washed and cleaned grain sacks

tuffed with hay and sewed together. The tumblers, trained by
he new principal, did well. The stage was cleared and the folk
ancers, boys and girls, also tutored by the new principal, came
n. They were somewhat stiffly reserved, but danced attrac-
vely in a lively square-dance choreography to the tune of
Captain Jenks of the Horse Marines," played by one of the
iddle-aged teachers. The applause was hearty, but the par-
nts and friends were self-conscious, too. Their community had
ot imagined their young people so wonderfully talented. It
as a tremendous, pattern-breaking evening. For an hour there
a that dreadful little back eddy of defeated generations, chil-
ren were bright and gay, and — more important — proud.

The guitar players brought down the house. This was enter-
ainment they knew. Tumbling and folk dancing were foreign
nd strange.

When my turn came, I talked of the small farmers of Scan-
inavia, and of how they organized into cooperatives, and
raded and marketed their products. I described Hitler and his
littering parade as he entered Vienna before the plebiscite of
he recent April. I told of how special units of Hitler Youth had
een brought from Germany, and of the boys and girls of Vi-
nna, the same ages as their own children who had just per-
rmed so well, were brought into the parade with them. I
ied to tell how they appeared, with banners flung out in the
inds of a raw, wet day, and of the hate songs they sang — of
eir frantic chant, "*Ein Volk, Ein Reich, Ein Fuehrer.*" I said
at wise and fearful men in Europe were afraid that all this
as another long step toward a war of dreadful potential. They
stened, and applauded, but I remember thinking as I talked
at the two old ladies in the front row likely had not the
aguest idea who Hitler was, and cared less.

It was a long ride back to Atlanta. I found myself wondering
ow many of these proud, excited young faces would grow old
efore their time on the small farms of the region and, within
ll too short a time, be sitting apathetically there in the old,

dimly lit gym watching their children in some school program
The population tide even in 1938 was running strongly to th
cities, and I tried to reach out to them in spirit, saying silentl
in the night, "Leave that awful place. Go as soon as you ca
and take that bright coin of your youth that shone so brightl
tonight and cash it somewhere else." I had seen enough youn
people corroded with hopelessness and the drab patina of noth
ingness, and they, taught by a young teacher to be tumblers i
new T-shirts and to dance merrily and gaily to "Captai
Jenks," had touched me deeply.

I knew, too, riding back through the soft night of early au
tumn that all over the South there were hundreds of suc
schools in which children were suffering cruel discrimination
There were poor schools in other regions of America, but non
had so many as in the Southeast. And nowhere were there s
many as shabby, barren, unpainted, bedraggled, disgracin
their state and their country's flag raised daily on the scho
grounds. Nowhere else were there so many meagerly prepare
teachers. No other region paid them so poorly, the good an
the inadequate. That the South should hold on so desperatel
with such pathetic, almost preposterous pride, to customs, tra
ditions, and a so-called way of life that kept them and the
children from equal opportunity, which is the basic promise
their country, seemed even more irrational on that long rid
home.

All along that stretch of almost thirty miles of dirt road lead
ing to the main highway, the moon softened the bleak ugline
of the small dark and silent farmhouses sitting close by the san
soft way. An impatient anger against the myth-South gre
within me. A part of Stephen Benét's description of the moo
soliloquy of the young planter and aristocrat Clay Wingate, i
John Brown's Body, ran through my memory:

> Fall of the possum, fall of the 'coon,
> And the lop-eared hound dog baying the moon.

Fall there is neither bitter nor swift,
But a brown girl bearing an idle gift,
A brown seed-kernel that splits apart
And shows the summer yet in its heart. . . .
A brief white rime in the red clay road
And low mules creaking a lazy load
Through endless acres of afternoon,
A pine cone fire and a banjo tune,
And a julep mixed with a silver spoon. . . .

Somehow there was a hound dog baying the moon in that mild and pleasant night. Summer was still in the heart of autumn. But there were no pillared mansions along that bumpy, pine barren road. There had been no such house in that part of the state, even in the heyday of cotton. They were shacks or near shacks, and their interiors were as dreary as their exteriors. There were children in them, and they were all being cheated (as their parents had been) of their national birthright by an irrational, inbred, estranged regionalism. The children of the South needed a helping hand reached out to them from some high place.

That's what the Supreme Court's school desegregation ruling, in time, proved to be. It was a decision about children. That's what the wise and moderate, long-overdue words of the nine justices were all about — the rights and opportunities of American children. This is one reason why it was so easy for the court to be unanimous — the Constitution of the United States is as concerned with the rights of children as with those of their parents.

It was not merely the original decision that recognized the needs of what Chief Justice Warren called the "hearts and minds of children." So were those that followed. I especially liked, and welcomed, the one that broke the backs of those who jeered at the Supreme Court and promised all sorts of sly, cynical and unworthy schemes to thwart the decision about children. It grew out of Governor Faubus's defiance at Little Rock and that of his lieutenants and others who took their cue from him. It was this:

> Cooper vs. Aaron, 358 U.S. 1, 17: The constitutional rights of children not to be discriminated against in school admission on grounds of race or color declared by this court in the Brown case can neither be nullified openly and directly by state legislators or state executive or judicial officers, nor nullified indirectly by them through evasive schemes for segregation whether attempted "ingeniously or ingenuously." Smith vs. Texas, 311 U.S. 128, 132.

The essence of this legal stroke, which deflated the demagogic windbags so thoroughly that for days after it was handed down winds blew over the entire Southeast, also was about children. ". . . the constitutional rights of children (are) not to be discriminated against. . . ."

History already is drawing a harsh indictment of those political leaders who, at all levels, took a decision delineating the rights of children and giving the South a God-sent opportunity to revise and elevate its long-inadequate school system, and dishonestly distorted it out of all its wise proportion and meaning.

Their defense is that they could not do anything else. This is not true. What they did was the easiest thing. But they know that for a few weeks after the court ruled there was almost a silence. There was resentment and anger. But it waited. "After all," people said, "it is the Supreme Court." "I wish to hell they hadn't done it," they said, "I don't want my kids to go to school with niggers, but it looks like they will." Had the governors, the congressmen, senators, and mayors in that time of pause, when emotions had not been loosed, when ears ached to hear from the South's leaders, spoken out and said, "The court has given us time. Local federal judges familiar with our problems will have authority to act"— had they done this, there would have been a different school story. The small hard core of violent ones would have given trouble, but it could have been controlled.

There was a will to proceed orderly and legally. Not long after the decision, the then chairman of the Atlanta School Board, Devereaux McClatchey, and the superintendent of schools, Mrs. Ira Jarrell, asked me to meet with them to discuss their problem. We met at lunch. Neither endorsed the ruling, but there was no idea of defying the court. What they wanted was help in obtaining a relatively small sum of money from outside sources with which to make a survey. Their thought was to begin in the high schools.

"Our problem will not be difficult," said Mrs. Jarrell. "The secondary schools are built where the people are. We can make a start without real trouble." Chairman McClatchey commented that there was really no choice but to make a beginning. The money was wanted to survey just how many Negro children might be resident near some of the all-white schools. Two weeks later, with the financing assured, the state moved. The politicians took over. Special laws were adopted making it a felony for a teacher to teach integrated classes.

Chester Bowles, then, as now, active in government and public affairs, recalls that he was in Roanoke, Virginia, to make a talk when the court announced its verdict. School leaders asked him what he thought the court expected in the way of a start. He replied that while he didn't know, he was sure it meant what it said, a reasonable start. The Roanoke officials told him they were sure they could integrate the high school — there were not many Negro children involved; and, perhaps, the first grade in the elementary school. They asked if he thought the court would consider this adequate. Bowles told them that he was sure this would be a wonderful start, but asked if they could make such a beginning. "Oh, yes," they told him. "We can do that without any real trouble."

But, even in Virginia, the political and civilian extremists took over. The voices of the school people were stilled. Here and there, in universities, professors spoke out. Almost all of these, in time, were forced out with various forms of coercion.

In the Deep South's public schools, elementary and secondary, many younger and better teachers left for other regions, once the 1954 semester was ended. In the border states of Kentucky, Missouri, North Carolina, and West Virginia, there were public school superintendents and teachers who spoke out. But none of these states had governors or public and political leaders who were damning the court and calling special sessions of legislatures to pass laws making it a criminal offense even to advocate desegregated schools.

"Never," was what they said in the Deep South, red of face, arms flailing, or fists clenched, pounding on tables or lecterns. "No Communist-led court would ever succeed in putting niggers in the schools. Not all the troops in the nation would be able to enforce such an order." (The sound of troops marching in the streets of Little Rock was but two years away.)

So it was, before the winter of 1954-1955 was done, that the hoodlums were fired up by the hot defiance from state capitals, city halls, the House and Senate office buildings. If "they," the power structure, could damn the courts and describe their actions as illegal, then the man who wished to dynamite or burn a church or school felt himself approved. He had been given a pat on the back. If the governor was telling the courts to go to hell, why that was all he, the criminal fanatic, needed. He had a license.

So it was that the controversy over school desegregation became almost entirely an exercise in abstractions. When children were mentioned it was in some abstract, irrelevant manner. Political and White Citizens Council leaders evoked Negro children with venereal disease who might use the toilets and infect Southern white children. There also were the statistical children of delinquency and illegitimate birth rates. The statistical Negro child who was "not prepared," or whose median achievement record indicated admission to schools would lower the I.Q., was for a while much used (and abused). This child, however, disappeared when it was realized that to admit the existence of such ill-prepared statistical children proved exactly what the Supreme Court had said about segregated schools.

The court, we may be sure from the understanding of the complexities of the problem implicit in the careful and wise phrasing of the decision, rationally anticipated that the knowledge and skills of educators, of school psychologists and of the social sciences, would assume direction of the processes of desegregation.

That this did not happen is a rebuke chiefly to the political and legal leadership of the states involved. In almost all the cases, school desegregation plans have been created not by educators, but political office-holders and lawyers. All the states involved hired legal help to bolster the staffs of the attorneys general.

Each plan so devised had the objective of preventing desegregation. This placated extremists. It obliquely encouraged the violent. The planners involved themselves needlessly with all the varied demands of local politics.

Not one of them planned simply to meet the undenied need of children who already were attending schools which, in every category, were below the national yardstick of excellence. Everything the politicians and their lawyers did prevented educators from meeting the needs of the children through a nondiscriminatory school system.

It was inevitable, therefore, that school plans drawn by political and legal staffs, rather than by experienced school people, were accepted by some district federal courts, even though they hardly met the test of equal protection of the law. Because of this, the task of seeking nonsegregated education was established as an exclusive responsibility of Negro pupils and parents. Negro applicants were subjected to placement criteria that included home environment, health, morals, per-

sonal standards and psychological adjustments. White students, many of whom had problems of environment, morals
and psychological traumas to equal those of any Negro pupils,
were admitted without question. The educator's responsibility
for setting up a workable system of classes was entirely by-
passed.

All these plans remained dormant, of course, unless Negro
parents and their children were willing to subject themselves
to hostile school boards, an antagonistic press, which often in-
flamed mobs by irresponsible comment, and, finally, violence.

Most of the so-called plans began at the top — that is to say,
at the twelfth grade — and worked backward. At this level
the achievement gap was greatest because of the cumulative
years of discrimination in inferior Negro schools. A further
psychological condition was that at the twelfth grade racial attitudes and images are more firmly established. This made adjustments much more difficult, as later events were to demonstrate. Critics gleefully made much of the occasional Negro
child who, admitted to high school, later asked to be trans-
ferred to an all-Negro school.

A further irony was that the popular assumptions about
nondiscriminatory education were supplied not by educators,
but by politicians, lawyers, and the speakers and publications
of Klans, White Citizens Councils, and other related organizations. Charges of lowered standards and pupil disciplinary
problems were freely made. They usually went unanswered
by educators because to dispute the power structure led to
harassments and dismissals.

For most teachers, including many of those who disap-
proved of the court's ruling, there began then a long period of
humiliation. They were not consulted. They, instead, had been
brusquely brushed aside by the politicians, local and state, as
unworthy of consultation. They were told, not asked. Not only
that, but the coercive, harshly restricting laws, so hastily and

angrily passed, plainly indicated that teachers were not to be trusted.

Two teachers from the Atlanta schools came one Saturday morning, in May, 1955, to my office to ask that a telephone inquiry in their behalf be made to another state.

"The situation is intolerable," they said. "Morale is very low. Except for those teachers whose hate and prejudices match those of the governor, the legislature and the states' rights councils, we all have a sense of shame. Some are ashamed of their state and the spectacle its leaders are making of themselves. But we are all, in one degree or another, ashamed of ourselves. We can't have pride in being a teacher. We are treated as if we were persons of no importance. Our professional advice not only was unsought, it was forbidden by law. The older teachers, with retirement payments made across a long period of years, and with families, can't leave. But many of us who are young enough to have little investment in pensions are leaving. That's why we are here to see you."

One night at dinner, in a private home, a highly respected woman, who had taught elementary grades for thirty years, began to talk of the fear that hung over the teachers. "There are a few," she said, "eager to run to the governor or some politician and report any teacher who questions what goes on or who says that desegregation is inevitable. It is very, very sad." She paused, began to weep, and left the table sobbing.

Some years were to pass before humor entered into discussions of the dilemma of those who taught and those who supported the court decision. Laughter came when the arrogance and power of the more preposterous governors were broken or reduced to terms of folly. The first three and four years after the decision were almost relentlessly grim.

In only a few states was there a voice or so raised to challenge the sensational assumptions and conclusions of the mob. In most of the Deep South states, public opinion itself became a sort of mob which terrorized or silenced any who might dare oppose it. There was no public dialogue. Those persons with open minds and a will to obey the law were offered no banner under which they could rally. This condition prevailed almost totally in four states: Mississippi, Alabama, South Carolina, and Louisiana.

Meanwhile, the facts stubbornly persisted and struggled for recognition. No study showed any significant deterioration of academic or disciplinary standards as a result of desegregation. In a few cities there was a temporary period of adjustment in which classroom standards declined. But they were soon repaired. The undisputed record is that reports of improved or unchanged standards outnumbered indicated losses. The Washington, D. C., school system was for a few months held up by extremists as a horrible example of desegregation. It soon solved its problem with intelligent educational techniques. Its academic achievement in most subjects then proceeded to rise above the national norm and delinquency rates substantially declined.

Despite the fact that educational leaders in general were barred from doing something about planning to implement the nondiscriminatory ruling, the politicians, lawyers and extremists were not wholly in charge. They could not, they soon learned, prevent the attention focused on the schools of the South. Nor could they deny the many studies of them, and the painful revelation of long-existing conditions of educational neglect and squalor — and the ill-met responsibility of legislatures and local boards.

This poverty of education was a wound which had long been draining away the strength of the region. As the extremists ranted, as the mobs rioted, and the apologists advanced the most irrelevant and preposterous sophistries and falsehoods, the wound could be concealed less and less easily. The sound and the fury served only to call more attention to it. The fact that many politicians and parents were willing to close the doors of schools to their own children rather than open them to innocent colored children, equally entitled to a share in their country's future, shocked world opinion. It sobered all but the more rabidly prejudiced. Even they showed signs of not being altogether happy with their own image.

The more intellectual among them went to great lengths to rationalize their unwillingness to accept the court's decision. Perhaps the most ludicrous of these was the doctrine of interposition. This was essentially an act of grave-robbing. It was necessary to exhume this pre-Civil War theory from the tomb of John C. Calhoun. The deed was done in what was described by some as darkness of soul rather than of night. Within a year after the court had spoken, interposition became almost fashionable. As proclaimed (chiefly by Virginians, apples of Senator Harry Byrd's eye), all that was necessary for a state to do was interpose its sovereignty between the courts and federal enforcement of the orders. That was all. It was really quite simple. (It did involve, of course, ignoring the historic fact that President Andrew Jackson had made John C. Calhoun back down on the same issue, and that General Lee had surrendered at Appomattox. It really was quite simple.) A year later, of course, it was difficult for anyone to believe that adults had not merely proposed such action but had made speeches about it and written ringing editorials and columns praising this escape from the authority of the federal Constitution. This childish bubble, of course, soon burst in the faces of the interpositionists, dampening their ardor and wetting down their oratorical and editorial powder. The United States Supreme Court (and the Virginia State Supreme Court) took them by the arm and led them out of their never-never land and turned their faces to the wall of reality. One could only presume they had the decency to place the theory back in the tomb to keep the great South Carolinian company. No more was heard of it.

The wound remained. Education in all states was in need. But nowhere was it so depressed, and in so many communities debased, as in the South. It was impossible to conceal this melancholy state of affairs. The children of the South, white and colored, were not being given a fair chance to prepare themselves for a life increasingly demanding more knowledge and skills.

Not until 1959 was it possible publicly to discuss the grievous lag in Southern education. (Since 1954 criticism of Southern education inadequacies had been equated by political and local extremist groups as a subtle argument for integration.) But as the decade of the 1950's drew toward its close, Atlanta's leadership had managed to discredit, with logic and facts, the propaganda of the segregationists.

Dr. James B. Conant's comprehensive study of American secondary education, titled *The American High School Today,* was published in 1959. The distinguished educator did not, of course, so intend it, but his book was a godsend to those who were fighting to save public schools. Organizations in Atlanta used Dr. Conant's documented conclusions to illustrate the crisis in all secondary education. They could then follow up with the deadly parallel offered by the statistics of the Southern region.

It then was suggested that if the book had been helpful, the man would be more so. There was by then a strong resolve to save Atlanta's school system. In the autumn of 1960, a group of businessmen sponsored an appearance of Dr. Conant in Atlanta. School superintendents and persons of stature from various regions of the state were invited to a luncheon. There was no mention of integration. Dr. Conant talked of the need to have our public school system attain and maintain high standards. He spoke of what had been learned in his studies of the nation's secondary system. He mentioned the need for competent, well-paid teachers. He recommended equal tax assessments (which the Southern states do not have) as the only fair basis for financing. He talked calmly, logically, and convincingly about our national lag.

By a stroke of luck, the National Education Association had released a report on support of education by the states just a few days before Dr. Conant's visit. It showed Georgia as fifth from last in support of schools. All the Southern states were at the bottom of the heap. People listening to Dr. Conant had those statistics in their minds as he talked. We saw to it that his talk was well publicized. State and local educators could, and did, talk with reporters about the state problem. So it was, that without ever so much as mentioning the problem of segregation, Dr. Conant, nonetheless, was one of the several factors that made possible the support of open public schools in Atlanta. He made plain the fact that the secondary-school student who did not receive adequate education was the victim of cruel discrimination.

Discrimination had been general. This was the key fact. The Negro, after all, is but roughly a third of the population. The greater crime, if one wished to dissect it only on the basis of numbers, was against the white children. Living closely with it, recalling in mind the wretched schools visited and the hopeful children, colored and white, one could not in honesty view the actions of the segregationist leadership as anything but monstrous deeds against children. Nor was this all. It was a cumulative thing. For generations Southern children had been sacrificed on the altar of a system that had perpetuated material and spiritual poverty. The best example of leadership — that of the revered Robert E. Lee — had been cast aside. Everything he had urged for the young people of the South, from his place as president of Washington College, was utterly ignored.

That the Lee who spoke from the small college then named for George Washington urged upon the South "the thorough education of all classes of people" as a primary need of the region, is all but unknown to the South of post-Civil War years.

The Lee who urged the Southern people to "abandon all their local animosities and make your sons Americans" is ignored. Instead, General Lee's name repeatedly is invoked by those who wish to make Southerners feel hostility toward their country.

The Lee who declared, in advice to the South, that a major aim of every Southerner should be to unite in "the allayment of passion, the dissipation of prejudice and restoration of reason," is the Lee largely unknown.

Yet, this was the real Robert E. Lee. It was this Lee who attempted to provide regional leadership in the years after Appomattox. That the passions of lesser men prevailed over the counsel of Lee is one of the saddest commentaries on those who have honored him only (or chiefly) in Confederate Memorial Day orations.

The South did not proceed, as he asked, in mighty efforts to educate all classes of its people, to allay passions and prejudice, to restore the rule of reason. It did not accept the advice of General Lee to "abandon all local animosities and make your sons Americans." The denial of the philosophy and principles of the real General Lee is, in a very real sense, a symbol of the South's post-Civil War history.

Many of the South's young people have not been taught to think of themselves first of all as good Americans. Rather, they have been conditioned to react as almost compulsive regionalists, or even more narrowly, as states righters in opposition to the Union, its courts and Constitution. This has fostered for some time a blind orthodoxy that causes them to defend even that which is unworthy merely because it is Southern. As a result, there are some who seriously believe they have "rights" not possessed by other Americans.

Truth born of experience requires one to say that the shibboleth phrases "states' rights" and "local control" are more falsely used than sincerely. They are used to cover rather than reveal. They used interchangeably. I must say that in more than thirty years of reporting and being a part of the Southern scene, I do not recall a single time when a politician's use of the phrase "states' rights" carried any ring of sincerity or made a single constructive contribution.

To look back at the past, therefore, is to experience both bitterness and inspiration. This was particularly true of schools. What education the region had in 1954 had come a long, hard path. Public education is, in fact, relatively new to the Southeast.

The report of the United States Commissioner of Education for the year 1900-1901 showed Southern schools to be wholly inadequate, poorly attended and poorly taught. The amount spent on public education was about a third of the national average. Then, as now, there was a greater proportion of children to adults than in the North. In addition to this, about eighty per cent of the Southern population was then rural and sparsely settled. School terms in agricultural areas were confined to a few winter months. (I will never forget my father, on a visit back to the old home place, taking me to see the one-room shack of rough, unfinished planks in which he went to school. I was then fourteen years old. The sagging old building, if such it could be called, was being used to store hay. The memory of it has been both an inspiration and an accusation.)

In 1900-1901, for example, Alabama's legislature gave the university a mere $10,000. Until 1904 Louisiana had a limit of $15,000 on annual appropriations for Louisiana State University. The total yearly state-provided income for the sixty-three colleges and universities of Virginia, North Carolina, South Carolina, Georgia, Alabama, Mississippi and Arkansas was $65,843.

We know, looking at history, that the damage done by the Civil War in property losses was intense. The poverty that followed was harsh, often brutal. Much has been made of the property destroyed in the wide path of ruin which Sherman's army cut from Atlanta to the sea. But the corrosive damage done the spirit and soul of the South was through lack of education. The children, the grandchildren and the great-grandchildren of the adults of those post-war years did not have a fair chance. I have known many men and women who were deprived of any chance at adequate education in those years. My own father and mother were two of them. Parents of those denied generations had almost a passion for educational opportunity for their children.

By 1901 the region's school situation was so desperately hopeless that it attracted the attention of Northern philanthropists. George Foster Peabody was first to help. John D. Rockefeller, Jr., and his father poured 53 million dollars into their General Education Board between 1902 and 1909 to help the South toward education.

The crusade for public schools slowly gained momentum. It was preached in evangelical fashion at barbecues, picnics, in churches, courthouses, schools, fairs, and camp meetings. There was strenuous opposition. Then, as now, there were persons of wealth, influence and learning who did not believe in free public education. Others did not want the Negro to have it. But the fight went on. "Outsiders" fought in it — and were welcomed. "Outsiders" contributed most of the money spent in the mighty effort for public schools.

Poverty lay heavily on the South. But nowhere was it as burdensome as on the farms — especially the many small ones. The wan man in the faded denim, his sunbonneted wife, and his pinched but eager children had already shown their many resentments in the Populist revolution. Walter Hines Page described them in a great speech for free education as "the forgotten man." Franklin Roosevelt, years later, was to take that phrase and make it a part of our political vocabulary.

By 1913 a certain momentum was attained. Standards of admission and graduation, which were widely debased, were tightened. Public education came to the South.

Teachers and parents have sacrificed and toiled for it. The despair of the first years of the century are but memories for the old or stories to be read in books.

There were many heroes of that period. Most of them are un-sung save in the small towns or rural areas where they lived and sacrificed to bring public education into being. Here and there one finds a school named for such a worker. Each state has its leaders, but in my years of traveling the South and writing about it, one man emerges from books and the memory of old men and women as the Southerner who provided the most inspiration and drive for the establishment of a system of state-supported schools. This man was Charles Brantley Ay-cock, of North Carolina. As a boy, attending a small, one-teacher "academy," he saw his mother make her witnessed mark on a deed because she could not write her name. This memory nagged at him as long as he lived. He graduated in law from the University of North Carolina in 1880. Like so many young lawyers, he went into politics. He began to talk free, public education. In the spring of 1900 he was unani-mously nominated for governor by the State Democratic Con-vention. He inherited the prejudices, the chaos, and the ha-treds spawned by the reconstruction. He was, of necessity, a candidate of the White Supremacy Party, which came to power at the end of reconstruction. He was not anti-Negro. He pledged, as governor, to obtain free schools for all.

When he was inaugurated in 1901, the plight of education in the Tarheel State was, in general, that of the whole South, save that it was not quite as wretched. Governor Aycock did not fail to put conditions before the people. The annual school term was less than four months; the monthly salary of teachers was twenty-five dollars; the schoolhouses were largely shacks; most of the teachers were untrained; and nearly a thousand districts had no schools at all. Almost a fourth of the white population was illiterate. Among Negroes, the illiteracy was estimated at ninety-five per cent. Governor Aycock had help from a number of men and women whose names are written high in the story of education. Rallies were held in each county. Men of public influence gave their time as speakers. The results in appropriations and establishment of schools were immediate.

Other states began to send for Aycock to rally them. (As late as 1919, Georgia's public school deficiencies were so enormous that a state illiteracy commission was created. Other Southern states were equally behind.)

In the ten years following Governor Aycock's administration, public school expenditures in North Carolina increased threefold; teachers' salaries were up fifty per cent, and some local systems were supplementing the state payments. There were 3500 more teachers and 3000 additional schools.

In the spring of 1912 Governor Aycock answered a call from the desperate and discouraged supporters of public schools in Alabama. On the night of April 4, he was introduced to a large audience in Birmingham as the beloved "educational governor" whose subject would be "Universal Education." Governor Aycock responded to an ovation with a few ad-libbed remarks and then turned to his prepared address.

"I always talk about education," he began — and then stopped, and fell to the floor, dead. The drama of his going lent further inspiration to those over the South who long had looked to him for that quality of leadership.

The late Josephus Daniels, who was editor and publisher of the *Raleigh News and Observer*, secretary of the Navy under Woodrow Wilson, and ambassador to Mexico under Franklin Roosevelt, was one of those who worked with Aycock and carried on after his death. It was from him that I heard many stories about the man who, perhaps more than any other, symbolized the heroes of the long struggle against apathy, greed, and hostility, in behalf of educational opportunity for the children and young people of the South.

Knowing all this, and having heard from fathers, mothers and grandparents many other heart-lifting stories of the South's tremendous struggle to establish public education, it was not easy to be patient in 1938 on leaving a wretched rural-slum school, or in 1954 when so much of the leadership began to urge the closing of schools and to damn a court for handing down a decision protecting the rights of American children. Nor was it possible to be unconcerned when men who knew better began to speak of interposition, of the right of voluntary choice of association, of setting up systems of so-called private schools, and of other schemes which would delay or detract from the education of children.

Men who in their own school days had held themselves aloof from most of their classmates, who had segregated themselves into clubs and secret societies to such an extent they hardly saw the general run of students, began to speak with horror of "forced mixing" as though going to school were a sort of ring-around-the-rosy game in which everyone held hands and went skipping from class to class.

There was such an unconscionable lot of irrelevant nonsense offered in support of destroying education so lately and laboriously won that it was difficult, indeed, to be patient. One could not resist pointing a finger at the most wicked and outrageous pronouncements and saying: "What you have said is not true. . . . What you have done is evil and wrong."

All the while there remained what was a great rock in an otherwise weary land. The facts of life about the South's schools could not be concealed. The fanatics and their rabble-rousers, the uninformed, the deeply prejudiced, the cynically expedient politicians, could not conceal the desperate plight of education. The more they shouted, deceived, and rationalized, the more the doubts grew.

The testing years for education and the Southern situation came and went. Names of tortured cities flamed in headlines and horror. Man at his best and worst became an almost daily part of the news. Governors arrogantly betrayed their oath to defend and support the Constitution of the United States.

In Virginia, a governor had the integrity to change his mind for schools and, with no assistance from the state machine, move courageously and successfully to save his state's honor.

In Florida, a governor, by the very force of his integrity, which the people answered, was able to prevent a legislature from voting itself the power to destroy public education.

Louisiana's legislature produced the morbidly hilarious drama of a crazed governor telling the people's representatives they had to learn to treat a Negro like a human being, and for his pains, being subjected to a fight for his political life. It was a story filled with all the action of one of the old *Perils of Pauline* movies, as "Uncle Earl," being hustled off to the booby hatch, escaped and returned like Napoleon from Elba, putting his enemies to flight. Death finally came for him, or he might, after all, have succeeded in allowing the Negro to vote — for Uncle Earl, which was, of course, what he wanted all along. Louisiana, fanatically opposing a court school order, proceeded to stage what came to be called the Shame of New Orleans.

Alabama, employing the political double talk called "Faubusian" after Arkansas's Orval Faubus, gerrymandered all Negro voters out of the city of Tuskegee, without, as a wit said, any reference to race, creed or color. The Supreme Court reversed that.

States' righters began to defend their conception of the special rights of Southern states by beating Negroes over the heads with clubs, or seeking to burn them in buses.

These were the fevers revealing the flare-up of an old and chronic infection.

But, always, when men took their eyes away from violence they were confronted with the problem of education.

An able reporter from a national magazine wrote a series of articles from the South in 1956, after a thorough tour of the region. Would schools be desegregated? His general title was: "The Deep South Says Never." Slowly developing events were to prove him wrong. Schools began to desegregate. But the mood of the articulate power structure continued to be "Never," and the pace was slow.

Education still could not speak for education — though a few in the field were doing so. Southern university faculties began to lose many of their better men. The public school systems began to find it more difficult to attract, and hold, bright young teachers.

If education could not speak, others could.

Gerald Johnson, one of the region's most articulate historians, wrote:

If the South is to survive as more than a mere Boeotia, as an effective participant in American civilization, it must make gains against formidable odds. Fortunately there are a few men who are aware enough and concerned enough to delineate the problems, and even a few who may attempt to solve them. It is a task for strong and determined men, for the South is a region where a tragic history has led to inertia and acceptance of the second rate. These conditions provide one of the least attractive backgrounds for constructive effort. But making such an effort is the only chance for increasing intellecutal capacity and accomplishment at a time when we are faced with a crisis that can be met only by a very significant increase of this kind.

By 1960 even the most intransigent Deep South governors privately were saying that at long last they recognized education as the central problem of their states and the region. Some, like Governor Faubus and Louisiana's Jimmy Davis, had learned it the hard way. Violence did not pay. Closed schools, or schools operated in the face of terrorism, were productive only of economic decay and public unease.

But the Deep South governors were prisoners of their own extreme words, pledges, promises. They had been tied down by the Lilliputs of Citizens Councils, Klans, and small-town politicians. Ironically, they had supplied some of the cords of fanaticism and irrational prejudice with which they were bound.

Governor Ross Barnett's bondage was tragically and unnecessarily dramatized by the shocking riots at the University of Mississippi. They began in the early evening of September 30, 1962, even as the President of the United States was making a televised announcement that the state of Mississippi had agreed to register Negro student James Meredith, whom the federal courts some time before had declared qualified for admission. While the President was saying the state of Mississippi had agreed to maintain law and order, an attack was launched on United States marshals by a mob composed of students, teen-agers, and adults.

General Edwin Walker, who had commanded the federal troops when they were sent to Little Rock in 1957, appeared as a seeming adviser of some of those involved in the mob. He previously had issued a call for massive resistance if troops were sent to Mississippi. Witnesses reported hearing and seeing him give instructions to some of those involved. It became necessary to bring in troops to restore order, which the courageous and all-but-overwhelmed marshals were unable to effect. The attorney general of the United States later charged that the promise of Governor Ross Barnett to provide adequate protection was not kept.

The possibility of violence in Mississippi had been one of the constant fears in the South since the Supreme Court decision. The White Citizens Council had originated in Mississippi. In time, leaders of this movement were to say publicly that they controlled Mississippi politics. Governor Barnett, himself, was a member of one of those Citizens Councils. In no state had the defiant word "Never" been spoken more loudly and more persistently than in Mississippi. In the days before the riots began, Governor Barnett had used state patrolmen to bar federal marshals seeking to carry out a court order to register applicant James Meredith. He had received almost unanimous support from the press of the state. Two newspapers in the capital at Jackson had been especially demanding of complete defiance of federal court authority. Once the governor himself was pushed to the edge of outright armed opposition to federal authority, he capitulated. The mob filled a vacuum.

One of the most hopeful signs was that none of the hotheads was able to have the university closed to prevent admission of James Meredith. A closed university is not good politics. The faculty of the University of Mississippi courageously denied Governor Barnett's charge that the United States marshals were responsible for the violence.

Mississippi's attitudes had been hardened by long years of abstinence from any forum in which the moderate voices of the state could be heard. But even so, there was evidence in the weeks following violence at Oxford that Governor Barnett's political prestige was falling and that support likewise was dropping away from him. More than one hundred businessmen of the state came forward with a statement asking for a return to law and order and common sense. These men admitted they were derelict in not having spoken earlier. There was hope that Mississippi's experience might be a catharsis that would discourage other leaders of defiance who were left. The moderate voices, however, were not many, and in the face of Mississippi's long years of defiance, the new policy of moderation confronted a long hard struggle. The violent voices were by no means stilled.

In Mississippi an old lesson had been relearned. It is that the white Southerner will not join in mob violence unless he believes that laxity in law enforcement will make it possible.

These governors suffered, therefore, from what might be called a political psychosomatic laryngitis, a condition which some saw as ironic, and others as retribution. It was best for them to remain silent about any move in the field of education. Happily, however, there was a respected organization which could serve as a faceless, nonpartisan mechanism — the Southern Regional Education Board. It had been created in

1947 by the Southern Governors Conference. The story of how it came into being is a somewhat typical one. It illustrated the power of morality, even when applied obliquely. The Supreme Court had then been making some of its early rulings in education. These concerned the right of the Negro to receive graduate-school training in his home state. There was, for example, no medical school in Mississippi or Florida. Some states did not have a veterinary, dental, nursing, or forestry school. Meharry, in Nashville, Tennessee, was the South's lone Negro medical college.

The original suggestion of the governors' meeting in 1947 was that the states get together and assist Meharry so they could then subsidize Negro applicants there and thus avoid possible attempts to enter white schools. It was a typical political answer to a problem which hadn't really arrived. A resolution to support Meharry was proposed. Newspapermen were present. The governors suddenly realized the ugly interpretations that would be made. There was an hour's recess. They came back with a broad proposal calling for an exploration of all educational needs, and the possibilities of exchange grants so that all states would not need to establish graduate schools in all fields, and this was the beginning of the Southern Regional Education Board.

There were, of course, then as now, those governors who were not willing to surrender to expediency and the pressures of prejudice. All through the years of the crisis in education there have been governors in the South like Frank Clement and Buford Ellington in Tennessee, LeRoy Collins in Florida, Luther Hodges in North Carolina, and Cecil Underwood in West Virginia, who were in office when confronted with the necessity for decision and who stood with the court and with the children. (In January of 1961, when Governor Ernest Vandiver of Georgia suddenly was confronted with an integrated state university, he, too, abandoned his former position and took one in support of maintaining the state school system and opposing any legislative effort to close or destroy it.)

The Southern Governors Conference, including Deep South and border states, has made its Southern Regional Education Board into the one organization that can, and does, act as a clearinghouse, and as a research agency for all states. Balanced as it is by the border states, the Board has been able to avoid ordinary pressures. It has been ably staffed and functions with integrity.

In late 1959 Southern governors, more and more disturbed by the urgency of their educational problem, began talking of a commission on goals. In the summer of 1960 Governor Cecil H. Underwood of West Virginia and Governor Buford Ellington of Tennessee appointed a commission.

Governor Colgate Darden, Jr., former president of the University of Virginia, and also a recent governor of the state, was named chairman. It was a most fortunate choice. He is one of those few men of whom Gerald Johnson wrote who is willing to work and speak honestly for his region.

His one public theme was this — delivered to legislatures, governors, and educators:

I have long felt that one of the things that we must get away from in the South is the willingness to come to terms with less than the best in our system of education. So frequently we say to ourselves, in looking over faculty appointments to be made in our universities, that if we can equal the pay schedules in a half-dozen good Southern universities, it will be good enough. I mean no reflection on our universities when I say that in this region that reaches from Oklahoma to Delaware we have reached a point where, unless we are willing to demand that we be judged by standards that are equal to those obtaining among the best in the nation, we are wasting our time, and wasting the time of our children. In the main this means that substandard faculty pay must go.

Nothing is more costly to a people than inferior education. No economy is dearer than that economy which is achieved by paring the cost of first-rate instruction because by so doing we diminish —

and diminish substantially — the opportunities of those generations who will come after us. Although the coming into the funds that are needed for the support of education in the South is not an easy task, it is by all odds the most important thing that we have in front of us. And unless we are willing, for we are able, to pay that price, we will seal the doom of this section. We shall end as a second-rate and mediocre section of the United States.

In early December, 1961, the long-awaited report of the commission was delivered in Louisville, Kentucky, before some two hundred and fifty leaders of government, education, and business.

Governor Darden's theme was, of course, written into it:

"We must cast away forever the traditional double standard according to which Southern institutions are compared only with others in the region. If excellence means anything at all, it is a universal concept, and we must insist that Southern colleges and universities be measured against the same criteria of excellence which are applied everywhere."

There was frank acknowledgment of the grim and demanding needs. Recognition of the region's deficiencies was declared an indispensable condition for improvement. There was high hope for what the South can be and what it can contribute to the nation. The South's opportunities stir the imagination. Higher education of superior quality is the one catalyst that can transform potentials, material and cultural, into actualities.

Can the South afford almost doubling expenditures in higher education?

"Yes," said the report.

The investment would be only 1.9 percent of the region's total personal income, less than "is now being spent for tobacco or alcoholic beverages."

A reporter for the *Baltimore Sun,* present for the delivery of the report, said in introducing its recommendations:

"A listener who closed his eyes and who could forget that

the accents were those of Dixie might have thought himself attending an earnest conference on education and national viability in Burma or India. Literacy of course is more common in the American South than in South Asia, and the chasm between actuality and aspiration yawns vastly wider there than here, but the calls for urgent betterment are sounded in the same words. The difference is not of kind but of degree."

For those present at Louisville, the report provided yet another hope. There were signs, still very faint in a few states, that the governors, senators, congressmen, small-town businessmen, and mayors were at last thinking about turning education back to the educators.

The politicians had done a bad job of it. Even they could accept the conclusion of the report:

If this report has failed to convey a sense of the urgency of our situation, it has fallen far short of its purpose. This is an hour of crisis for our nation, and the South must help provide the leadership to meet it.

Above all else, we need a new sense of mission, a new dedication to excellence, a new determination to help our democratic South succeed in a world filled with uncertainty. . . .

Taking a plane back home in the evening after the day of discussion at Louisville, I found myself thinking of the shack where my father had obtained all the schooling available to him, and of the boys and girls whom I had seen folk dancing at the first parents' night their wretchedly poor and inadequate school had ever held. Maybe, one thought, the report would prove the necessary catalyst to precipitate a decision to make education equally and adequately serve all the children and the young men and women of the South. One held to hope.

XVII

The Agony of the Church

IN THE MONTHS which followed closely on the U. S. Supreme Court school decision, during which the Bible-committed segregationists sought a way out of their dilemma, I found myself thinking often of Darling Jill, Pluto, and Ty Ty, and the capture of the "all-white-man" albino in Erskine Caldwell's *God's Little Acre*.

The moral weight of the court's rule fell even more heavily on the Christian church and its clergy than on education. Southern educators were pushed brusquely aside as the politicians and their extremist associates and supporters took charge and thereby assumed responsibility.

The Christian, however, could not easily evade the moral issue so starkly raised by the judicial order. (A few rabbis remained silent, but most of them openly supported the court. This in part explains the anti-Semitic outbursts and attacks on temples and synagogues which were a feature of the more violent resistance to desegregation.)

The White Citizens Councils, the Klans, and hate organizations in general, all insist they have God on their side. Indeed they employ God and Christ somewhat as cosmic bellboys. They invoke both as they burn crosses or plan the bombing or burning of a church or school.

The moral question raised by the Supreme Court made it

necessary for them to find the symbolic equivalent of Ty Ty's "all-white-man" in the ranks of the clergy. The "all-white-man," Pluto assured Ty Ty, could "divine" where to dig for gold. The white supremacy groups felt they had to have an "all-white-man" preacher to divine for them that God was really the first segregationist, the true founder of the White Citizens Councils, Klans, et cetera. Some of the more eager spiritual albinos were able to provide extra comfort for the brethren by assuring them that Jesus of Nazareth was not really a Jew.

The groups that attained the services of these divines thereafter considered themselves eminently respectable. It should not be thought that all these men called of God, and the hate groups, were from poor and illiterate churches of the more obscure holy roller sects. Most of them were from this category. But there were a few who came from ultra-conservative churches of substance and standing. The truth was, and is, that many congregations contain men and women just as eager as Ty Ty to have a conveniently captive "all-white-man" to do their divining.

Their psychological need really explained the success of rabble-rousers such as John Kasper, a satanic young man, who appeared violently on the segregation scene in 1957. For a few brief months, before the processes of law and reality reduced Kasper to the status of a shopworn failure, he was regarded as a sort of Citizens Council Moses come to lead his people to the Promised Land.

He preached dynamite with the lighted fuse. He ascribed Negro blood to Presidents, judges, and cabinet members. He wrapped President Eisenhower, Vice President Nixon, former President Truman, the Supreme Court, Jews, Negroes and his critics into one vast Communist plot.

He was a fearfully articulate man who knew the value of the extreme shock. "Hang the nine swine," he would shout, in describing the Supreme Court as Jewish-Communist controlled. His audiences, fed on the narcotic of abusive invective by their local spellbinders, came to Kasper for the big fix. The bombing of the schools at Canton and Nashville, Tennessee, was, in the opinion of law enforcement officers, carried out by persons who had been fired to criminal violence by Kasper's words.

Those who saw Kasper in Florida and Tennessee noted the careful, possessive attention given him by older, less articulate men who used him. They did not keep a shotgun on him, or lock him in the barn as Ty Ty did his "all-white-man" albino. But his managers did treat him as a valuable piece of property. He could do what they could not. His extreme, fiery phrases, smoking with hate and outrageous abuse (which all those listening knew to be untrue, but which they were excited and thrilled to hear), translated into sound and fury all that stewed in less agile brains.

Preachers often appeared on platforms with him. They could not say what Kasper said — but they sat with him and nodded approvingly as Kasper predicted blood in the streets and obliquely referred to shotguns and explosives.

"My approach is different," they would say, but "I believe he [Kasper] is a good man, moving in the right direction."

The ministers who preached God as a segregationist and a spiritual Citizens Council member declared they preached "the Bible-truth." Others, they said, used a "Red" Bible. Few, if any, of these had studied Greek or Hebrew. They used the King James version found on most of the nation's pulpits. What they apparently meant was that only their interpretation of it was truth — all else was Communist.

In Nashville, for example, there was an active, self-described "truth-preaching" reverend whose activities in that city's desegregation action of 1957 led to his and nine other men's being enjoined against further interference with school authority plans. One of his signs read:

COMMUNISTS!
INFILTRATED OUR CHURCHES
NOW IT INTE GRATES
OUR SCHOOLS.
2ND PETER, 2:12

"Go home and read the word of the Lord," he exhorted parents bunched outside the school. "Be prepared to die for the Lord."

"I preach only what the Bible teaches," he insisted.

A handbill distributed for a Kasper meeting at which the reverend would also speak urged readers to:

Hear How: The Commies have taken over the Churches
in Nashville and How the Nashville Association of
Churches is Poisoning the People Of Nashville against
Bible teaching which Prohibits intermingling of the races.
Find Out: What we are going to do about the Niggers
in White Schools.

This Christian brother attacked evangelist Billy Graham as "an integrationist," and roundly condemned the World Council of Churches and the ecumenical movement.

In Columbus, Georgia, in the early summer of 1959, the pastor of the First Presbyterian Church was dismissed from the pulpit he had filled for almost seven years. His friends in the church said the "Spanish-Inquisitionlike hostility," as they described it, was led by a hard core "of about fifty church members."

The minister, Alabama-born, Southern reared and educated, had never once used his pulpit to urge integration. His handful of bitter enemies never so charged. In a magazine article published in May, 1957, he had suggested that a "creative contact between the races" was a necessary approach to "racial harmony and Christian duty."

From that day on that mild comment triggered some in

his church to a remorseless drive to oust him. His friends, and reporters who talked with some of his opposition, said that the brutal elements of hatred, malice, half-truth and falsehood were ill concealed, if at all. There were some who were quoted as saying that "no nigger would ever darken the door of the church." Others said, "If a nigger comes, I go."

Three days after the pastor's dismissal, he suffered a severe coronary. Some of the more relentless opponents in the congregation seemed to gloat, saying that "the Lord finally had taken care of him."

Other members of the congregation, however, manned a reception table outside his hospital room from early morning until late at night to register visitors and protect him against intruders. Special prayers were said in hundreds of homes. His attractive wife and three children were never without friends. Love was all about him, and them.

A leader among those who opposed him, once satisfied that the desperately sick man would not contest the dismissal but would, on recovery, accept one of the several offers made him was quoted as saying, "Now we must find a preacher with the right kind of religion."

In the summer of 1960, while covering the Kennedy-Humphrey primary in West Virginia, I stopped off in Charleston and visited with the young minister and his family. He was an assistant pastor. Still weak in body, his spirit and his Christianity still were strong and unshaken. The experience had, of course, been a traumatic one. But he remained the quiet, gentle man he had always been. He had only compassion for those who had so remorselessly hounded him and his family. "They must live with themselves," he said. "And God is merciful."

His home was high on one of the mountain slopes that rise above the valley of the Kanawha River, in which Charleston is located. We sat on a porch that looked out over seemingly endless folds of the Appalachians and admired their beauty. "This state has become a refuge for Southern ministers," he said, smiling. "There now are three of us in this area, dismissed for the offense of suggesting that Christianity could not overlook its duty to participate in the South's major social problem."

A year later, the pastor to whom he was assistant reached retirement age and the young exile was elected to fill the pulpit. The ailing heart now and then gave trouble, but he went on his way, a good and useful man, whose life illustrated his faith and principles.

This story of a Christian minister in Georgia, whose own life had reflected the two great Commandments as specifically stated by the Nazarene, is not an unusual one in the South. In varying degree it has been encountered by all Southern ministers and priests who have had the courage to defy extremists. Some lost pulpits for the offense of saying publicly that the race problem is a Christian responsibility.

Pressure from some of the more influential, major financial props of churches has, in many instances, taken on almost incredible un-Christian aspects. Repeated telephone calls in the dead of night, the ugly, whispered filth, threats of violence, social ostracism, and obstruction make a pattern familiar to all those in the South who have sought to uphold moral and secular ethics and law.

At the national level, however, all major church organizations have supported the United States Supreme Court's decision. The problem lies within the communities where congregations and ministers are in furious disagreement with the national officers.

It is estimated that the total number of churches of the more established sects in the states of the Confederacy is somewhere around 55,000. This would include several hundred small mission churches. It does not, however, count 4000 or more churches of the various Pentecostal groups, some of which spring up overnight like mushrooms in empty store spaces and residences. In the twelve Southern states, the Baptists have a commanding lead of more than 20,000 of the total churches. The Methodists follow next with roughly 8000. In these states the combined Baptist-Methodist total of the entire church population runs from fifty per cent to more than ninety. The Roman Catholic Church total in the twelve states of the old Confederacy is roughly 2200.

The net effect of national policy statements on most of these churches, more particularly the rural, was to increase bitterness and defiance. Ministers, like football coaches and baseball managers, are expendable when local support fails, or a hard core of members sets out to "get" the pastor.

Churches in the South that have had the least trouble are the Episcopal and Roman Catholic. Neither was split into Northern and Southern divisions by the Civil War. Their bishops have authority. Yet, neither denomination has been spared trouble and embarrassment. Three or four Episcopal priests have become darlings of the White Citizens Councils, and their statements and sermons are published and commended in their publications. A Roman Catholic layman's organization in New Orleans angrily and publicly defied local church authority and appealed directly to the Holy Father himself, following an order against diocesan segregation. The Vatican took a "serious and most unsympathetic view" of the appeal. A high Vatican source said the New Orleans group had committed "a grave error" in thinking it conceivable that the Holy See could declare itself against integration. This could never be, it was said, because the church is concerned with souls and all souls are "equally dear to her." "It follows," the Vatican source said, "that the church is unalterably opposed to all forms of discrimination — in New Orleans as much as in South Africa."

The agony of most Southern ministers has been, and is, undenied. They know that, in general, the church has failed to speak out as it should have in time of crisis.

One city, Atlanta, offered something of an exception.

In November, 1957, eighty Atlanta ministers signed and gave for publication what came to be termed a manifesto calling for communication between the races, maintenance of public schools, and obedience to law and the courts. A year later, three hundred twelve ministers and rabbis, representing sixteen denominations, issued an even stronger statement. While the Catholic bishop did not sign it, because the ministers had signed as individuals, and not as representing their congregations, which he could not do, he did give public endorsement to the principles contained in it. In many other Southern states, ministers and church organizations have later published similar affirmation of Christian policy. None doing so escaped criticism and harassment.

Resentment against the more than three hundred Atlanta ministers stewed until late March of the next year before it could be translated into action. In that month a newly created Evangelical Christian Council issued a statement signed by fifty-three ministers. These signers asserted their belief that integration of the schools is "satanic, unconstitutional, and one of the main objectives of the Communist Party."

The purpose of the Evangelical Council was, their paper said, "to advance evangelical Christianity, and to give to Bible-believing conservatives a voice and an agency through which we may speak and work unitedly."

There was only minor response to this attempt to counter the manifesto signed by an overwhelming majority of Atlanta's best-known ministers. The latter received signed support from a heavy majority of the faculties of the major educational institutions in the state.

Extremists, in and out of White Citizens Councils, repeatedly urge that "weak-kneed preachers" be "whipped into line" by withholding contributions. They sneer at the clergy of all faiths, saying, "Money talks and they all listen."

Lay attacks on ministers, however, rarely are so virulent as those which attracted national attention in Columbus, Georgia. They usually take the form of relentless, petty harassments and a steady erosion of the pastor's program. Some of the "big givers" reduce their pledges and let their action and dislike become known. Others move to another church where the "religion" is the "right kind," and seek to take others with them. The meetings of the church board suddenly begin to produce budget wrangles and decisions which, while not so stated, have the effect of wrecking the pastor's program. The congregation of an Atlanta church, for example, sensing the intention of some of those hostile to the pastor to reduce their giving, bestirred itself to extra effort and sacrifice and turned in the full amount of the budget anyhow. The irritated board promptly found a need for an unneeded, expensive addition to the physical equipment of the church. By this and other devices they so depleted the budget that the pastor's program was nullified.

During those years I talked with many distressed pastors of churches, large and small. "The thing that gets me," said one of these, a man who had occupied his pulpit for more than thirty years, "is the silence I encounter. Now and then I deliberately seek out members of my congregation whom I know to feel strongly on the subject so that we may talk. They won't. There is some ostracism. Old friends who used to come to call or invite us to a dinner, cease to do either. They reject our invitations. But the silence is worst. Then, too, it is distressing to see members who are adult business and professional men, old friends and strong financial supporters, one day become cold and aloof because the minister voices the opinion that a colored person is a child of God and has a right to worship in any of God's houses. Meeting one of these you want to kneel and pray with him or to put your arms around him and say, 'Please, old friend, what is it in your heart that makes you so stubborn and afraid?' But today, too many men are wrapped in the armor of unreasonable fears and anger."

"I reluctantly have come to a conclusion," said another. "It is one that causes me deep grief. It is that many people love their church, but not the Christ and His teachings.

"I would never have believed," he said, "if I had not seen it happen, that for many professing Christians 'the church' is the building, the Sunday meeting with old friends, the association in the men's and women's organizations. That the church also means Christ does not seem to occur to them. There is a wide gulf between what some mean when they say they love the church and what others, for whom Christ has validity, convey by the same words. It pains me to learn how many persons do not want Christ to intrude on them, indeed, will not permit it, if He makes them uncomfortable."

A few Southern churches adopted resolutions which called for the dismissal of any church officials (including the pastor) or Sunday school teachers using the facilities of the church to practice or advocate integration.

The most prophetic words were those of a minister who said:

"We are all integrated . . . every one of our churches is integrated. The faces in the pews may all be white. But the Negro is there. He is present in the angers and guilt of some of the congregation. He is present in the consciences of many. He is present in the fears of the ushers who wait each Sunday to see if one will come. He waits in the wings, invisible, but present just the same. God is at work. Some of the churches may become private clubs and establish rigid rules against the presence of nonmembers. They will never be happy. They will never know peace. We are all integrated and there is nothing we can do about it save ask God's grace to make us see the fact of it."

Perhaps the severest distress is felt by younger ministers and theological students. I attended, as a speaker, panel discussionist, or guest, quite a number of meetings of ministers of all major denominations. Their private conversations were often depressing. One encountered the agony of spirit, the sense of shame and self-accusation. Younger ministers, seeing for the first time the callous pragmatism of some older men in the pulpit and congregations whom they had regarded as beloved Christian leaders, had stories to tell which, while sometimes wryly humorous, were always sad with shock and disillusionment.

Many a minister refused to "preach segregation" when urged by his congregation. He developed a technique of survival, merely because he did not want to desert those in the congregation who depended on him and needed him. These often would plead with him to stay. "If you go, what will happen to us?" they would ask. So, silent on the subject, he stayed on.

It was not all negative. Despite the lack of resolution, the Christian church in the South has reversed history. In 1861 about ninety per cent of the clergy in the South, and an even larger total of the congregations, urged the South on to war, proclaiming that God had ordained slavery.

In 1954, and the years thereafter, the opposite was true. Those ministers who shouted that God was the first segregationist and a spiritual member of the Klans and Citizens Councils, were few. They were viewed by intelligent, thoughtful persons with a mixture of melancholy and contempt. A current story about the formation of a White Citizens Council in Mississippi may be merely apocryphal, but it has relevancy. A suggestion was made that a well-known minister in the town be asked to give the opening prayer. "There ain't a damned bit of use sending for him," interrupted the organizer. "He holds the Christian viewpoint."

Every minister with any shred of sensitiveness understands that just as the racial issue is the paramount political issue before the world today, so it is for Christianity. If the first commandment, and the second which is like unto it, have no validity in the minds of church members, then their churches are finished, or eventually will be.

There were always enough shockers to embarrass both the neutral ministers, the "truth-preachers," and the spiritual albinos. There were the shrewish women in New Orleans, their faces contorted with hate, screeching and spitting at a tiny Negro child on her way to school. The same vulgar crowds cursed and jeered a white Methodist minister taking his child to classes. A Roman Catholic priest was called a Communist and roundly cursed. Anniston, Birmingham, and Montgomery contributed some frightfully inhuman acts of bloody violence.

Against all, there was the Negro leadership as symbolized by the nonviolence of Dr. Martin Luther King and dramatized by the Freedom Riders and the sit-in students. The NAACP contributed able legal direction. It dynamited no churches, burned no buses, organized no mobs.

The Negro pastors who provided this courageous, impressive, nonviolent resistance were often magnificent in their dedication. They made their churches literal centers of teaching and inspiration to their people. They taught prayer for one's enemies. They managed to teach a disciplined attitude of nonviolence which was so absolute that it drove mobs to an excess of fury.

In Montgomery, Alabama, a young man from the United States attorney general's office found himself in the midst of violence. A white girl, one of the Freedom Riders, was walking along the sidewalk before him, being beaten by a heavy, middle-aged woman. This rage-crazed female was swinging, like a bludgeon, a heavy, well-filled leather handbag, her face distorted with fury, her mouth spitting curses.

The young man took the girl under attack by her arm and urged her to get into his car. The woman halted, cursing both.

"Mister," said the battered girl, "you leave here. You will get hurt trying to help me. I am not leaving."

At that moment a blow above the right ear felled the attorney general's representative. He dropped to the street, unconscious. The girl was driven to her knees with blows, and then sprawled out, also unconscious.

The mob, meeting with nonviolence, became the more brutal because of its own knowledge of guilt.

Negro ministers made their people understand that the church was fighting for a moral principle, that religion was a vital force in their lives.

I recall at least three white ministers whose comment, in general, was this: "These Negro preachers have scored a tremendous victory. They have managed to translate it into action which makes people feel that religion has tangible meaning. They have managed to make it a positive, inspiring thing. We have badly missed the boat in our own churches."

Actions of Southern extremists were, in a sense, invaluable in that they revealed with terrible and accusing clarity the mind and the character of those who opposed the courts, the moral demands of judicial decisions. Nonviolence frustrated them and left them naked to the judgment of civilization.

More and more it became impossible for the Christian church and its ministers to anesthetize their consciences.

The same was increasingly true for individuals.

One remembers small happenings that made the going more tolerable. In the summer of 1961 one young Negro boy, aged eleven, a communicant of a long-established, segregated Episcopal church, applied to attend the diocesan camp maintained in north Georgia by the churches of the Diocese of Atlanta. He was accepted. There was some concern that a few parents might withdraw their sons. None did. Counselors were well briefed before the boys arrived. The two weeks spent there by this lone Negro boy, the only one to apply, was a huge success. He made a good camper. His personality was a happy, excellent one and he became quite popular.

Later that summer I was in Philadelphia. An able young Negro newspaperman, with whom previously I had worked on an assignment, met me at my hotel for a visit. At its conclusion he remarked that he was to pick up his son who was returning from a camp. I told him my son was due back home the next day from our church-maintained camp where he had worked all summer as a counselor. (The conversation earlier had developed the fact we both were Episcopalian communicants.) And so, reminded of our first Negro applicant, I told him about it. He was astonished.

"We could not do that here," he said sadly. "The paradoxes of the South both dismay and excite me. I really cannot comprehend some of the terrible things which are so foreign to the story of the young boy at the church camp."

I assured him we who had been born in the South and who had spent all our years there equally and continually were frustrated by the contradictions, some of them so preposterous as to be unbelievable.

There are, nonetheless, certain conclusions which emerged out of the paradoxes and the trials and errors of the years after 1954. One was that the ideology of moderation was mostly myth. The practicing moderates contributed largely to the undoing of a fine, honorable word. As events developed in the South's travail of race, the self-styled moderate turned out to be one who stood on the sidelines wringing his hands and urging both parties in conflict to be calm. There is nowhere on record a single constructive plan or action proposed by so-called moderates. Moderate businessmen, clergymen, editors, and educators remained aloof while affairs drifted into crisis. The moderate was almost sure to say, when a neighboring city had, after extreme difficulty, arranged to desegregate its department and variety store lunch counters, "We are delighted, but, of course, we can't do it in our city." This was precisely what the hoodlum elements were saying. It could not be done in their city because they had not from the beginning offered an opposing voice and alternative to the political leadership, which deliberately deceived the people.

A few Southern Episcopalians, concerned with the paralysis of Christian action, formed an independent organization, the Episcopal Society for Cultural and Racial Unity. Its members participated with student sit-ins and the Freedom Riders, seeking to identify the moral weight of religious conviction with the effort to end segregated practices.

The Southerner is reared with a consciousness of the Bible. His region historically has been subject to Calvinist and other fundamentalist doctrine. The Southerner is apt frequently to quote Scripture and to have a fondness for the more articulate charlatans in religion as he has for his more preposterous, rascally politicians.

Hence, it was no surprise at all that the sit-in students came clad in the armor of the Lord, offering the story of Shadrach, Meshach, and Abednego as prime Biblical illustrations of civil disobedience. They also were armed with Thoreau and with Sophocles's play *Antigone.*

The students were quick to understand the hypocrisy that developed when they began to violate hastily enacted trespass laws. Those Southern newspapers and segregationist leaders who had been urging defiance of the federal court orders professed to be shocked by the refusal of the students to obey ordinances hurriedly designed to maintain segregated lunch counters.

The spiritual leader of these students was the Reverend Mr. Martin Luther King. His statement on civil disobedience was widely accepted. He said, and put in writing:

We will take direct action against injustice without waiting for other agencies to act. We will not obey unjust laws or submit to unjust practices. We will do this peacefully, openly, cheerfully because our aim is to persuade. We adopt the means of nonviolence because our end is a community at peace with itself. We will try to persuade with our words, but if our words fail, we will try to persuade with our acts. We will always be willing to talk and seek fair compromise, but we are ready to suffer when necessary and even risk our lives to become witnesses to the truth as we see it.

The way of nonviolence means a willingness to suffer and sacrifice. It may mean going to jail. If such is the case the resister must be willing to fill the jail houses of the South. It may even mean physical death. But if physical death is the price that a man must pay to free his children and his white brethren from a permanent death of the spirit, then nothing could be more redemptive.

Nonviolence, like Christian soldiers in the old hymn, went on "to victory and to victory." Within eighteen months more than two hundred Southern cities had altered in some degree their pattern of segregation. The sight of well-dressed Negro couples in department store tea rooms no longer caused eyebrows to lift or hot Southern pulses to pound even in the old Confederate capital of Richmond, or Atlanta, the modern capital which arose, as the municipal seal attests, phoenixlike from the ashes of fires set by General William T. Sherman's troops.

In none of these, sad to say, could the established church point to any direct contribution. The victories had been won by students who had picketed, and by the boycott which supported them. This withdrawal of trade was assisted by a surprising number of white sympathizers, though, to be sure, most of it was Negro. The majority of the ministers who became at all articulate on the subject, condemned both sit-ins and Freedom Riders. The fact that many of the youth groups in churches were ideologically sympathetic was lost on the men who indicted from their pulpits. Many a publicly silent minister, however, lent private encouragement to the militant individuals and organizations. In some churches lay leaders spoke out and small groups were formed to press for an end to discriminations. But in the main, the churches were on the sidelines.

Martin Luther King, with characteristic candor, put the crusade in proper perspective. "The one thing a business community understands," he said, "is the sound of the cash registers."

It would be comforting to say that moral right had shown effective power in the swift changes taking place in the South. It cannot be said. But without question, morality has been one of the many factors that moved to end segregation or make a beginning. Even so, there is no blinking the fact that in general, the Christian church has been either in retreat or standing afar off wringing its hands in an agony of spirit and guilt. This unhappy state was, of course, worsened by the religious albinos who dressed God out in a Klan robe or put into His mouth the most extreme prejudices and shibboleths of the more fanatic and blindly defiant. Save for these persons, there was general awareness that the established churches, Protestant and Roman Catholic alike, were embarrassingly on the defense.

There was the other side of the coin. The symbolic albinos were the exception, not the rule. And if the majority of Southern ministers were expediently silent or in strategic retreat, they were not, as were their predecessors in 1861, supporting an immoral and un-Christian position.

There was yet another constructive asset. Those ministers who had come to grips with the issue, and used Christian faith and principles in contending with it, were not inclined to pass judgment on those who had not. They see the church fulfilling its greatest role in the years ahead, that of binding up the spiritual wounds and of moving mankind another inch or so toward an acceptance of the two greatest Christian commandments.

XVIII

Compensations

ONE RAINY Saturday night about 11 o'clock, in the spring of 1961, my wife and I heard what sounded like a short, somewhat muted, string of firecrackers exploding. We wondered out loud what children in our neighborhood could possibly be out with firecrackers at that hour and at that time of year. We went on to sleep. But it so happened that across the street a young lady of fourteen, who, on the morrow, was to participate prominently in an outdoor school program, had at that moment awakened and gone hopefully to her upstairs bedroom window to see if the rain showed any signs of ending. Looking down into the well-lit street, she saw a cream-colored station wagon draw up by our mailbox and witnessed the flashes as a six-shooter was emptied into it.

The slugs cut six ugly gashes in the box and until a new one was installed, it was much admired by the neighboring children and visitors.

On other evenings garbage was dumped on the lawn or in the drive of our small brick house, which sits about one hundred twenty-five feet back from the street.

These were among the more curious revelations and reactions of the Klan and White Citizens Council mentality. One wondered without answer what they sought to demonstrate by firing into a mailbox or gathering up garbage and transporting it in boxes to be strewn on a lawn or drive.

On another occasion a .22 rifle was fired from a passing car. It put a neat hole in a window pane. No one was home when it happened and not until a window drapery one day was pulled back was the hole seen, and the bullet found in the back of a chair. This was a more serious thing, but still a puzzling, though somewhat revealing manifestation of the minds of the extremist groups which were, in many areas of the South, urging and employing violence as protests against the U. S. Supreme Court's decision banning segregation in the schools.

The anthropologist Margaret Mead has written that Americans join lodges and veterans organizations because there is created thereby a feeling of security by stressing a communal past. Status in our extremely fluid society, she concludes, depends not on birth, but on achievement. Social classes have been eliminated by highly temporary pecking orders.

The Klans and the various citizens councils in their beginnings attracted a gaggle of men whose sense of insecurity has remained embarrassingly obvious, as exposed by their publications, speeches, and deeds. Those organizations assuredly stressed a communal past which, if largely mythical and not therefore of their members' experience, nonetheless repeatedly was reasserted as a sacred tradition or way of life. Members could attain status by achievements such as dynamiting a school or home, by violent acts of terrorism, or by minor acts such as shooting into a mailbox or throwing garbage on a lawn. A fine manly council member might need to explode dynamite. His wife, on the other hand, would feel important if she shrieked curses and spat on school children and their mothers as did the harridans in New Orleans when the schools were desegregated there in the fall of 1961.

All too often in the years when fanatic adults set the ugly and irrational examples in the violence-ravaged cities seeking to obey court orders and desegregate their schools, one saw the sins of the fathers reflected in youthful efforts at emulating parental "achievement." One of the more dreadful features of Southern racial riots has been the high percentage of teen-agers in brutal mobs — bent on injury and murder. On the summer night in 1961 when only the presence of federal marshals in Montgomery, Alabama, prevented a mass attack on a church filled with praying Negroes, thereby saving the lives of many, a local partisan source estimated that ninety per cent of the murder-minded mob of over two hundred persons was made up of teen-agers.

When the University of Georgia was desegregated in January, 1961, a shrieking mob enjoyed a few hours of infamy. (The shock of this was good therapy, enabling common sense to come into play.) This student-led demonstration was triggered by adults who assisted, financially and emotionally, the young men responsible. A leading merchant, from a town near the university, stood on the fringes of the riot, publicly encouraging the rioters and loudly offering to put up bond for any student arrested. The fact that the overwhelming majority of students at the university had not participated was largely overlooked.

Admission of Charlayne Hunter and Hamilton Holmes to the university became more than the story of the first Deep South state university to be integrated. It was, of course, compensation for much of the clamorous tirades of abuse which those who had supported the court orders had so long endured. But the mob made the two students and their admission into an exciting drama of America at its best, which was not at all what the rioters or the adults involved intended it to be.

All the university students, their parents, and the almost four million persons in the state, saw the Bill of Rights transformed, in the fast-driven drama of court tests, from printed words to action. The whole process of how our system works to protect and project the rights of the citizen was brought to focus in the swift series of events growing out of the desegregation order.

On Friday, January 6, 1961, the Georgia legislature, gathering in Atlanta for its annual session to begin on the following Monday, anticipated no emergency. It believed the severely restrictive segregation statutes enacted by previous legislatures made new action unnecessary. Had any person in the hours before mid-afternoon of that day, suggested that before the legislature would be called to order two young, superiorly qualified Negro students would be sitting in classes at the university, he would have been dismissed as preposterous. Had it been further predicted that the legislature would remove all segregation laws from the books and enact legislation allowing local boards to desegregate or close schools, such a prophet would have been laughed down.

But even as the Assembly leaders were being interviewed and expressing the views the up-coming session would be a quiet one, a court case, long under consideration, was decided one hundred miles away.

At 3 o'clock that afternoon a law clerk in the District Court at Macon, Georgia, routinely released a judicial order. Reporters read its relatively brief content and excitedly telephoned newspapers and wire services. Bells soon began to ring in Atlanta hotel rooms where legislative leaders were registered, and at the governor's office.

The order said that Charlayne Hunter and Hamilton Holmes were qualified students and were being deprived of their constitutional rights by being denied admission to the university. They were, the court said, to be admitted at 9 o'clock on Monday, January 9, when the new term began.

A shocked and somewhat awed legislature found itself, to its own surprise, without words. There privately was general acknowledgment that an era had ended. Members met in quick caucuses. Save for a few die-hards, all recognized the fact they were up against the Constitution of their country and its guarantee of equal rights before the law for all citizens. For the legislators, too, the Constitution that day ceased to be merely words and was present in the form of physical meaning.

On Monday morning the two students dutifully were admitted. But at the same hour two automobiles hurried toward Macon. In one was a state attorney, who was to make one last face-saving effort. He asked for a delay in admitting the students so that an appeal could be made. The Negro attorney, who had been in the second car, opposed. The District Court reflected and then granted a delay. The two cars moved again. In Atlanta, a hundred miles north of Macon, an appeals judge heard the constitutional arguments. He ruled there was no constitutional basis for a delay, since the issue had already been covered in previous decisions. The students remained in school.

It was in the next act of the civil rights drama that "the bad ones" had their inning. The mob was organized. But of seventy-five hundred enrolled students less than five hundred participated. Among the mob were Klansmen, seven of whom were arrested. When order belatedly was obtained, the two Negro students, who had remained quietly in their rooms, were suspended because of the threat to law and order. By morning the drama was back in the courtroom. The Constitution was there, too. It presumed that law enforcement agencies would prevent violence. It further declared that the rights of some could not be suspended while the rights of others were maintained. So Charlayne Hunter and Hamilton Holmes went back to their classes.

The swift moves from court to court, the solemn arguments, the decisions based on the equality of citizenship, the acceptance of court order by the Georgia legislature, and the elimination of state segregation laws all combined to reveal the essential ingredients and meaning of our national principles. It did something else. It made plain the fact that under segregation the Negro citizen had been deprived of a just share in those principles.

In two great wars the American soldier was classified by many observers in Europe, Asia and Africa, as a confident, assured man — too damned much so, some said. He had grown up with no worry about liberty, individual rights, and full exercise of citizenship. It was a part of the national environment. We have been late to see that the American Negro has been excluded from the inspiring, developing psychology of American life. This exclusion was greatest in the South, though it existed everywhere. The school cases dramatized this fact. To see the Constitution function to give to the Negro citizen a chance to share in the assurance of the rights of citizenship was rewarding compensation.

The courage of the Negro children involved in the initial desegregations of schools was heartening. Many of them were too young to really comprehend the issues involved. But each knew enough to understand that something momentous was occurring and that they were a part of it. The first day in school is always a testing time for any child. But for those who had to go through police lines or be escorted by officers, the test was something more than going to school. It was an experience of very real courage and faith. The children in elementary and secondary schools and the young men and women who desegregated colleges and universities knew loneliness and hurt. But they stayed the course.

There has been criticism of what has been called "tokenism." Use of this word has cast a shadow over some of the school integrations. I do not agree that small beginnings were unwise or that they were in any sense tokens. What happened in Atlanta and other Southern cities where children were admitted in desegregation actions was that pupils selected under the placement acts had been carefully screened. It was important for them, and for those who would come after them, that they be children who would not fail. Had there been larger, unscreened admissions there inevitably would have been a number of failures. There would have been unavoidable charges of discrimination. Therefore, it seemed to me that it was the better part of wisdom to select students for the precedent-breaking changes who would be able to hold their own. In all Southern states where such admission policies were used the results have been good. It was possible then to build on this and to admit a larger number in the next year's classes. I have always regretted that the word "tokenism" came to be applied to many of the beginnings of school desegregation.

By 1962 there was evidence of some Southwide organization of a hard-core hate group. Members of it seemed to be available on call to travel to distant states. Thus, when the Albany, Georgia, troubles reached the stage of violence in the late summer of 1962, Klan groups came from neighboring Alabama and South Carolina to participate in demonstrations. "Outsiders" were reported by police in almost every instance of racial violence in the South. This, of course, reached its climax in Oxford, Mississippi, when a considerable number of armed men appeared on the scene. Some of them were quoted as saying that they had come in response to General Edwin Walker's plea for supporters to join him there. Some of these men were found to have as many as three rifles in their cars.

Another melancholy development has been the mobility of teen-age toughs who have been on the move from state to state whenever violence seemed likely.

This fast-moving continuity of events has provided exciting experiences though, to be sure, there have been days of near-despair and sadness. The young toughs are perhaps the saddest of all spectacles.

Almost without exception the youngsters recruited into hate groups come from homes where they grew up hearing it. A ghastly sort of classroom for corrupting young minds exists, for example, in the homes of those adults, men and women, whose "achievements" are of the lowest grade — the anonymous telephone callers. They are so utterly common and vulgar, and so completely lacking in any quality save that of coarseness, that they become interesting because of their petty viciousness and the meagerness of their imagination and the poverty of their vile vocabulary.

They are, first of all, obsessed with sex. Females of this species, for example, regularly would telephone my home. If my wife answered they would speak in an absurd, stereotype Uncle Remus dialect and demand to know, with the most vulgar phrases, why I had not kept a date and was I coming. If I or my son answered, the approach was slightly varied. Often some of the men would call and, speaking in the preposterous phrases of the old minstrel show blackface acts of bygone generations, would say they had a daughter who wanted to marry a white nigger-lover. There were some who were simply psychopaths who spewed sex filth into the phone. A few who called dealt in threats of death and bombing. The mind pictured children listening to papa and mama, and the satisfaction of papa and mama over their "achievements."

There were those who telephoned at intervals all through the night. Pairs, or teams of them, harassed all those who publicly supported the courts and the morality of the school decision. Once during the desegregation of the University of Georgia, we had nineteen abusive calls between 7:30 and 9 P.M. In addition, there were those who saw in any effort to assist the Negro to have simple justice, the right to vote, and equal use of public services, a Communist plot. Some had to endure this idiocy in telephone calls and letters to the editor.

My experience with this sort of thing began in the early autumn of 1938. I had returned from Europe to be made executive editor. I was soon honored with a parade — about seventy-five or so robed and masked Klansmen paraded around the Constitution building one Saturday night carrying placards denouncing the paper and me.

From that time until the early spring of 1961, when my wife's increasing illness made an unlisted phone imperative, the number was in the book. In those years we were educated in how a Klansman, a White Citizens Council member, or plain vicious hater, attained status by achievement. For the more cretinlike, a filthy telephone call would suffice.

There were, of course, wonderful, warming, comforting, and strengthening compensations. One of these was almost weekly abuse by the Georgia equivalent of the White Citizens Council publication. It featured red and black type and its headlines were eighty-point bold and in the reddest of ink. I treasure, as a heritage for my son, certain copies of that paper. I knew we had it and its editor off balance and on the run as early as October, 1957, when the banner ribbon read: "Ralph McGill Menace to Georgia: South's Worst Foe Since Thad Stevens." I was sure of it when the top red lines read "Ralph McGill Deliberately Lies Again; Tries To Scare South into Race Mixing" (Nov. 4, 1957); "McGill Continues to Deceive the People in Effort to Break Down Segregation" (Nov. 18, 1957); "People of Atlanta Will Not Be Tricked by Editor McGill." . . . (March 2, 1959); "Ralph McGill Is 'Just a Carpetbagger' Greensboro, Alabama Paper Charges" (March 9, 1959); "Georgia Politicians Had Better Beware the Siren Song of McGill, Hartsfield" (April 13, 1959); "Rastus McGill, Atlanta Constitution, Led People of Atlanta into a Boghole" (Jan. 11, 1960). In September of 1962 came the real accolade. The White Citizens Council choice for governor was defeated in the Georgia primary by a huge majority. Their headline, in red ink, read: "McGill's Race Mixing Philosophy Won Sweeping Victory Sept. 12." I had this issue framed as a sort of diploma.

There were other compensations. Letters of support and encouragement came, not too surprisingly, from small rural towns where the extremists ruled. Some were sent to neighboring towns to be mailed. Others were brought to Atlanta on a shopping tour and mailed there. One Thanksgiving eve a lady brought to my door a package of more than two hundred personal letters of thanks, and they were from white and colored citizens, teachers, professional and business people.

There were small, simple compensations which touched the heart with their sincerity. Frequently in restaurants an unknown Negro waiter or waitress would, in putting a plate of food on the table, whisper, "Thank you, sir, for what you write." Now and then a Negro cloakroom attendant would refuse the proffered tip, and say, "Please, sir. Let me do this for you."

There were compensations when the Atlanta bus lines were desegregated. To see the self-consciousness of most of those who boarded a bus and sat at the front or center, after a lifetime of going to the rear, was both an accusation and a compensation.

For some, the first experience of taking any available seat in a trolley bus was one of intense excitement. A college professor told me, "I was angry with myself for being self-conscious when I took a seat midway up a bus. But unless you have lived all, or most of your life, on a strictly segregated, separate basis, you simply cannot comprehend what it means suddenly to be able to sit in the middle of a bus."

John Hope, a distinguished member of Fisk University's faculty, said that he, and many of his friends, would now and then take a plane to New York just to escape the pressurized chamber of the South's segregation.

"I could never understand those white persons who would say, with apparent sincerity, that they couldn't see why segregation really made much difference," said Hope. "It never seemed to occur to them that a Negro might like to take his family out to dinner or lunch at a decent restaurant. He could not do so in the South. Or, he might wish to take his wife to a

movie or concert without going down an alley to an entrance
and climbing two or three flights of stairs to a seat. The average nonhostile white person never seemed to comprehend
that his enjoyment of such simple services might not be experienced by a Negro."

When the buses, the libraries, the department store restaurants, and golf courses were desegregated one could not avoid
the feeling of guilt which came with the knowledge that fellow human beings had for so long been denied. There was an
unexpected dividend for me in the desegregation of buses.
Years ago I gave up driving a car, and almost daily ride the bus
some eight miles to and from the office. In the first months after
restrictions ended, I usually was able to get a seat beside some
Negro man or woman. Some perplexed, or stubborn, white passengers would be standing in the aisle, themselves self-
conscious about the change. This did not long endure. All too
soon for my own selfish comfort, the old Southern custom lost
out to tired feet and weary legs. The sight of Negro and white
persons sitting together ceased to be a novelty on my route.
This, too, was a compensation.

But greatest of all compensations was to be one of the many
who worked long and patiently at the arduous job of seeing to
it that the people of Atlanta knew the facts and the alterna-
tives. To see the golf courses, transportation, eating places,
libraries and schools desegregated without an incident but
rather with understanding and good manners was a warm and
rewarding experience. There is almost an ecstasy which is
quite indescribable, in seeing, and feeling, a city slowly but
surely reach a decision and act on it. For a time, one lives a
shared existence which is deeply rewarding.

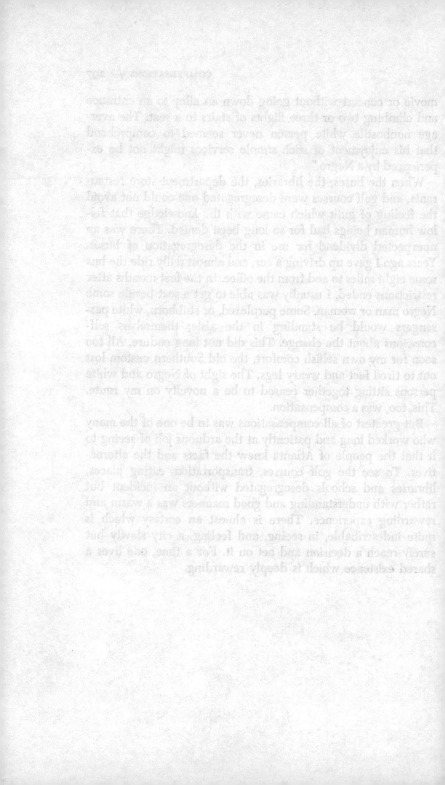

Index